American Genesis

American Genesis

The Antievolution Controversies from Scopes to Creation Science

JEFFREY P. MORAN

OXFORD

UNIVERSITY PRESS

OXFORD
UNIVERSITY PRESS

Oxford University Press, Inc., publishes works that further
Oxford University's objective of excellence
in research, scholarship, and education.

Oxford   New York
Auckland   Cape Town   Dar es Salaam   Hong Kong   Karachi
Kuala Lumpur   Madrid   Melbourne   Mexico City   Nairobi
New Delhi   Shanghai   Taipei   Toronto

With offices in
Argentina   Austria   Brazil   Chile   Czech Republic   France   Greece
Guatemala   Hungary   Italy   Japan   Poland   Portugal   Singapore
South Korea   Switzerland   Thailand   Turkey   Ukraine   Vietnam

Copyright © 2012 by Oxford University Press, Inc.

Published by Oxford University Press, Inc.
198 Madison Avenue, New York, NY 10016

www.oup.com

Oxford is a registered trademark of Oxford University Press

Earlier versions of chapters have appeared as "The Scopes Trial and Southern
Fundamentalism in Black and White: Race, Region, and Religion," *Journal of Southern History*
70, no. 1 (February 2004): 95–120, and "Reading Race into the Scopes Trial: African American Elites,
Science, and Fundamentalism," *Journal of American History* 90, no. 3 (December 2003): 892–911.

Library of Congress Cataloging-in-Publication Data
Moran, Jeffrey P.
American genesis : the antievolution controversies
from Scopes to creation science / Jeffrey P. Moran.
p.   cm.
Includes bibliographical references and index.
ISBN 978-0-19-518349-8 (hardcover)
1. Evolution (Biology)—Study and teaching—United States—History.
2. Evolution (Biology)—United States—Religious aspects—Christianity—History.
3. Creationism—United States—History. I. Title.
QH362.M67   2012
576.8—dc23   2011037435

1   3   5   7   9   8   6   4   2

Printed in the United States of America
on acid-free paper

Dedicated to
Susan, Hannah, and Rebecca

Contents

Preface

WHEN I MOVED to Kansas in 1998, I thought the antievolution movement lay quietly in the past. Like many of my generation, I had read *Inherit the Wind* in high school, but considered its treatment of the Scopes antievolution trial of 1925 to be more of an attack on American intolerance in general than on antievolutionism per se. Like Arthur Miller's *The Crucible*, the play said more about modern McCarthyism than about its ostensible historical subject. When I taught my undergraduate classes about the 1920s, I paid due obeisance to *Inherit the Wind*'s original 1925 inspiration, but I described the Scopes trial more as a historical curiosity—a piece of Jazz Age Americana that, like goldfish-swallowing and the Charleston, remained safely in the past. Like so many teachers before me, I could not resist using the trial to illustrate the clash between traditionalism and the inevitable rise of a more modern, secular, and urban culture during the Roaring Twenties.[1] Besides, students relished the story of how the three-time presidential candidate William Jennings Bryan led the prosecution of John Thomas Scopes for violating Tennessee's law against teaching the theory of evolution, only to run up against Clarence Darrow, the notorious attorney and agnostic whom the high school teacher had retained for his defense. As I pointed out, the jury in Dayton, Tennessee, ultimately found Scopes guilty, but the spectacle of Darrow placing Bryan on the witness stand and exposing his ignorance about science and the Bible led many Americans of liberal sympathies to proclaim the trial a ringing triumph of progress over the forces of obscurantism. When Bryan died mere days after the jury's decision, antievolutionism seemed to have followed him into the grave. End of lecture.

That was 1998. In 1999, the Kansas State Board of Education made international news when the conservative majority voted to remove evolution from the state's educational standards, leaving the question of whether to teach the subject up to local school boards. Contrary to most reports, the state board did not directly banish evolution from the classroom, but the majority of its members clearly hoped their decision would have the same effect, as teachers and local boards could now sidestep the controversial topic if they wished. This minor decision touched off a massive response. Editorialists throughout the United States invoked images from *The Wizard of Oz* and a back catalogue of rural caricatures to deride the ruling. Foreign correspondents particularly wanted to know how the most technologically advanced society in the world could also host so many citizens who were hostile to science. In the next election, irate Kansans threw out the antievolutionist majority, but the lesson was clear: the antievolution impulse, first visible in 1925, had never died out. It had gone underground and changed leaders and strategies, but it remained alive.

By now, scholarly studies of the Scopes antievolution trial and the antievolution movement that followed have well exceeded the word count of "300 volumes of 3000 words apiece" that one social scientist estimated journalists filed from Dayton, Tennessee, in July 1925.[2] The deluge should not be surprising. The struggles over evolution open a window onto American culture, for the question of evolution has exposed and exacerbated extant social tensions throughout the twentieth century and beyond, and the American environment in turn has shaped the antievolution impulse.

In a diverse culture that prizes both science and faith, that has the most advanced scientific infrastructure as well as the highest rate of church adherence among developed nations, the issues raised in the antievolution controversies touch the heart of our collective and individual identities. Therefore, while most works on the subject tend to focus on courtroom battles or the relation between science and faith, this book broadens the inquiry to argue that social forces such as gender, region, and race have intersected with the antievolution impulse in ways that shed light on modern American culture.

Although the book is not primarily about the Scopes trial, the battle at Dayton threads its way through the chapters, for the themes first sounded during that trial continue to resonate decades later in the disputes over teaching evolution in the public schools. At the same time, the book makes clear that the Scopes trial cannot be simplistically connected to recent controversies, a point underlined by the nuances of the labels used in these pages. As a general rule, the book refers to the antievolution "impulse" rather than the antievolution "movement," for while *movement* applies to the fairly coherent crusade at the time of the Scopes trial, it implies a greater coherence than has historically existed among evolution's various opponents. *Antievolutionism* and *antievolutionists* refer to umbrella categories, but those can be roughly subdivided into a small number of groupings. The book employs the term *creationists* to designate those who specifically disallow the Big Bang theory and evolution; early in the century, they generally based their arguments on purely religious grounds, as when the Tennessee legislature in 1925 rejected evolution on the simple basis that it "denies the story of the Divine creation of man as taught in the Bible"—that is, it contradicts a literal reading of the first chapters of Genesis, which record the story of God creating the universe by fiat in six days. Many creationists at the time maintained some interpretive latitude, as they differed over the actual length of these days, or posited the existence of a vast chronological "gap" between the creation of "the heavens and the earth" recorded in Genesis 1:1 and the much later Edenic restoration, including the appearance of Adam and Eve, beginning in Genesis 1:2.[3]

By the 1960s, however, their creationist heirs had embraced the narrowest interpretation of the creation, holding that God created the universe and all life on earth in six days of exactly twenty-four hours apiece, approximately six thousand years ago. This more rigid interpretation was reinforced by the efflorescence of various species of "creation science," which sought to employ scientific arguments to substantiate what they called the "young-earth" position. This book occasionally treats intelligent design (ID) as a variant of creation science, but tensions exist between the two approaches, and many ID proponents protest being lumped in with orthodox creation scientists, for ID draws partly on an independent philosophical background and allows for the possibility of an older earth and a more flexible reading of Genesis. Still less does the "creationist" label fit those who, like the prominent modern scientist Francis Collins and the leaders of the nation's old-line Protestant and Catholic denominations, see God's hand behind the Big Bang and evolution but do not call for their theological interpretation to be taught in science class; they are exempted from the creationist category altogether. Finally, like many of the people examined here, the book generally employs the terms *Darwinist, Darwinian,* and *evolutionist* interchangeably, except where a fine distinction needs to be made between those who believe in Darwinian evolution and those who accept evolution as a general proposition but largely reject Charles Darwin's specific mechanism of natural selection. Historical taxonomy may be an imprecise science, but its distinctions will prove useful.

Acknowledgments

I AM MOST grateful for the support of my immediate family. My wife, Susan Kang, and our daughters, Hannah and Rebecca Moran, have supported me every plodding step of the way, providing joy, companionship, inspiration, and the occasional nudge. I appreciate the love of my extended family as well, radiating from my parents outward to the far branches of the family bush. Like almost everyone else working in this field, I owe a great debt to Ronald L. Numbers for his extraordinary intellectual and professional generosity; his influence is apparent on all the good pages. A late reading by Jon Roberts pulled me back from the precipice of numerous errors. I have been buoyed by a number of others working on evolution and creationism, including Edward J. Larson, Constance Areson Clark, Jonathan Zimmerman, and James Ivy. Most Americans might associate the University of Kansas primarily with basketball, but I also have found at KU friendship and support from my good friends Bruce Lieberman and Paulyn Cartwright, as well as my colleagues in the History Department, particularly Don Worster, Jonathan Earle, Kim Warren, and Paul Kelton. I wish to thank the anonymous readers at the *Journal of American History*, the *Journal of Southern History*, and Oxford University Press, whoever and wherever they are under their cloaks of invisibility. For permission to reuse excerpts from my published material, I thank the *Journal of American History*, the *Journal of Southern History*, and Bedford/St. Martin's Press. My editor at Oxford University Press, Susan Ferber, has been a demanding critic at all stages of this project, and her high standards have much improved the book. For sharing their time and many of their materials, I am grateful to Glenn Branch, Eugenie Scott, Howard J. Van Till, Eric B. Verhulst, Ken Miller, Wesley Elsberry, and Nick Matzke. Mike Vorenberg's friendship has been a treasure all along, and Charles Conrad and Franco DeMonte have given me life-sustaining support for years. All these good people have helped make this book. For any errors herein, I would like to blame society, but the responsibility surely rests with me alone.

American Genesis

Introduction

DARWIN COMES TO AMERICA

THE DURABILITY OF antievolution sentiment in America has reinforced the idea, first popularized in the late nineteenth century through such works as John William Draper's *History of the Conflict Between Religion and Science* (1875), that the entire history of science "is a narrative of the conflict of two contending powers, the expansive force of the human intellect on one side, and the compression arising from traditionary faith and human interests on the other."[1] The antievolution controversies, in this view, are only the latest battles in an enduring war between science and religion. The drive to burn Giordano Bruno at the stake for heresy in the sixteenth century was the same impulse that led to the arrest and prosecution of John Thomas Scopes for teaching evolution in Dayton, Tennessee, and the same motivation that spurred the Kansas State Board of Education to strike its comparatively mild blow against evolution.

This interpretation has launched several best-selling books and numerous symposia—not to mention lawsuits—but the idea of an eternal opposition between science and religion ignores the multiple roles that the theory of evolution has played since Charles Darwin published *On the Origin of Species* in 1859. In particular, the warfare metaphor overly simplifies the specific historical forces that have shaped the antievolution impulse in the United States, and it also obscures the ways in which evolution intensified extant cultural divisions. Far from epitomizing an eternal stalemate, the reception of Darwinism worldwide and in America has been contingent on a complex interplay of timing, nation, and culture.

This interaction becomes much clearer at the bookends of American antievolutionism. The Scopes antievolution trial of 1925 was the first widely noticed clash in the evolution controversy, and it established themes and strategies that were to resonate nearly a century later, with the rise of scientific creationism and the emergence of the present-day conflict over teaching evolution in the public schools. In both eras, the antievolution controversies were inextricably linked to broader cultural turbulence, such as the "New Morality" of flappers and feminists in the 1920s and the "culture wars" at the turn of the next century. History is an unreliable guide to the future, but analyzing the events and themes bracketed by these confrontations may be helpful not only for understanding cultural changes in modern America but also for grappling with a conflict that seems likely to endure in the years to come.

This is an American story, but the roots of the antievolution struggle run deeper and wider. Every human society has a creation story to answer a series of series of inescapable philosophical questions: Why does the world look as it does? How did our tribe or our world get here? What is our purpose? The chapters in Genesis that have been the central issues in modern antievolutionism describe a single omnipotent God creating the heavens and the earth; this is "the divine story of the creation of man" that John Scopes allegedly contradicted when he taught his students about evolution.[2] Other cultures have developed their own stories in keeping with their separate experiences in the world.[3] The ancient Greek myth passed on by Hesiod in the eighth century BCE features a more explicitly and humanly sexual mother figure embodied by Mother Earth, who begets her own husband, "starry Heaven," and with him conceives Titans, gods, Furies, nymphs, and the rest of the constellation of Greek mythological figures.[4] In the Bantu tradition, the original god, Bumba, copiously vomits forth the sun, the creatures of the earth, and men. The Mayan Popol Vuh records the gods creating man only after blundering on three previous attempts.[5]

Scholars of religious texts would assert that the question is not whether one creation story is more "true" than the others. Scientific truth was not their purpose. Rather, the intent of creation stories in the oral cultures that gave them life has usually been to instruct in morals and to buttress community traditions. If the stories accomplished these goals and fit with the community's changing experience, then they remained in the oral tradition without being questioned or challenged. As the historian of science David C. Lindberg explains, "There are no rewards for skepticism in such a social setting and few resources to facilitate challenge."[6] On the contrary, oral cultures produce no written record that would freeze the continuous flow of invention into a single form that is subject to dispute. When faced with a deep challenge to its explanatory power, the oral tradition can simply evolve to account for new circumstances, and few will find the new explanation to be somehow a betrayal or contradiction of the old.

Such plasticity characterized the original oral tradition from which the book of Genesis was constructed. The reputation of Jews as a "people of the Book" has often obscured the Hebrew Bible's roots in an older oral culture, but Judaism had flourished for several centuries as an oral tradition among various Hebrew tribes. Like most other creation stories, the primeval story or stories in the Hebrew Bible evinced all the advantages and weaknesses of orality. Inconsistency and even great internal contradictions in the story flourished alongside the strengths of adaptability and communal self-reinforcement in the oral transmission of Jewish culture. As is common during the transition from preliterate to literate societies, though, written forms such as scrolls began to gain authority over oral recitations. Having discarded the traditional view that Moses was the sole author of the Torah, or the first five books of the Hebrew Bible (also known as the Pentateuch), scholars have disagreed vigorously over the process by which scribes wrote down and put together the various creation stories, genealogies, laws, and poetry that were to become the Pentateuch. Most agree, however, that the various scrolls and tablets of the Pentateuch remained scattered and unrelated for centuries and were not bound together as a single holy book until around 450 BCE, when the Torah took more or less its final form, with its aura of holiness as a book—as Scripture. It was a monumental achievement, but the transition from the oral tradition to a written form also meant the sacrifice of some of orality's flexibility. A book is open to challenge in a way that an oral tradition is not. As an account of natural history that could potentially become open to other standards of proof, the first verses of Genesis were like a time bomb ticking away very, very slowly.

The first hints of this kind of danger came with the flowering of scientific reasoning among the ancient Greeks. Around 800 BCE, widespread literacy gave birth to an intellectual elite of unprecedented vigor and sophistication. Pythagoras, Heraclitus, Plato, Aristotle—these men from the golden age of Greek thought were able to develop rules of argumentation and standards of proof by which they could evaluate the truth of statements about the external world.

While to modern eyes the philosophies that they practiced resembled theology more than science, they were the first to begin searching for natural explanations of natural phenomena.[7] For example, at the same time as the Greeks continued to evince a general belief in the ancient myths of Zeus and Hera, generations of philosophers engaged in an intense dialogue over the nature of the universe and divinity. The inquiry began with the pre-Socratic philosophers, who claimed to find no evidence of divinity or purpose in the universe. The capriciousness of life, they argued, came not from the playful gods on Mount Olympus but from the essential aimlessness and contingency of nature. Plato disagreed strongly, arguing that the disjunction between the earth's imperfection and the universe's orderliness pointed toward the existence of a Creator—the Demiurge, in Plato's language—who had constructed the cosmos as an imperfect replica of the eternal ideas and shapes that existed in the world of forms.[8] Similarly speculative was Aristotle's conclusion that, logically, the universe could only be eternal, for something could not come from nothing.[9] This does not look much like modern science—even Aristotle spent more time in rational speculation than in observation of natural phenomena—but the Greeks had begun a tradition of logic and inquiry aimed not at communal solidarity but at skepticism. The evidence of the senses and the rules of reason began to trump or at least contend with inherited wisdom and faith.

Although later generations mistakenly were to consider Greek science to be the first salvo in a centuries-long war between science and religion, Western science in the millennium between the ancient Greeks and the modern Darwinians existed primarily to support religion rather than to challenge it. During the medieval era, for example, scientific inquiry was mainly the province of churchmen, and their chosen subjects were, not surprisingly, religious in nature. Perhaps the best example of this is the flourishing of "angelology" in the thirteenth century. Often caricatured as a debate over how many angels could dance on the head of a pin, angelology was in fact a scientific inquiry, using rules of logic and proof inherited from Aristotle via the Muslim world. Leading scholastics such as St. Thomas Aquinas (1225–1274) and St. Bonaventure (ca. 1217–1274) posed a series of Aristotelian questions that delved deeper and deeper into the mysteries of the angels: Did angels have a temporal nature, or were they eternal? Could angels have an emotional nature? Scholasticism was, in the words of one Bonaventure scholar, an "expansive" approach: "It led the scholastics to further questions, more detailed considerations, and specific chains of logic"—a far cry from the rote repetition of biblical formulas.[10] Nor was the scholastic project concerned solely with theology. Even the caricature of monks debating the number of angels dancing on the head of a pin was based on the scholastics' legitimate inquiry into whether angels possessed mass or displaced space, and angelology was inextricably linked to questions about the fundamental nature of such

categories as space and time—the stuff of which the universe is made.[11]
In its methodology and much of its subject matter, angelology was indeed
a science, and it was science in the service of religion. This is not to say
that science and church doctrine did not occasionally run afoul of each
other. But for centuries, scientists and church officers managed generally
to accommodate each other. In fact, they were usually the same people.
Although Nicolaus Copernicus's 1543 *De Revolutionibus Orbium Coeles-
tium* (*On the Revolution of Heavenly Orbs*) challenged the orthodox Catholic position that the earth was the immobile center of the universe,
Copernicus was himself a canon in a monastery, and his book featured a
dedication to the reigning Pope and a preface (added without the author's
knowledge) stressing that the book's heliocentrism was merely a mathematical hypothesis. Only in the early 1600s—half a century after Copernicus's death—did real trouble begin to percolate between Copernicanism
and the Church's terracentric orthodoxy. The object lesson for adherents
of Draper's argument about religious intolerance was the Church's persecution of Galileo for proving that Copernicus's "mathematical hypothesis"
was actually an empirical fact.

In all of his efforts, however, Galileo saw himself as a devout Catholic.
He put forth what one historian calls the "ancient argument" that God was
the author both of nature and of Scripture, and that the proper understanding of one could only lead to a better appreciation of the other.[12] If the
Bible seemed in error on a matter involving the natural world, Galileo
believed, then the fault lay with the interpreter, not with Scripture.
Throughout his career, Galileo had a great many friends among church
leaders (including the man who, as Pope Urban VII, would later condemn
him), and the Jesuits initially feted him for his pioneering work with the
telescope. Galileo did not see his work as a blow for intellectual freedom
against the tyranny of religion.[13]

Even after the scientific revolution in Europe created the concept of
"scientific truth" and developed tools for investigating it, few scientists
and theologians saw any difficulty in accepting Genesis as a valid account
of the creation of the universe. Scholars in the Western tradition generally
adhered to a two-tiered worldview in which natural science below supported biblical revelation above. In this system of "natural theology," a
study of the natural world revealed God's glory through his design of the
universe.

In the decades before Darwin, the most influential exposition of the
ways in which science supported religion came from the pen of William

Paley, the Anglican archdeacon of Carlisle, England. Born in 1743 to a family of middling wealth in the north of England, Paley made a fair showing as a student and then tutor at Christ's College, University of Cambridge. But rather than pursuing higher status in the metropolitan areas, Paley was set on being a "country parson," a vocation well suited to his personality and his desire to write.[14] Thus it was from a series of semi-rural posts in the north that Paley published such liberal, temperate works as his *Principles of Moral and Political Philosophy* and *A View of the Evidences of Christianity*. Paley was not an original thinker—on the contrary, his work was influential precisely because it repeated themes and ideas that already commanded general acceptance—but he was an able writer, and his piety was impeccable. Paley's best-known book, the 1802 *Natural Theology: or, Evidences of the Existence and Attributes of the Deity, Collected from the Appearances of Nature*, resuscitated the "argument from design" that Cicero, the Roman orator, had first put forth in 44 BCE.[15] Suppose, Paley argued in his updated version, that in crossing a heath you were to come across a watch lying on the ground (Cicero had postulated a sundial).[16] On closer inspection, you discovered "that its several parts are joined and put together for a purpose, e.g., that they are so formed and adjusted as to produce motion, and that motion so regulated as to point out the hour of the day."[17] Such a discovery pointed in only one direction: "The inference, we think, is inevitable; that the watch must have had a maker; that there must have existed, at some time and at some place or other, an artificer or artificers who formed it for the purpose which we find it actually to answer; who comprehended its construction and designed its use."[18] Paley connected his analogy to the proof of God's existence in nature. "Every indication of contrivance, every manifestation of design, which existed in the watch," he wrote, "exists in the works of nature; with the difference, on the side of nature, of being greater and more, and that in a degree which exceeds all computation."[19] The scientific examination of nature, in other words, involved an ever greater appreciation of the wonders of God's design, from the ways in which every part of the human eye seemed perfectly contrived for the function of sight to the magnificent order of the solar system (Copernicanism by this time having become generally accepted). Like many other works in this genre, including the American Cotton Mather's 1721 *Christian Philosopher*, much of *Natural Theology* consisted of cataloguing the wonders of nature, always referenced back to the glorious plan of the Creator.[20] This plan, Paley concluded, was surely a benevolent one, for if God had bestowed this kind of attention on even "the minutest parts" of creation, such as "the hinges in the wings of an *earwig*, and the joints of its antennae," then humans had "no reason to fear, therefore, our being forgotten, or overlooked, or neglected."[21]

Once a reader accepted the proof of God's existence as revealed in the design of nature, then he or she could turn to the words of the Bible to learn of God's ultimate design for humanity.[22] Building on the two-tiered worldview he had inherited, Paley's argument from design harmonized the two realms of knowledge and suggested that no real conflict could exist between the Bible and the study of nature.

Most scientists and theologians accepted this formulation. Despite occasional hints of conflict in the past, at the dawn of the nineteenth century William Paley and his numerous allies had every confidence that the scientific ferment they were living through would continue to buttress their vision of a purposeful universe, presided over by a benevolent, knowable God.

When Paley died in 1805, many of his books were firmly ensconced on the required reading lists of English universities, and *Natural Theology* was particularly popular at his alma mater, the University of Cambridge. Perhaps it was merciful that he did not live to see the convulsions that half a century later were to shake his two-tiered model. After taking most of his evidence for God's existence from the world of plants and animals, Paley would have been shocked to find that the greatest scientific threat to his argument had burst out of the realm of biology.[23]

The source of that threat, Charles Darwin, gave few early indications that his life's trajectory was to collide with Christian orthodoxy. Indeed, Darwin's physician father, on perceiving that his son did not have the stomach to follow him into medicine, suggested strongly that he become a minister, and Darwin entered Cambridge in 1828 intending to do so.[24] Like other university men of his generation, Darwin at Cambridge was required to familiarize himself with Paley's work. Although later in life Darwin was to publish an explicit refutation of Paley's argument from design, he nevertheless testified that the "careful study" of Paley's books at Cambridge "was the only part of the Academical Course which, as I then felt and as I still believe, was of the least use to me in the education of my mind."[25] During Darwin's time at Cambridge, the call of geology grew stronger than the call of the pulpit, so when Captain Robert FitzRoy in 1831 put out inquiries for a young naturalist to join him on the voyage of the *Beagle*, Darwin eagerly accepted.[26]

The story of the voyage of the *Beagle*, with its captain chronically depressed when not enraged, and its young naturalist soaking up the words of Charles Lyell's *Geology* as well as the natural wonders of the land and sea from Tierra del Fuego up to the Galapagos Islands, is well known. But with regard to Darwin's religiousness, it is noteworthy that, at least early in the voyage, the young man was still "quite orthodox," as he remembered, and he amused the ship's officers on at least one occasion by quoting the Bible "as an unanswerable authority on some point of morality."[27] Nevertheless, as England receded into the distance, Darwin's orthodox belief seemed to recede with it, to be replaced by his intense observation of natural phenomena and, eventually, by his conviction that the natural world was not the handiwork of Paley's "designer," but rather the constantly evolving product of natural forces.

Just what those forces were, however, was not immediately clear. During the voyage, Darwin had been struck by several observations, including the discovery of fossils of large armored animals resembling armadillos; the ways in which closely "allied" animals replaced one another as he traveled southward down the continent; and then the glorious diversity of the Galapagos Islands, on which most of the flora and fauna seemed South American in character, but with slight differences from island to island.[28] Different species all seemed admirably adapted to their physical environments—they seemed to have been modified to fit into various niches—but Darwin, like the handful of other naturalists who suspected that species had been modified over time, was still at a loss to explain the mechanism by which these living forms might have changed.

During the twenty years after his return from the *Beagle*, Darwin published occasional scientific pieces and, in his slow, methodical way, ground through the reams of notes he had taken during the voyage. Around 1856, he began writing what was to be a massive volume—at least four times the size of the book he eventually published—incorporating all of his observations and his theory about the causes of species variation. It is unclear whether this book ever would have appeared or, if it had, if anyone would have had the fortitude to read it. Fortunately, in 1858 Darwin was prodded into action and blessed brevity by news that another naturalist, Alfred Russel Wallace, had independently reached the same conclusions as Darwin about the modification of species.[29] Alarmed, Darwin worked quickly with the mass of material he had already assembled, and in 1859 he published *On the Origin of Species by Means of Natural Selection, or the Preservation of*

Favored Races in the Struggle for Life. With this compendium of empirical observation and hypothetical deduction, the English naturalist wrought a revolution in science and helped touch off as well a radical revision in the status and content of Christianity.

Scientifically, *On the Origin of Species* provided a powerful framework for explaining phenomena that had puzzled scientists for generations, particularly the exceptional diversity of living organisms and the history of life recorded in the fossil record. Although some natural scientists around this time accepted that life on earth had existed for perhaps millions of years, they were prevented from developing greater insight into organic development by the general belief that species were fixed for all time, so any variation within a species constituted merely a deviation from the species's "ideal form." Thus natural scientists could attribute the appearance of new species in the fossil record only to separate, divine creations. A trilobite, in other words, was always a trilobite, and if a fossil was found of a trilobite with twelve segments rather than eleven, then that represented either an accidental deviation from the "true" trilobite form or a separate species of trilobite created by God.[30] Many scientists were growing dissatisfied with this explanation, but Darwin was among the first to make the conceptual leap to the idea that a "species" constituted not a fixed Platonic ideal but rather a shifting, fluctuating population of closely related organisms. The rest of the so-called Darwinian revolution spread from this insight.[31]

Once he accepted that species were not fixed, Darwin was free to seek other explanations for the problem of the multiplication of species. Rather than having been created separately by God, could not species have developed—evolved, diversified—from common ancestors? Indeed, Darwin even suggested that all organisms were related to one another at the earliest branching of the family tree.[32] Thus far, Darwin's ideas found ready acceptance: with the death in 1873 of Harvard's Louis Agassiz—the last of the scientific true believers in God's separate creation of fixed species— every American natural scientist of any repute had come to agree with Darwin that species were mutable and that the fossil record demonstrated the evolution of species from earlier species.[33] Freed from their belief in the fixity of species, natural scientists no longer focused on merely cataloging the earth's flora and fauna into static divisions but could turn to the work of connecting species through history. Darwin's fundamental insight opened up for science what he called a "grand and almost untrodden field of inquiry."[34]

Accepting the fact of evolution, however, did not mean that scientists accepted Darwin's explanation of how evolution worked. For reasons both scientific and theological, Darwin's theory of natural selection—his proposal that species evolved because the "struggle for survival" in various locations made animals with certain traits more likely to survive and pass on their advantageous traits to offspring—was not to find general scientific acceptance until the "evolutionary synthesis" of the 1930s and 1940s. Indeed, Darwin himself waffled on the role natural selection played in evolution; he sometimes viewed natural selection as sufficient in itself for evolution, and sometimes supplemented natural selection with more Lamarckian ideas about "use-inheritance" (for example, a father who lifted weights would sire more muscular offspring, or creatures that strained their necks to reach fruit on a tree might eventually found a line of giraffes).

Natural selection provided a powerful explanation for organic evolution, and it undoubtedly played a large role in the acceptance of Darwin's work, but it also became a focus of tremendous opposition. Even Darwin's scientific supporters were far from unanimous in their approval. Many produced technical objections to natural selection, based either on relatively rapid transitions evident in the fossil record or on a general misunderstanding of inheritance in the era before the science of genetics had developed.[35] Other scientists confessed that they were still flummoxed by such questions as how small, undirected changes could produce such complex structures as the eyeball. Evolutionists suggested alternative mechanisms of evolution, such as the inheritance of acquired characteristics or the sporadic appearance of advantageous mutations. Little wonder that Darwin himself sometimes wavered in his commitment to strict natural selection.

The objections were not merely technical. From the first, many commentators also considered the theory to be a "moral outrage."[36] Darwinian natural selection, based on "the war of nature," seemed an immensely cruel process, a law that operated randomly and created tremendous waste by killing off the "unfit" by the millions. Darwin saw in the fossil record and the living world no overt evidence of an intervening intelligence, no indication of a trend toward greater perfection among organisms. Natural selection thus seemed to contradict the argument from design. Darwin now seemed to be suggesting that nature revealed a God who was either cruel and wasteful or else absent altogether. Having reluctantly set Paley aside in favor of the law of natural selection, Darwin concluded late in his life, "We can no longer argue that, for instance, the beautiful hinge of a bivalve shell must have been made by an intelligent being, like the hinge of a door by man. There seems to be no more design in the variability of organic beings and in the action of natural selection, than in the course which the wind blows."[37]

Darwin's theory also struck more directly at certain foundational Judeo-Christian beliefs.[38] The melancholic Captain FitzRoy, who had given Darwin his berth on the *Beagle*, became one of Darwin's numerous acquaintances who showed open hostility toward the naturalist for the irreligiousness of *On the Origin of Species*.[39] Although Darwin must have appreciated having an excuse for avoiding the volatile FitzRoy, he had to agree with the captain and others that his theory held some disturbing implications. Most obviously, the theory of evolution was incompatible with a literal reading of either of the two creation stories in Genesis, for it contradicted the story that God created the earth and subsequently stocked it with living creatures within six literal days, and the theory's suggestion that humans and animals shared a common descent contradicted the account of Adam and Eve as the first humans on earth. By lumping humans together with all other animals as products of evolution, rather implicitly in *Origin* and then explicitly in *The Descent of Man*, published in 1871, Darwin further undermined the Christian ideal of humanity's special relationship to God.[40]

Finally, Darwin seemed to weaken Christianity simply by ignoring it, deeming it irrelevant to his scientific endeavor. In Darwin's opinion, the scientist's task was to seek out the natural causes of phenomena without falling back on supernatural explanations; Darwin followed his own rule and largely omitted God from his work. In this respect, *On the Origin of Species* was the culmination of a process that had been building, unevenly, since at least the seventeenth century, as scientists attempted to formulate hypotheses that, if they did not necessarily rule out God, at least did not directly invoke him as an explanatory mechanism.[41] But Darwin's challenge cut deeper. Strictly understood, Darwin's work seemed to make God, as Christians (and devotees of other religions) had long understood him, not merely unknowable but also unnecessary. Such issues touched off repeated public debates and scholarly controversies in the decades after *Origin* was published.

Prior to the Scopes trial in 1925, the most famous public clash over evolution and religion was the legendary debate between Samuel Wilberforce, the Anglican bishop of Oxford, and T. H. Huxley, whose pugnacious defense of evolution eventually was to earn him the nickname "Darwin's Bulldog."[42] Memory, legend, and fact have become mixed together in accounts of their encounter, but this much is certain: On June 30, 1860, the British Association for the Advancement of Science, a mixed group of professional and amateur scientists, held a meeting to discuss Darwin's recent book. The site, appropriately or ironically, was the Oxford Museum, a Gothic shrine to natural history and anthropology that had just been built out of the profits Oxford University Press made from sales of the Holy Bible. Riding on the excitement over Darwin's book, the meeting was overcrowded. Clergy, students, and scientists had to adjourn to the museum's great library in order to cram themselves in. Darwin himself was absent; following a difficult year of controversy after the publication of *Origin*, the neurasthenic scientist was in no condition to court disputation in person.

According to the legend, after a "somewhat dry" address from the American John William Draper, the Anglican bishop "Soapy Sam" Wilberforce rose to deliver a defense of Christian faith and a mocking, sarcastic criticism of Darwin's hypothesis, to the delight of the many clergymen in the crowd. But then the bishop made a grave tactical error. Turning to Huxley, Wilberforce is supposed to have asked whether it was "through his grandfather or his grandmother that he claimed his descent from a monkey."[43] While it was bad enough to smear Huxley's grandfather, to impugn his grandmother was stepping over a very real boundary of Victorian etiquette. Sensing the bishop's vulgar mistake, Huxley is supposed to have muttered, "The Lord hath delivered him into my hands."[44] The least reliable but most concise version has Huxley then rising to proclaim, "I would rather be descended from an ape than a bishop."[45] Huxley himself later claimed that he had said only that he would rather have an ape for a grandfather than a man "highly endowed by nature and possessed of great means of influence and yet who employs those faculties and that influence for the mere purpose of introducing ridicule into a grave scientific discussion."[46] The words were less pungent, but the resulting legend was the same. In general shock from the repartee, Lady Brewster fainted; others cheered, and Huxley immediately became the toast of Oxford. Huxley— and by extension Darwinism and science in general—had vanquished "Soapy Sam" Wilberforce and religious obscurantism. The Oxford Museum debate cleared Darwinism's path to victory in England.

The legend of Huxley and Wilberforce at Oxford is meaningful, but not because it is true. Bishop Wilberforce was no narrow-minded religious zealot; indeed, as an amateur scientist, he had published a lengthy critique of Darwinism on purely scientific grounds, and he confined his Oxford talk almost exclusively to scientific matters before entangling himself in his ill-fated attempt at humor, which may or may not have been directed at Huxley. As for Darwin's bulldog, what he said or did not say was lost to posterity because young Huxley could not project his voice over the large crowd. Reporters who were present for the debate took no particular note of the supposedly climactic exchange between Wilberforce and Huxley. Indeed, contrary to legend, Wilberforce and his supporters came out of the meeting as convinced of their own victory as the Darwinians were of theirs. Only gradually was the story of the night recast as a ringing triumph for Darwinism and science. By the dawn of the twentieth century, the established clergy in England had come to accept the basic tenets of evolution, making it easy for many to "remember" the legend of Huxley vanquishing Wilberforce in 1860 as an inevitable triumph of reason over superstition.

Although Darwinism's victory in England suggested that evolutionary theory was to follow a clear path from initial resistance to inevitable acceptance, the reality was far more complicated. While the acceptance or rejection of evolution is perhaps the most important question for observers and activists in the present day, the question does not capture the rich variety of Darwin's early reception. In every country, the impact of evolutionary thought depended on the contingencies of the nation's religious structures, racial composition, scientific establishment, chronology, and culture. In Spain, for example, anarchists embraced Darwinism as pointing the way toward a cooperative society; in Bolivia, social and racial elites invoked social Darwinism to justify their privileged position in society, at least until the country lost its own "struggle for existence" in a war with Chile, thus calling into question the reliability of evolutionary theory as an explanation of superiority.[47] The labor movement in Germany invoked evolution as a justification for liberation. As different peoples put Darwinism to a variety of purposes, the truth or falsehood of the doctrine became almost beside the point.

The reception of evolution in the United States was more complicated yet.[48] In the initial stages, discussion was generally limited to scientists and elite theologians, whose tone was usually moderate. Indeed, many decades before liberal theologians such as Shailer Mathews at the University of Chicago rose to national prominence, numerous leading theologians were already committed to what was known as "modernism" or

"theological liberalism." They had become sympathetic to the "higher criticism" of the Bible—in which scholars studied the Bible not just as the
revealed word of God but as a historical artifact, a piece of the past that lay
open to historical, linguistic, literary, and archeological investigation. The
higher critics believed the Bible employed symbolic and allegorical
language to convey God's meaning in a way the ancient chroniclers could
understand.

For the mostly German scholars who pioneered the higher criticism as
well as for their English-speaking disciples, following the literal words of
the Bible was less compelling than uncovering what Mathews came to call
the "spirit and purpose" of Jesus Christ's moral teachings.[49] Despite the
potential threat that *On the Origin of Species* posed to a literal reading of
Genesis, therefore, most of the leading liberal Protestant theologians in
England and the United States were able to adapt to the new Darwinian
environment in the decades after 1859. They achieved this accommodation both by tailoring their own aspirations to fit with the new evolutionary
consensus and by adjusting Darwin's theories to suit them better. Modi-
fying both Darwin and the tradition of the two-tiered worldview, leading
liberals came to pronounce the existence of separate spheres for science
and religion.[50] Theology was to give up its former status as arbiter of both
the natural and supernatural and henceforth confine itself more closely
to the arenas of faith and morality. There, beyond the reach of scientific
inquiry, religion could survive and perhaps, they hoped, even thrive.

At the same time, modernist theologians and natural scientists, the
vast majority of whom remained pious Christians, chose selectively which
elements of Darwin's theory to accommodate. Even as they accepted the
fact of organic evolution, they often threw aside natural selection, for its
alleged cruelty and directionlessness contradicted their belief in a caring
and immanent God. As one historian notes, Darwin in the second edition
of *On the Origin of Species* left a narrow opening for a Creator, and his
American followers crowded into the breach.[51] Theological liberals such as
Henry Ward Beecher retreated to the shelter of "theistic evolution," claiming that evolution was the working out of God's blueprint for the universe
and that natural history revealed clear evidence of organic progress toward
perfection. The argument from design, they believed, still held, though
God now seemed more a warm, immanent spirit than an all-powerful
deity continuously involved in human history.[52] Some theologians and scientists tried to split the difference, accepting the general validity of evolution while asserting that humans were not part of the evolutionary process

but a separate creation by God. At any rate, mainstream theologians largely made their peace with Darwinism.

The theistic, sanitized version of evolution began to make its way into textbooks and classrooms at the university and secondary levels in the 1880s. The generation of scientists and educators trained after *Origin* began to write textbooks that largely discarded the older theory of special creation in favor of an evolutionary framework.[53] Biology education at the college level, including institutions with a religious affiliation, reoriented itself around the central concept of organic evolution. Educators were more hesitant to introduce the theory to high school students, partly because science education at this level was generally more practical than theoretical, partly because the subject might have seemed too difficult for secondary school students. Although none of the books for the high school market around the turn of the century presented a particularly good explication of evolution, almost all of them included the concept.[54] Nor was the spread of theistic evolution into these niches particularly controversial. To be sure, universities were careful not to flaunt their evolutionary teaching, especially in the South. But in general, by the turn of the century public disputes over evolution seemed to belong to the past.

In the first years of the new century, however, a set of unique American characteristics began to assert themselves over the reception of evolution, taking the hypothesis down a very different path than in Darwin's England. The distance between the two countries may be measured in the general indifference American fundamentalists met when they tried to spark antievolutionist crusades in England.[55] It is surely an oversimplification, but in the United States, the particular direction that antievolution controversies have taken has been determined by three major cultural characteristics: the dominance of Protestantism, the traditions of democracy, and the unique cultural diversity of the nation itself. These forces laid the groundwork for the Scopes trial, and they have continued to provide a framework for antievolution controversies through today.

Militant Protestantism has been the most conspicuous element of the antievolution movement. Although the nation's Founders pointedly rejected the idea of establishing a state religion, Protestant Christianity was from the beginning central to the culture. The Puritans were by no means alone in their religious fervor, and the intensity of Protestant faith among the colonists lived on into the following centuries. In the nineteenth century, a majority of Americans belonged to one Protestant denomination or another, and the language of the King James Bible suffused the rhetoric of public life. Protestant ministers were leaders at both the local and national levels, and Protestant values such as temperance, individualism, and a veneration of "pure" womanhood structured private life as well as public life. Despite the increasing visibility of Jewish and Catholic immigrants over the course of the nineteenth century and into the next, Protestantism remained a dominant force in the nation's religious and cultural life. To use only numerical measures, from 1906 through 1958 Protestant church members consistently made up approximately 60 percent of all church membership, and the actual figure is likely several percentage points higher because most Protestant denominations employ a fairly restrictive definition of membership.[56] Despite an overall decline in churchgoing in the last fifty years, Protestants still make up the largest body of American Christians, and self-identified Protestants constitute about half the population.[57] Further, of the Protestant denominations in recent decades, the more conservative congregations have experienced the strongest growth—Southern Baptists, for example, have grown much faster than the more liberal American Baptists.[58]

Conservative Protestant institutions kept alive the antievolution impulse during the long years between Scopes and the rise of creation science, and antievolutionism continues today to be almost exclusively a Protestant preoccupation. The Institute for Creation Research, for example, is a purely conservative evangelical project, as are all similar organizations such as Answers in Genesis and the Center for Science and Culture (formerly the Center for the Renewal of Science and Culture) at the Discovery Institute.[59]

The reason for this alignment has a theological basis, but the theology makes a practical impact well beyond the walls of the seminaries. At the heart of Protestantism lies the doctrine of *sola scriptura*, the belief that the Bible itself is a necessary and sufficient guide to salvation. Neither the Pope, his priests, nor the theological traditions of the Church hold more authority than Scripture. This doctrine, promulgated most famously by Martin Luther, touched off the Protestant Reformation in the sixteenth century and crossed the Atlantic with the Puritans. Two elements of *sola scriptura* were to play a crucial part in the antievolution battles. First, the instability of interpretation based on *sola scriptura* called forth early in the twentieth century a countervailing demand for orthodoxy, or at least a search for it. Second, the primacy of the Bible implied by *sola scriptura* developed into a belief in the inerrancy of the Bible during this time, and this more rigid approach to Scripture made accommodation with evolution a trickier proposition.

Orthodoxy had always represented a problem for Protestants, especially at the turn of the twentieth century. While Protestant theologians argued that readers of the Bible could all discern its fundamental truths, no central authority existed to rein in the proliferation of individual readings. In practice, wrote the intellectual Walter Lippmann in 1912, this exercise of private judgment led only to "schism within schism and heresy within heresy."[60] Baptists, in particular, had seen their policy of individual and congregational autonomy lead to innumerable variations—Primitive Baptists, Hard-Shell Baptists, Sovereign Grace Baptists, Free Baptists, and on and on. Catholicism, by contrast, suffered less splintering because it was structured as a stable hierarchy with the Pope at the apex; although the Bible was obviously a central component of the Catholic faith, Roman Catholicism held that the Church had existed prior to the writing of the Gospels, and thus the teachings of the early Church fathers and the authority of the Church itself could corral the wilder tendencies of individual biblical interpretation. Conversely, in the United States, where the Protestant idea of a "plain reading" of the Bible took a particularly strong hold, the tension between individual latitude and the need for orthodox boundaries was especially strong.

The threat of evolution in the schools really became an issue around the turn of the century, just when the push for Protestant orthodoxy was intensifying, and evolution further galvanized the search for theological order. By contradicting the literal truth of Genesis, the theory of evolution buttressed the higher critics' contention that the Bible should not be accepted as a literal account of history but rather should be understood in historical context. The menace these forces represented, as well as competition from Catholicism, Spiritualism, and skepticism, prompted a number of leading conservative Protestants to publish, from 1910 through 1915, *The Fundamentals*, a series of mass-circulation pamphlets outlining the "fundamental" doctrines that any orthodox Christian should subscribe to, such as the authenticity of miracles and the doctrine that Jesus died for mankind's sins.

Primary among the doctrines insisted on by the fundamentalists, as they came to be known, was the second crucial element in *sola scriptura*: biblical literalism, including the Bible's account of historical events such as the origin of life on earth. Although evolution was not a prominent theme in *The Fundamentals*, the literal reading of Genesis directly contradicted several scientific discoveries—particularly the theory of biological evolution. Thus the demand for orthodoxy, prompted by the doctrine of *sola scriptura*, propelled conservative Protestants toward their confrontation with evolution. Beginning around 1922, leading fundamentalists such as William Jennings Bryan, William Bell Riley, and Billy Sunday began a national crusade against the heretical doctrine, crisscrossing the country to speak to congregations and legislatures about the threat Darwinism posed to the Bible and their faith. It was this militancy, this willingness to do battle within the denominations and in the broader culture, that differentiated fundamentalists from merely conservative evangelicals.[61]

The confrontation over biblical literalism and the others that have followed were shaped by the second major American characteristic—a democratic tradition that has provided a structure, a rhetoric, and a strategy for antievolutionism. Unlike the reception evolution received in Bolivia, say, or even in England, the conversation over evolution in the United States by the 1920s was not limited to a small cadre of elite scientists but rather involved a broader public that included not only the leaders of the American Association for the Advancement of Science but also ordinary citizens. Newspapers, journals, and public lectures spread word of evolution and its discontents to a wide circle of Americans, with striking results. Only in the United States did evolution become a subject of broad public interest. Only in the United States did evolution become a matter for legislation and lawsuits—both of them, for better or worse, democratic institutions.

The Scopes trial embodied this democratization and set the populist tone for future antievolution activity. In 1925, inspired by the fundamentalist crusade against evolution, a rural Tennessee state legislator named John Washington Butler, a Primitive Baptist, proposed a bill to make it a misdemeanor offense to teach in schools receiving state funding "any theory that denies the story of the Divine creation of man as taught in the Bible, and to teach instead that man has descended from a lower order of animals." The law's target was to become a familiar one. Public schools have proved to be the central battleground of the antievolution disputes, for Americans use the schools not only as imparters of information but also as political institutions that exist to pass down community values to the malleable next generation.[62] With little dissent, the Tennessee House and Senate passed the bill into law.

In New York City, the newly founded American Civil Liberties Union (ACLU), which had been created in response to majoritarian abuses during the Great War, determined that this law was both a violation of academic freedom and an attack on the rights of labor. Rejecting the strategy of convincing Tennesseans to repeal the law, the ACLU advertised in Tennessee newspapers for a teacher who would help them launch a test case to determine the law's constitutionality. Only in the small town of Dayton, Tennessee, did the ACLU find a willing candidate. Although it is unclear whether John Thomas Scopes had ever taught about evolution in Dayton's high school, local boosters pressed him to admit he had in order to generate publicity for the town.

The publicity stunt immediately ballooned into a national sensation. Under prodding from William Bell Riley and other prominent fundamentalists, Bryan himself signed on to join the prosecution. The "Great Commoner," as he was known, was rusty in the practice of law but still supple in his ability to move a crowd with his eloquence. For his defense, Scopes hired the celebrated attorney Clarence Darrow, whose notoriety as a radical and agnostic prompted the ACLU to engage in a series of comic maneuvers to elbow him aside, but Scopes, anticipating a "down-in-the-mud" fight, clung to his "Indian fighter."[63] Darrow was joined by his associate Dudley Field Malone, a wealthy divorce attorney from New York City. The ACLU managed to insert local counsel John Randolph Neal and Arthur Garfield Hays, another rich radical attorney from New York who, like Darrow, had learned a deep distrust of majority rule as a result of defending unpopular cases. Their chief antagonists for the prosecution were Bryan and the sober young attorney general for this circuit, Tom Stewart, who spent much of the trial trying, unsuccessfully, to steer the arguments away from religious and scientific speculation and back to the narrow channels of the law. Anticipating fireworks, more than one hundred reporters descended on Dayton, and a Chicago radio station set up the first-ever network hookup to broadcast the trial. During the trial that followed, European reactions focused on the democratic peculiarities of the American situation. The London *Evening Standard*, for example, suggested the American antievolution conflict demonstrated that "an ultra-democratic policy may co-exist with the narrowest tyranny and intolerance."[64] The London *New Statesman* concurred on the cause of the "heresy hunt" in Tennessee: "The United States has been from the beginning the land of the merciless majority."[65] In France, even Marie Curie signed a letter of surprise and dismay at the "oppression of science and thought in America."[66]

Under the guidance of Judge John Raulston, the trial did not disappoint. The validity of employing the fundamentalist interpretation of the

Bible as the basis for the Butler Act was the central issue. The defense lined up a team of experts from such institutions as Harvard University and Johns Hopkins University to testify that Genesis could not be taken as a factual account of the creation of the world and the diversity of life. The prosecution, having failed to rustle up any reputable experts of its own, took the strategy of arguing that no experts were needed to understand the plain language of the Butler Act or of the Bible, and further, no one from what Bryan called a "little oligarchy of self-styled 'intellectuals'" had the right "to demand control of the schools of the United States" against the wishes of the Tennessee majority.[67] Raulston allowed several days of skirmishing over these points but ultimately ruled for the prosecution and disallowed testimony from almost all the experts who had traveled to Dayton to defend the validity of evolution. Only Maynard Metcalf from Johns Hopkins managed to take the stand.

Stranded without their main tool for defending Scopes, the defense experienced an epiphany: after Raulston blocked the defense's expert witnesses, the only real "expert" left in the courtroom was William Jennings Bryan, who had long portrayed himself in speeches and articles as something of a Bible scholar. Thus, on the celebrated seventh day of the trial, Darrow called Bryan to the stand as an expert but unfriendly witness on the reliability of the Bible as a book of fact. Incredibly, Bryan agreed to cooperate and Raulston chose to allow the examination. Fearing that the courthouse floor would collapse under the weight of the spectators, the judge moved the trial outdoors for the afternoon, and there, for two hours under a pitiless summer sun, Darrow grilled Bryan about the literal construction of the Bible. Under this pressure, Bryan finally made the seemingly damaging admission that the Genesis account of creation might not have involved six literal days of twenty-four hours apiece, but rather each of the "days" actually could have been thousands or even millions of years long. Bryan's answer was a common fundamentalist interpretation of Genesis, but the defense pounced on it as evidence that the Bible could not be understood literally; the Book needed interpretation, and so the antievolutionists could not use the literal words in the Bible to oppose the teaching of evolution in the public schools. By the end of the examination, Bryan and Darrow were shouting, red-faced with anger. "The world shall know," Bryan proclaimed, "that these gentlemen have no other purpose than ridiculing every Christian who believes in the Bible." "We have the purpose of preventing bigots and ignoramuses from controlling the education of the United States," Darrow shot back, "and you know it."[68]

Despite Darrow's spirited fight, he knew he actually needed to lose the trial at Dayton in order to be able to appeal his case to higher courts that could invalidate the Butler Act. On the day after his joust with Bryan, therefore, Darrow stood before the jury and essentially asked them to find his client guilty. In only nine minutes—the time it took jurors to push through the crowd to the deliberation room and back—Dayton and the world had a verdict: guilty as charged.

Both sides claimed victory in the case, but the antievolutionists' jubilation was short-lived; five days after the trial, while Bryan took an afternoon nap in Dayton, his Creator carried him off to eternal rest. Although some supporters believed that death had come because "the agnostics and atheists unmercifully nailed our Great Commoner to a cross of calumny and vituperation," he most likely died of complications arising from diabetes.[69] The defense suffered its own setback in appealing the case to the Tennessee Supreme Court. The court said nothing about the constitutionality of the Butler Act and threw out Scopes's conviction on a technicality, so the ACLU no longer had a losing case to appeal to the U.S. Supreme Court. Moreover, the court extracted from the prosecution a promise not to pursue the case further. "No more baffling legal wet blanket could have been contrived to smother the famous case," observed one reporter.[70] Four decades were to pass before an antievolution case reached the U.S. Supreme Court.

Despite Bryan's death, the antievolution movement pressed ahead, mounting strong campaigns to ban the teaching of evolution in the following years. Although the example of the Scopes "circus" fight helped defeat antievolution proposals in North Carolina, Kentucky, Florida, and other states, Mississippi and Arkansas eventually passed bans on teaching evolution, and the governor of Texas, Miriam "Ma" Ferguson, ordered her state textbook board essentially to take a razor to the chapters in state texts that treated the descent of humans. Meanwhile, textbook publishers muffled their treatment of evolution, and the conservative evangelicals who opposed evolution gradually withdrew from public notice, even as they quietly built their own institutions—seminaries, churches, interdenominational fellowships, and others—outside the corrupting influence of the secular world and its apparent ally, theological liberalism.

In the late 1960s, evolutionists and creationists met again in the nation's court system. By then, the U.S. Supreme Court was in the habit of applying the First Amendment's establishment clause—the doctrine of church-state separation—directly to the states, and in a series of decisions

from 1968 onward, various courts rejected both obviously religious attempts to teach biblical creationism and the less blatant strategies that
invoked the relatively new concept of "scientific creationism." Despite set-
backs, creation science remained a powerful force, and it was joined in the
1990s by the movement to teach intelligent design (ID), which makes the
argument that certain elements of life and the universe are too complex to
be the result of purely material forces such as evolution; in this updated
version of Paley's natural theology, the complexity of the universe and significant unexplained gaps in the fossil record testify to the existence of
some sort of "designer" whose methods cannot be discerned through the
lens of scientific naturalism.

These transitions have not disrupted the strong continuities in American antievolutionism. Darwinism has highlighted conservative Protestantism's contested but still dominant position in American life. Although
scientific creationists occasionally claim the status of oppressed minority,
democratic majoritarianism still suffuses their arguments and their strategies. But Protestantism and the democratic tradition are only two of the
major forces determining evolution's reception. The third characteristic of
the American context is the nation's cultural diversity. Responding to foreign condemnations of American intolerance in 1925, the editor of *Outlook*, a prominent American periodical, bristled at the implication that
America was all of one piece regarding evolution or any other matter. "It
is as idle to draw conclusions concerning the whole country from what has
happened in Tennessee as it would be to draw conclusions concerning the
whole British Empire from some case in Canada or New Zealand," he
wrote.[71] The editor was thinking in terms of regions in the United States,
but he could have cut his distinctions more finely, for the antievolution
controversies have laid bare a multiplicity of divisions in American culture. Far from being one more battleground in a war between faith and
science, the fight over evolution in America has been a mirror, however
distorted, of the culture itself.

This project aims to trace those reflections, but it also examines the
active role that evolution has played in several cultural arenas. Evolution
has served as a weapon, as an enforcer of identity, as a rallying issue, and
as a polarizing force within and without the churches. In order to convey
this complexity, the book ranges across the last century roughly from the
Scopes trial to more recent controversies, but the interconnected studies
are structured more by theme than by strict chronology, and the careful
reader will note that major figures and events occasionally reappear in

different chapters, their multiple facets illuminated by light from a different direction.

Chapter 1 of this book locates one of the foundations for fundamentalism and antievolutionism in a crisis over gender and sex roles in the years before Scopes. The role of women in the antievolution controversies has seldom been discussed, but women as activists and as symbols have played an important part in the conflict, even as the first wave of fundamentalists and the more recent leaders of creation science have tried to disentangle their mission from the tendrils of a feminine, sentimentalized Christianity.

Chapter 2 looks at the geography of antievolutionism—particularly the ways in which a movement born in the urban North came to be associated with the American South, and the consequences of this shift. Antievolutionism threw into higher relief the continued cultural divisions between North and South and prompted many regional representatives to emphasize these differences in an attempt to define and clarify their own local identities. Northerners employed the image of rural southern intolerance to underline their own vision of the North—especially the urban North—as an embodiment of the spirit of enlightenment and progress. In response, many southerners, exemplified by the literary "neo-Confederates" who made up the "Fugitive-Agrarians," defended their region by equating it with true religiousness and by embracing mythical southern values as an antidote to the secular individualism of northern industrialism. In the process, they came close to proudly associating their regionalism with a willful anti-intellectualism—a connection that remains important in the modern antievolution impulse. The chapter explores the ways in which ruralism and the rise of suburban antievolutionism in recent times complicate these regional identifications, but offers the conclusion that the South remains a geographical stronghold of Darwin's detractors.

Related in part to the southern focus of chapter 2, chapter 3 analyzes the ways in which African Americans, most of whom in the 1920s still lived in the South, found that the question of evolution forced them to examine more carefully the character and future of the race. Race occasionally showed up in the Scopes trial itself, and African Americans were deeply interested in the issue and its implications. Antievolutionism exposed a deep gulf between conservative black piety—embodied at the extreme by self-proclaimed black fundamentalists—and a smaller group of intellectuals, including W. E. B. Du Bois, who linked the future of the race to the secular forces of scientific progress. Although the racial elements of the evolution dispute have become muted, evolution continues to highlight social conflicts within African America, and race in turn plays a regular rhetorical role in debates over Darwinism.

Chapter 4 first traces the strong continuities in antievolutionist ideology and then charts the strategic flexibility antievolutionists have developed in defending this vision. Discussions of antievolutionism focus, by definition, on the antievolutionists' defense of Genesis, but from the first decades of the twentieth century to the first decade of our own, their defense has been motivated primarily by their need to safeguard the full Christian narrative of fallen humanity and its redemption through Christ. Similarly, antagonism toward the theory of common descent has also run unbroken through the antievolution impulse over the last century. Creationist complaints that Darwin "made a monkey out of man" are not just rhetorical flourishes but expressions of a deep uneasiness over where evolution places humanity in the scheme of the universe. The final thematic continuity in antievolutionism has been a fear of social disorder, which first shocked William Jennings Bryan into action and continues, in a variety of guises, to propel modern antievolutionism. Opposition to evolution might not be the central concern of modern social conservatives engaged in the "culture wars," but it continues to serve political purposes for conservative evangelicals, as it reinforces the existing boundaries between their vision of a Christian America and a culture they see as degraded and overly secular—a culture in which the scientific naturalism embodied by Darwinism undermines the religious foundations of morality. This chapter also investigates the strategies antievolutionists have pursued against the Darwinian threat, with particular attention to their claims of scientific expertise. More recent versions of creationism have met limited success in the courts, legislatures, and schools and provoked ridicule in the broader culture, but they have achieved victories even in defeat, for such opposition bolsters creationists' conception of themselves as critics standing outside a degraded secular culture. At the same time, antievolutionists can claim identity with the majority of the population, for well over half of Americans profess belief in some form of divine creation for life—mostly through the procedure outlined in Genesis. Antievolutionists gesture toward such figures as proof that conservative evangelicals are, in fact, an embattled majority in a culture that has been hijacked by the forces of scientific naturalism. Ranged against them is a small but powerful cabal of scientists, judges, and liberal elites who seek to foist upon the nation evolution and its secularist hatchlings—abortion, crime, homosexuality, and other social ills.

Militant creationists of the late twentieth and early twenty-first centuries have achieved much success in narrowing the grounds for accommodation between religion and science, to the point that many Americans believe one must choose definitively between evolution and Christianity, but creationists have not always been able to translate this progress into tangible victories in the nation's classrooms. They have oversold the dangers that evolution poses to young people, and despite their superior numbers, they have run into spirited opposition not only from the so-called elitist cabal but also from ordinary parents, business leaders, and even their fellow evangelicals.

Chapter 5 explores with several leading activists and scientists, including a number of avowedly evangelical scientists, the impact the antievolution crusade has made on their teaching, their research, and their sense of civic engagement. Here, as elsewhere in the book, evolution illuminates cultural tensions that already existed, and it has also played a dynamic role in widening the divisions. Darwinism did not come to America so much as it came to a fragmented collection of Americas, each with its own unique developmental path.

I

Monkeys and Mothers

GENDER AND THE ANTIEVOLUTION IMPULSE

REPRESENTATIVE JOHN W. Butler offered a straightforward explanation for why he had introduced his law against teaching evolution in the public schools of Tennessee: "As a little boy I was taught by my mother to believe in the Bible."[1] During the debate over the bill, the Speaker of the Tennessee state senate, Lew D. Hill, proclaimed he had been petitioned to support the bill by "the women of the state and the teachers association." The bill was, he continued, a last stand for Christianity, civilization, and motherhood.[2] Another senator poignantly gestured toward a mother in the gallery "whose son had been made a confirmed infidel by having been taught evolution in a high school."[3] Letters to the newspapers in favor of the Butler bill were almost always sent by women, while letters against the law tended to come from men. As Mrs. E. P. Blair of Nashville proclaimed in a poem supporting the Butler bill, the fight against evolution was being waged "for country, God and mother's song."[4]

This "mother's song" was hard to ignore. In 1925 and afterward, women played important roles in the antievolution controversy, both as symbols and as flesh-and-blood activists, and they were not divided on the issue. Although male leaders such as William Jennings Bryan and T. T. Martin were more prominent, one editorialist estimated in 1925 that 70 percent of the antievolutionists were women.[5] Further, the male fundamentalists' involvement was entangled with their relations to women and gender roles. Questions about masculinity and negotiations over the new world of gender relations in the early twentieth century were surprisingly significant forces in bringing about the Scopes trial. Evolution continued for the rest of the century to shine a light on the mismatches and complexities that characterized the collision between an aggressively traditionalist antievolution impulse and a culture undergoing rapid changes in its social and sexual organization.

Changes in women's societal roles fed into the antievolution controversy. Most obviously, women came to participate more directly in politics, and they generally ranged themselves on the side of conservative morality. Further, women played indirect roles in pushing Christian men into fighting Darwinism as a way of solidifying their masculine identity. At the same time, antievolutionism called forth opponents—exemplified by the Scopes defense team—who aimed to liberate society from what they considered an outmoded Victorian maternalism. These gender negotiations were to remain important in the antievolution controversies and in conservative Christianity in the century that followed the clash in Tennessee.

The jostling over the Butler bill was not an anomaly but rather an episode in women's continuing involvement in American religion and politics. While they were barred from most pulpits and nearly all elected offices, many women in the nineteenth century fashioned themselves as active agents of morality. Held up in the popular culture as inherently virtuous, white middle-class women pursued their mission of maintaining domestic morality by passing on to their children the lessons of the Bible and by reining in what was commonly considered to be their husbands' innate tendencies toward greed and vice in an untrammeled free market.[6] Women also proved adept at redirecting this domestic mission toward church work at levels below the ministry and toward local levels of political activity. Nevertheless, the white middle-class ideal presented a clear division of labor: for men, the public world of work and politics; for women, the domestic world of maternity and morality.[7]

Toward the latter decades of the century, however, women begin to trespass more openly on the male public domain. Secure already in their church work, female activists increasingly wielded their moral authority to carve out a larger place for themselves in politics. But they did not simply throw themselves into the hurly-burly of masculine party politics. Rather, beyond fighting for suffrage itself, these Victorian reformers directed their political energy toward goals that were consistent with their traditional roles as conservators of the home and family. The struggle against prostitution, campaigns to secure child protection laws, and, above all, the crusade against the saloon embodied this feminine politics of home protection. The Woman's Christian Temperance Union (WCTU), founded in 1874, became the largest women's political organization of the century.

Before women earned the national right to vote in 1920, their political activity usually took the form of pressure on male politicians through organizations such as the WCTU; sometimes the activity came from the small number of women who had won political office, and sometimes the activity took place at the ballot box in localities and states that already allowed female suffrage. In either case, observers were confident that the female vote was a vote for moral reform. After Illinois granted women suffrage in 1913, female voters played a major part in voting twenty-two Illinois counties entirely dry. Various towns and counties in the state saw women vote against the liquor trade in overwhelming percentages: in Galesburg, 90 percent of the women's vote was dry; Atlanta registered 96 percent dry. Ella Seass Stewart, a suffragist, temperance advocate, and political scientist, noted with pride, "In Virginia, a county seat town, not a single woman's vote was cast for the saloon."[8] The results prompted Stewart to observe that "the forces of evil" in the liquor trade had good reason to fear the women's vote.[9]

Female voting was not quite as monolithic as Stewart reported. Women could be found on both sides of the temperance and suffrage movements.[10] Fewer women than expected voted after the Nineteenth Amendment was passed, and some reporters accused those who did vote of casting their ballots in 1920 for Warren Harding because he was handsome. Most observers, however, agreed with Stewart's evaluation that women would vote for moral reform. They would vote as "citizen mothers" and as avatars of Protestant Christianity.[11] Indeed, women's political pressure proved crucial in the passage of such acts as the Sheppard-Towner maternity and infancy protection law in 1921 and a series of measures to defend and enforce the Prohibition amendment.[12] Even if the "woman vote" did not usher in the new millennium, it could not be ignored.

By itself, this new political empowerment would not have become part of the crusade against evolution, but in conjunction with what many historians have labeled a "gender crisis" among white Protestants, the specter or the reality of this new voting bloc was to play an important part in Tennessee's dalliance with antievolutionism. The path that led from the gender crisis to the antievolution movement was a crooked one. It began with the ways in which the dangers of effeminacy bolstered the development of fundamentalism. At the same time as women were emerging as political actors in the early twentieth century, women's changing roles also contributed to what many men feared was the increasing "feminization" of middle-class culture.[13] The turn of the century marked a vulnerable moment.

The older ideal of the independent male producer was being eroded by a series of economic shocks, such as the depressions of 1873 and 1893; in both North and South, the man's central identity as breadwinner and protector of the family was being threatened by forces beyond his control and even his comprehension. The rise of factory work and industrial dependency further eroded the sense of manly independence. Even men who made successful transitions to the new economy, such as clerks, accountants, and salesmen, could be troubled on some level by the lack of solidity in their work.

This new economic world offered middle-class white men mixed compensations. They had new opportunities for leisure and consumption, for example, but these were realms of activity that, like religion, had long been considered feminine. Physicians and other observers at the dawn of the twentieth century believed that these cultural changes went so deep that they affected male bodies as well. Doctors began to diagnose American men—especially men from the upper and middle classes—as suffering from a variety of physical disorders that undermined their masculinity: "neurasthenia," or nervous exhaustion, was a diagnosis that doctors had usually assigned to women, but now they increasingly diagnosed modern men as neurasthenics whose vitality was being sapped by modern conditions. Similarly, complaints about "overcivilization" highlighted the growing sense that middle-class white men could no longer find proper outlets for their natural impulses toward physical activity and aggression; sometimes the term was simply a code word for creeping effeminacy. In the worst-case scenario, many white middle-class men suspected that they were in danger of becoming like women.

The threat of feminization generated a wide range of secular responses. For example, the sudden popularity at the turn of the century of bodybuilding, college football, and boxing testified to the broad search for masculine pursuits, as did a novel romanticization of working-class toughness.[14] Teddy Roosevelt's emphasis on the "strenuous life" was tightly bound up with this broader cultural concern about the feminization of American life, especially among the "better classes." For Roosevelt, hunting, imperialism, and a preoccupation with "virility" were necessary demonstrations of manliness in the face of an emasculating civilization.[15] Even Roosevelt's temperamental opposite, the philosopher William James, responded to the threat of overcivilization with his much-misinterpreted call for the "moral equivalent of war."[16] The phrase meant, in James's original formulation, a *moral* outlet for the natural human impulse toward aggression and not, as many use it, a designation for something that is just as immoral as war; that is, the anti-imperialist James sought to replace war and violence with benign outlets that would be their equivalent in masculine strenuousness, such as conservation or civic activism. Whatever forms their reaction took, many white men at the dawn of the twentieth century shared a deep concern about escaping the snares of a feminized, overcivilized culture.[17]

Religious men were perhaps particularly sensitive to suggestions that they were less "manly" than they should be. Their tenuous relation to masculinity had for decades been imperiled by women's prominence in church work. Women in America have always attended church more often than men, and usually with deeper commitment. From the creation of the Puritan colonies to the recent rise of megachurches, women have consistently made up 60 to 70 percent of the churchgoing population.[18] Ignoring the longer history of this ratio, R. W. Conant, a Chicago author, suggested in 1904 that the imbalance was an alarming recent trend, a development so clear that one did not even need statistics to be convinced. "Any one can easily verify the statement himself in any congregation," he observed. "The women in attendance always outnumber the men, often by several hundred percent." Further, Conant noted, many of the men attended "merely to please women or children in whom they are interested."[19] The reason for this imbalance, he believed, was "so obvious it seems to escape observation—the Feminizing of Christianity." This feminization was not merely a matter of demographics but was bound up in the dominant messages of modern Christianity. "When you stop to think of it," he wrote, "what is there in the personality of Christ, as usually presented, to attract the interest or inspire the enthusiasm of hard-headed, practical men?"[20] Conant was a very middling author—published, but not particularly original and not well known outside of Chicago. His views were well in keeping with the thought of the time, for though male Protestant leaders had for decades been aware of the significant role women played in the church, only toward the turn of the twentieth century did they begin seriously to fear that this gender imbalance affected their own identities and reputations.

To defend their character as men in a society that valued manhood so highly, Protestant leaders pursued two strategies, both of which became key components of fundamentalism. First, these men emphasized the masculinity of Jesus and, by extension, his male followers and church work in general. One expression of this desire to take the churches back for men had roots in the English movement for "muscular Christianity," which flowered in the United States as a movement to unite sports and Christianity.[21] Another was the Men and Religion Forward Movement of 1911–12. Under the motto "More Men for Religion, More Religion for Men," this primarily Protestant association excluded women from membership and focused its popular revivals on developing a masculine image for men in the church.[22] More than a million people attended the revivals, and the organization found strong support from such groups as the Young Men's Christian Association (YMCA), the Gideons, and a variety of other middle-class male associations. Despite this support, the Men and Religion Forward Movement was a short-lived crusade—probably because its leaders barred the very women who would have done so much of the organization's work. The impulse behind the movement, though, took other, more durable forms.

The early twentieth century witnessed a spate of books and articles that proclaimed the message that Jesus himself was a manly Messiah.[23] Even one of the foremost theological liberals, Harry Emerson Fosdick, felt compelled to pen a book, *The Manhood of the Master*, that discounted the sentimental images of Jesus as a "pale Galilean," a meek sacrificial lamb, in favor of a joyful Jesus, a Messiah of vigor and strong personal character.[24] Fosdick's Jesus was a man whose activity against the moneychangers in the temple, as recounted in John 2:13–17, was meant to inspire young men to enter active lives of civic and political reform against "the corruption of our city governments and the spoiling of our great democracy by graft."[25] It was no coincidence that Fosdick's book grew out of a series of lectures to young men in the YMCA.

In 1925, an advertising executive named Bruce Barton updated Fosdick's ideas in his best-selling book *The Man Nobody Knows*.[26] Like Fosdick and Conant before him, Barton rejected the common portrayal of Jesus "a pale young man with flabby forearms and a sad expression," preferring instead to underline Jesus' position as "the founder of modern business" and a true man's man. But where the progressive Fosdick drew on John 2:13–17 to emphasize Jesus' righteous anger against "legalized graft in God's temple," Barton cited the passage to emphasize Jesus' physical power: "Physical weakling! Where did they get that idea?" he asked. "Jesus pushed a plane and swung an adze. . . . His muscles were so strong that when he drove the money-changers out, nobody dared to oppose him!" Although Barton, as a business booster, was probably distressed on some level by Jesus' attack on the ancient banking system, he was nevertheless deeply impressed by the Messiah's toughness and hard-headedness. Not only was Jesus strong enough to clean out the temple, but he also had the power and vision to have "picked up twelve men from the bottom ranks of business and forged them into an organization that conquered the world." Church work was not so very different from the male world of business after all. The religious historian R. Laurence Moore sums up the central message of this literature: "Jesus was no sissy."[27]

In addition to emphasizing Jesus' manliness, several Protestant leaders pursued a second strategy to "rescue" Christianity from the dangers of effeminacy: they stressed the creedal aspects of Protestantism. Christianity, they implied, was not a sentimental religion of the heart, with its feminine associations, but rather a masculine religion of the head.[28] The publication from 1910 to 1915 of *The Fundamentals*, which played such a central role in the development of antievolutionism, was a watershed in this movement toward doctrinal purity. While the threat of feminization was not the sole or even the dominant factor in the development of fundamentalism's conservative shibboleths, the new emphasis on doctrine contrasted with the "feminine" Christianity that was stereotyped as overly emotional and sentimental. The concern for doctrinal purity and the conservative impulse to remasculinize Christianity made congenial bedfellows.

In comparison to this more doctrinal approach to religion, the few denominations that allowed women to take leadership roles tended to be unconventional sects more concerned with the experiential aspects of Christianity. Alma White, for example, in 1918 became the first female bishop in the United States in the little-known sect she had largely created, the Pillar of Fire, which was an offshoot of the Wesleyan/Holiness tradition.[29]

More influentially, Ellen G. White (no relation) became a major figure in Seventh-day Adventism, which distinguished itself with a novel theology as well as its better-known preoccupation with the digestive system's baneful influence on the sexual impulse. White's "visions" from God and her many publications eventually became central to the faith.[30] Her prophetic visions were officially subordinate to the Bible, but the indefatigable prophetess was the unquestioned guiding spirit of her sect. She could never have achieved such a position of leadership in even the most liberal of mainline denominations. In this rival sect, however, White's sex did not present an obstacle. Nor did it preclude her from opposing evolution; adding complexity to the story of gender and antievolution, White was actually the godmother of scientific creationism, which grew directly out of the sect's doctrines that God created the universe in six days of twenty-four hours apiece, exactly as Genesis reports.

Representing in some ways a modernization for the 1920s of Ellen White's position, "Sister" Aimee Semple McPherson's Pentecostal Church of the Foursquare Gospel also offered a combination of female leadership and experiential Christianity. Although she certainly was a doctrinal fundamentalist and fought vigorously against modernist theology, McPherson focused her ministry far more on receiving the gifts of the Holy Spirit than on the intellectual business of defending the "fundamentals" of the faith. In truth, McPherson devoted at least as much energy to putting on a good show for her Los Angeles congregants, who turned out year after year for McPherson's stationary revival at Angelus Temple. "Her Sunday evening service is a complete vaudeville program, entirely new each week," explained Sarah Comstock, a reporter for *Harper's Monthly Magazine*.[31] According to Comstock, McPherson's sermons were suffused with "the type of sentimentalism styled as 'sob sister' . . . a mass of commonplaces, melodrama, tawdriness, and cheap emotionalism."[32] Behind the scenes, Sister was an iron-willed leader—star, director, and executive producer—but for public consumption the self-proclaimed "world's most pulchritudinous evangelist" emphasized more conventionally feminine qualities. Her message was very much within the tradition of Victorian sentimentality, one that many conservative male Protestant leaders were eager to escape.[33] Fundamentalism helped provide them an exit.

Thus in the 1910s and 1920s the masculine "Christianity of the intellect" converged with the more obvious reaction to the gender crisis—the emphasis on manly Christian vigor. Together, they fostered the combative style that was to distinguish fundamentalism from its equally conservative variants. The combative style would also, not coincidentally, distance fundamentalism from the potentially effeminate taint of church work.[34]

Although in many ways sui generis, the career of J. Franklyn Norris epitomized this new, aggressive strain of Christianity. Born in Alabama in 1877 and later converted at a Baptist revival, Norris became the most notorious fundamentalist of his time. Indicted for burning down his own church and blaming it on his enemies, and acquitted for shooting a man dead, Norris saved his real firepower for doctrinal controversies. From his pulpit at the First Baptist Church in Fort Worth, Texas, Norris thundered against liberal ministers who believed in modernism and evolution. When he faced the problem that such heretics were in short supply in the conservative South, his biographer explains, Norris "in effect created his own enemies by portraying himself as the defender of orthodoxy and everyone who opposed him personally as an enemy of the faith."[35] Often these "enemies" were Norris's fellow Southern Baptist ministers, men he found insufferable or guilty of differing with him over a point of Baptist doctrine. Like many other conservative Protestants, Norris was tortured by the fact that a "plain reading" of the Bible occasionally led some Christians to believe erroneously that the Book said something at odds with his own rigid interpretation. At other times, Norris simply railed against unnamed (and probably nonexistent) modernists who were loose in the region. When he did dredge up a flesh-and-blood opponent, Norris attacked with extravagantly violent rhetoric, and he pressured churches and universities—even conservative Baylor University—to fire anyone he suspected of modernist or Darwinian sympathies. Norris was not above hiring detectives to trail and investigate his opponents.[36]

Norris's close ally John Clover Monsma excused Norris's pugnacity by comparing him favorably to a true picture of Jesus—not the Jesus painted as the "feminine type of the old Italian school," but the Jesus who was "a real he-man, as they say on the streets, a man robust and strong, fearless in his whole demeanor."[37] Norris, like the "true Jesus," was no sissy. His own daughter called him "a dictator," but in his combination of masculine aggressiveness and narrow orthodoxy, he was also the wave of the fundamentalist future.[38]

The preacher with the fewest worries about his own manhood was probably Billy Sunday. A former major-league baseball player turned revivalist, Sunday combined a straightforward defense of the fundamentals with aggressive rhetoric and an athletic virility in the pulpit.[39] He jumped on tables, shook his fists, and shouted down the threats to America and Christianity in huge revivals across the nation. One of his well-known stunts was to knock on the floor to invite Satan up for a fight. As one reporter described the result:

> Billy admits his own fearlessness and when the bid to Beelzebub is not accepted the audience shares with the champion the delight and conquering pose. Cheers ring for the tower of physical strength and spiritual righteousness whom the Boss of Hell dares not meet in combat.[40]

His biographer estimates that such antics allowed Sunday to convert one million Americans in the course of more than three hundred revivals.[41] Billy Sunday was no intellectual, and defiant about it; he claimed proudly that he didn't "know any more about theology than a jack-rabbit knew about ping-pong."[42] But he knew evolution was wrong.

William Jennings Bryan was in many ways the exception that proved the fundamentalist rule. Although he often cooperated with fundamentalists such as Norris and Sunday, Bryan "usually took a warmer, even maternal approach to moral reform," according to one biographer.[43] Bryan's frustration during the Scopes trial eventually boiled over into fist-shaking vitriol, as when he denounced Darrow as "the greatest atheist or agnostic in the world," but his rhetoric, even on the subject of evolution, was notably more temperate than the language used by his fire-breathing allies. Further, Bryan openly acknowledged his reliance on his wife, Mary, and had for decades cooperated with women's groups in the campaigns for temperance, suffrage, and other reforms.[44] The Great Commoner seemed untroubled by the gender crisis. Norris, for his part, occasionally found Bryan to be insufficiently aggressive, and fired off letters urging his fellow fundamentalist to join the fray with greater vigor.

In light of this concern with manliness among the early fundamentalists, it was ironic that their greatest public crusade was to come in the traditionally female mission of protecting the home. Tellingly, home protection was not antievolutionists' initial focus. At first, the men who were to earn the label of "fundamentalist" concentrated on the narrower goal of purifying the denominations. Norris, Bryan, and their most committed allies, including Minnesota's William Bell Riley, attempted to make a public confession of belief in the fundamentals and rejection of evolution a condition for ordination and employment in the Presbyterian and Baptist faiths. These were bitter struggles. In the 1923 Presbyterian General Assembly, for example, Bryan sought to be elected moderator, a position that would allow him the opportunity to purge the seminaries of theological liberals, especially evolutionists. The Presbyterian election ended in yet another political defeat for the Great Commoner, but like his other losses, it did not deter Bryan from continuing the struggle. On the contrary, Bryan and his allies began to push their crusade beyond the boundaries of the denominations.

As with the earlier reaction against the feminization of religion, gender played an important role in galvanizing conservative Protestants into wider action in the 1920s. Indeed, the historian Betty A. DeBerg maintains that female threats to the Victorian patriarchal order were more important than theological disputes in creating the fundamentalist movement. DeBerg's exhaustive reading of fundamentalist newspapers and periodicals has at the very least unearthed an obsession with the upheaval in gender roles at the turn of the twentieth century; the fear of female emancipation through work, activism, and sexuality intensified greatly over the following decades as young women, in particular, shook off the bonds of Victorian gender roles. This crisis in sex roles and sexual morality propelled thousands into the fundamentalist fold. In DeBerg's view, fundamentalists did not "discover" a moral crisis among youth; rather, the moral crisis itself first breathed life into the fundamentalist movement.[45]

Whereas the first stage of fundamentalist activity primarily involved the churches, the rapid transformation of American culture, especially changes in the behavior of young women during and after the Great War, prompted conservative evangelicals to turn their attention to the purification of American society.[46] Religious leaders found much to worry about. The notorious flapper of the 1920s flaunted her lipstick and rouge, and often coupled these accessories with overtly sexual attire, including blouses that exposed naked arms and a hint of clavicle, and hemlines that soared up almost to the bottom of the knees.[47] Not surprisingly, young women who were willing to expose themselves in such a manner also seemed to engage in more overtly sexual activities, such as dancing or "parking." Flapperism was not limited to colleges and big cities. Even the young women of Dayton, including the daughters of the judge in the Scopes trial, sported the more openly sexual dresses favored by flappers, and rolled their stockings in the approved "daring" manner.

FIGURE 1.1 Some young women in Dayton came down squarely on the side of the monkeys. Image courtesy of Bryan College.

As observers cast about for the causes of this moral anarchy, some identified women's suffrage as the culprit; others blamed the Great War itself, the automobile, or Sigmund Freud. Many conservative evangelicals eventually settled on evolution as the main culprit.[48] They tended to lump evolution together with the other depredations of the era: theological modernism, German militarism, and the more obvious sexual sins. Fundamentalists argued that evolution was at some level responsible for all of these moral offenses. By sapping popular belief in the truth of the Bible, it threatened the only reliable foundation of morality, while reducing humans to the level of amoral animals. No wonder sexual morality was receding at the same time as Darwinism was flooding the nation. But this perceived connection, by itself, might not have been sufficient to raise a public controversy over evolution. It was one thing to purge the seminaries of modernists and evolutionists; it was quite another to awaken the broader public to the Darwinian threat.

Fundamentalists finally made the transition to public activism when they discovered that a connection between evolution and America's declining morals ran right through the public schoolhouse. It was here that American youth were learning what Billy Sunday called "that God-forsaken, hell-born, bastard theory of evolution"; it was here that young people were losing the faith their mothers and fathers had bequeathed to them.[49] And it was here that the antievolution movement discovered the power of the nation's mothers as activists and as symbols.

Antievolutionists therefore shifted the battleground from the churches to the public schools. "The teaching of Evolution," complained the evangelist T. T. Martin in his tract *Hell and the High Schools*, "is being drilled into our boys and girls in our High Schools during the most susceptible, dangerous age of their lives."[50] For the sake of their children and their faith, antievolutionists drew a line at the schoolhouse door.

Teaching Darwin in the high schools had hardly been a public issue in the late nineteenth century, when each year only about two hundred thousand youth, or less than 5 percent of high-school-age children, attended secondary school. By 1920, however, attendance had shot up to nearly two million students per year, making the public schools an institution of great political and social concern.[51] Intense public controversies broke out over such topics as sex education, teacher radicalism, and the patriotism of history textbooks, as the content of the curriculum affected so many more children and their families.[52] The proliferation of public schools similarly brought thousands of "impressionable" high school students into contact with evolutionary science for the first time, alarming many parents and religious conservatives. Thus, when fundamentalists around 1922 made eradicating evolution in the schools their central theme, many Americans were ready to listen

The antievolution campaign fit well with the maternal ideal. Although they tended to hold traditional values about a woman's place in the home and society, antievolution women claimed the right to participate in this public crusade because evolutionary teaching affected children, and rearing the next generation was primarily a mother's responsibility. Indeed, the Victorian tradition particularly idealized the mother's role as caretaker of her children's moral and religious development. Female antievolutionists repeatedly referred to their status as mothers and lamented that evolutionary teaching interfered with their right to bring up their children "on the Bible," as one Nashville mother put it.[53] Mrs. E. P. Blair noted in the *Nashville Tennessean* that she and other mothers had long been distressed by children learning in school that evolutionary science had proven the Bible wrong. "What are mothers to do," Blair asked, "when unwise education makes boys lose confidence in the home, the bible, the government and all law?" The Butler Act, she hoped, would prevent this "unwise education" from "acting as a wedge" between children and mothers, and between Americans and their "moral and spiritual" values.[54]

As the school system mushroomed into a central institution in American society, tension between mothers and schools became unavoidable. In many localities, especially in the South, the teaching of evolution only increased this strain. But women in Tennessee and elsewhere sought to ease the tension by transforming the schools into allies rather than competitors. Once the Butler Act expelled evolution from the classroom, the schools could again become instruments of traditional morality. Mandatory school prayer and instruction in temperance, for example, were far more proper subjects for students than was evolution.[55] Although women could be found on both sides of the temperance movement that preceded it, antievolutionism was more clearly a female-dominated reform movement that enlisted the state as an extension of maternal influence.

Antievolution strategists in Tennessee, not surprisingly, relied heavily on women. In letters to newspapers and legislators, women publicized the dangers evolution posed to a Christian home life, and they complained that evolution threatened their own status as arbiters of morality. Always the specter of their political power loomed in the background. Many of the legislators, and certainly Governor Austin Peay, were privately tepid toward the Butler Act, but they were more uneasy about what outright opposition might do to their political careers. "Women have not extensively availed themselves of the right to vote," explained Rollin Lynde Hartt in the *Nation.* "But politicians know that on one issue appearing to involve a defense of Christianity, so called, against atheism, so called, the threat to 'get out the woman vote' may well be taken seriously."[56] Further, Hartt noted, politicians had before them the example of women's influence through the Anti-Saloon League and other temperance organizations: when unable to exercise their power at the ballot box, women proved they had learned very well the lesson of "coercing the men already in office."[57] For his part, Governor Peay needed the support of the "church people" in order to pass his ambitious plan for modernizing Tennessee's educational system, so he could take no chances with the female voter, however nebulous she might turn out to be.[58]

Peay's gambit paid off. Even as they became the targets of mockery from all over the country, Peay and the legislators reaped praise from many of their female constituents. For example, Mrs. Jesse Sparks, from the small town of Pope, Tennessee, applauded the legislators' action. "I for one felt grateful for their standing for the right against all criticism," she wrote, "and grateful, too, that we have a Christian man for governor who will defend the Word of God against this so-called science."[59] With help from "church people" such as Mrs. Sparks, the legislature duly passed Peay's school bill, and women's support for the governor and the Butler Act only grew as the Scopes trial progressed.

While the fundamentalists and the Tennessee legislators were generally ridiculed throughout the Scopes controversy, the involvement of Tennessee's women and mothers called forth opposition that focused particularly on the role of their sex in the struggle. "The whole Dayton episode would be a subject for mirth," opined one C.D.H. in the New York *World*, "were it not for the fact that the Nineteenth Amendment has added so many to the electorate who are intensely controlled by their emotions and sentiments. Sensible people must keep their eyes open and be ready to meet this danger."[60]

More enlightened than C.D.H., the defense attorneys did not attack actual antievolutionist women so much as they participated in what one historian has called the decade's "symbolic matricide."[61] Rather than insulting mothers directly, Dudley Field Malone at first attempted to enlist the symbols of motherhood on the side of Scopes's defense. Malone, a prominent divorce lawyer, took the common antievolutionist argument that schools were interfering with mothers' right to rear their children and turned it on its head: "The women of America," Malone intoned, "can take care of the morals of their children without the help of Mr. Bryan or state legislatures."[62] The defense went further and attempted more broadly to undermine the Victorian tradition of maternalistic reform. Scopes's team thus joined with the cultural rebels of the 1920s—including Malone's wife, the prominent feminist Doris Stevens—in attacking the moral ideals represented by their stereotype of the Victorian matriarch: gentility, religious sentimentality, and the kind of busybody reformism that had pushed Prohibition into the Constitution. Contrary to what reformers believed, young people did not need to be "protected"—not by their mothers, and certainly not by a maternalistic state government. "The trouble with Mr. Bryan," Malone maintained, "is that he has not the confidence in the young people that I have. . . . Mr. Bryan thinks they're all going to hell unless he does something about it."[63] Not surprisingly, Malone found that many members of the self-aware "Younger Generation" agreed with his analysis. "Is independence a crime?" asked Regina Malone (no relation), a writer in her early twenties. "Logically, an age of freedom always follows a period of artificiality and repression. . . . Is not this independence of our Youth of today little more than a swing of pendulum from Victorianism, with its laughable prudery and absurd conventions, to an ultra-sophisticated and brutally frank age of Modernism?"[64] The two Malones expressed their faith that the rising generation would be able to pick its way between these two extremes without constantly being "mothered," if only they were given access to the knowledge they needed. Perhaps the antievolutionists were right: the modern era, with its glorification of science, education, and individualism, did threaten to tear children away from the shelter of maternalism.

Not surprisingly, women and mothers did not disappear from either antievolutionism or fundamentalism, even as both of these movements entered a decades-long period of public anonymity a few years after the Scopes trial ended. The retreat from public view allowed many observers, especially in the North, to believe that the conflict in Dayton had vanquished the antievolution movement and, with it, its female supporters. The antievolution impulse, however, never died out, and it continued to be associated with feminine values and occasionally with actual women. Aimee Semple McPherson, for one, led a huge rally in support of her friend Bryan's efforts in Dayton and pressed hard in 1926 for California's

Proposition 17, which would have required Bible readings in the public schools, with the clear intent to push evolution out.[65] McPherson's influence was limited, however, because she was in the midst of a sensational scandal in which she seemed to have staged her own kidnapping in order to cover up a romantic tryst. Proposition 17 qualified for the ballot but failed in the general election. A follow-up effort to pass a law based on the Butler Act went nowhere, despite McPherson's support. McPherson did continue to oppose evolution publicly, with an enthusiasm that grew out of her own youthful crisis of faith when she first contended with the implications of Darwinism.[66] Evolution never became a major issue for her, though, and her pronouncements on the subject were mostly warmed-over themes derived from antievolutionists more in the "doctrinal" stream of fundamentalism.[67] Whether her motivation came from a determination to shield the next generation from the doubts she had once entertained or from her enduring instinct for showmanship, McPherson occasionally squared off against evolutionists in public venues. Her notes for one debate explained "that a gossipy woman can make a story from a word, a look, or imagination."

> BUT BEHOLD THE EVOLUTIONISTS! They have taken
> 1. a rag
> 2. a bone
> 3. a hank of hair, so to speak
> AND HAVE MADE FOR US AN ANCESTOR.
> They don't call it gossip.
> They don't call it imagination.
> [THEY] CALL IT BY [THE] DIGNIFIED TITLE OF "PALEONTOLOGY."[68]

Based on such flimsy evidence, she lamented, evolutionists would have Christians give up their Bibles and accept the implications of Darwinism, including the thesis that man sprang from a "ghastly grimacing gorilla" rather than from the "HAND OF GOD, a creature of the holy eternal creator." The implications went further yet. Accept evolution, Sister said, and thereby accept that there will be:

> No more Easter.
> No more Thanksgiving.
> No more church choirs.
> No more sacred music.

Like other antievolutionists, McPherson protested spending taxpayers' money to support the teaching of such an irreligious theory; further, she argued that evolution was "not conducive to good American citizenship." Although Sister continued to fight the good fight against evolution from her position at the head of the Church of the Foursquare Gospel, her leadership role in her church continued to be the exception rather than the rule for women throughout American Christianity, and especially in the conservative denominations that hewed closely to a literal interpretation of the Bible's strictures against female leadership, such as the Southern Baptists.

Nevertheless, as fundamentalist institutions proliferated after the 1920s, fundamentalism was sometimes more open to female participation than was mainstream Protestantism. Many women flocked to fundamentalist teaching institutes, including McPherson's own LIFE Bible College. Although generally barred from the pulpit itself, they often took up positions in the middling ranks of missionary work and teaching, and they continued their tradition of keeping the religious organizations running on a day-to-day basis.[69]

Thus, when the antievolution impulse reignited in the 1960s, it was not surprising to see women involved. Women continued to act as foot soldiers for antievolution, and women continue to profess significantly greater hostility toward evolution. In one of the few opinion polls that tracked responses by gender, a 2005 Kansas survey that asked whether evolution should be taught in the public schools found that 74 percent of men answered yes, while only 58 percent of women did so. Asked whether it was "possible to believe in both God and evolution," 73 percent of men agreed, while 57 percent of women answered in the affirmative.[70] The size of the gender gap rivals the difference similar surveys have found between college graduates and Americans with high school degrees or less.

The modern creationist movement owes its existence in part to two women, Nell J. Segraves and Jean E. Sumrall. Segraves was a conservative Baptist mother from southern California, and like so many conservative activists in that seedbed of the New Right, she sprang into action because of what her children were learning in the public schools. For many of the newly awakened conservatives, sex education was the schools' primary offense. For Segraves, the problem was evolution.[71] With her friend Sumrall, a Missouri Synod Lutheran and dedicated creationist, Segraves helped pioneer the strategy of demanding "equal time" in the public schools for what came to be called "creation science."[72] She allied for a time with Henry Morris to create the Creation-Science Research Center (CSRC) until Morris split off to found his own Institute for Creation Research (ICR), which was to become the leading organization for scientific creationism.[73]

Although Segraves and Sumrall were exceptions to the rule that creationism's modern leaders were men, gender continued to play a critical role in the antievolution movement from the 1970s onward. This element was underscored, in particular, by creationism's alliance with the New Right. While the antifeminist crusader Phyllis Schlafly and such groups as Beverly LaHaye's Concerned Women for America (CWA) focused their attention primarily on sexual issues—the dangers of homosexuality, in particular, but also feminism, pornography, abortion, and sex education—they made room for evolution on their list of threats to American culture. As the CWA explained in 2002, "Evolutionary thought has shaped our Western conscience. Abortion, pornography and homosexual behavior would not be rampant had we not dismissed the truth of our origins."[74] Only by diminishing Darwin's influence would American culture restore sexual relations to their traditional order—sexual impulses confined to heterosexual marriage, men and women fulfilling complementary but separate social roles, and popular culture reinforcing these values. Creationists have occasionally chafed at what they see as the New Right's underemphasis on evolution, but these movements' shared commitment to conservative evangelical Christianity and traditional sexual values has generally reduced this friction.[75]

Nevertheless, in some ways the antievolution movement has diverged from the New Right's treatment of gender. As creationism has grown more "scientific," it has become in certain ways less receptive to female participation. Despite the early contributions of Segraves and Sumrall, women are largely missing from the leadership of modern creationism. According to the Answers in Genesis (AIG) website, the "most prominent woman in creation science" is probably Margaret Helder, a Canadian botanist who is also, the website adds, "a mother of six."[76] Helder has published in a number of creationist organs and has served as vice president of the Creation Science Association of Alberta, Canada, but she seems to have few American counterparts outside of AIG's Kelly Hollowell and Georgia Purdom. Developments in the American creationist movement have not changed that dynamic. While women continue to participate actively in the most recent antievolution struggles, they do not lead them.

As Eugenie Scott, one of creationism's major public opponents, observes, "Antievolution is very much an old boys' club, and an old white boys' club at that."[77]

Further, women as symbols have largely faded from the public rhetoric of antievolution. This change began in the 1960s with the rise of scientific creationism and has reached its apogee in the intelligent design movement. Despite the contributions of Segraves and Sumrall, as creationists increasingly portrayed their movement as challenging evolution on purely scientific grounds, they were no longer as free to employ the powerful imagery of motherhood and children, at least in public or legal settings. Where once the antievolutionists waved the flag of "country, God, and mother's song," their modern heirs present disquisitions on flood geology and the wily flagellum. The development was perhaps symbolized by Morris's relief when his departure from Segraves's CSRC allowed him to place much greater emphasis on scientific rigor and scientific leadership in the ICR.

In private antievolution circles, women as activists and as symbols have remained an important force, but for public consumption the modern creation science movement has dropped the ideal of maternalism as thoroughly as Scopes's defenders ever could have hoped. For a movement that has roots both in the reaction against effeminization and in the defense of motherhood, the meaning of this development is properly tangled.

2

Regionalism and the Antievolution Impulse

REFLECTING BACK ON the Scopes trial half a year afterward, the fundamentalist minister John Roach Straton still marveled at the "colossal vanity" that had impelled men from the vice-ridden, irreligious cities of the North to "invade" the South, a land "where women are still honored, where men are still chivalric, where laws are still respected, where home life is still sweet." As Straton saw matters: "A group of outside agnostics, atheists, Unitarian preachers, skeptical scientists and political revolutionists . . . swarmed down to Dayton during the Scopes trial and brazenly tried to nullify the laws and overthrow the political and religious faiths of a great, enlightened, prosperous, and peaceful people."[1]

Far from needing to be saved from itself, Straton argued, the "chivalric South" was needed to "save America from the sins and shams and shames that are now menacing her splendid life."[2] Little matter that Straton himself held a pulpit in New York City. He voiced a common opinion held by southerners who felt the Scopes trial had loosed an attack on their region by northerners and elitist intellectuals. The Scopes trial exposed and exacerbated sectional divisions between the traditionalist South and a rapidly modernizing North. Although neither region was monolithic, many opponents of the Butler Act mocked its southern supporters as typical rural ignoramuses and in the process defined their own identities as modern, urban, and tolerant—everything they said the South was not. In response, many southerners, especially in Tennessee, defended the peculiarities of their region, and ironically, they came close to identifying themselves with the northerners' caricature.

This caricature of the South has remained critical in the antievolution controversies. Even today, when a significant percentage of antievolution "flare-ups" occur outside the South and suburbanization threatens to rival regionalism as a geographical determinant of antievolution activity, the antievolution movement has been unable to shed its image of southern yokelism. The durability of the image owes a great deal to the Scopes trial, which for many Americans set the framework and the vocabulary for understanding the antievolution impulse. But the reportage of the Scopes trial is not solely responsible for this persistence. On the contrary, the South has played a crucial, concrete role in sustaining antievolutionism, from providing leadership and a network of fundamentalist institutions to furnishing a rhetoric of antielitist populism. Modern allusions to the Scopes trial may give too much prominence to the southern roots of antievolutionism, but regionalism has always been a significant factor in the struggle over evolution.[3]

Although the antievolution movement was to find its greatest success in the South, southerners in general had been slow to awaken to the Darwinian threat. Outside of small knots of scientists and theologians, most southerners before the 1920s were not aware that a controversy existed between their religious views and the scientific theory of evolution. The fundamentalist crusade was confined initially to the North, simply because that was where modernism was making its greatest advances. Harry Emerson Fosdick proclaimed the modernist creed from his pulpit at New York City's prominent First Presbyterian Church. Another leading theological liberal, Shailer Mathews, spread the word from his position at the University of Chicago Divinity School, where he served as dean for twenty-five years. Conservative evangelicals grew alarmed that their own institutions were being turned to the purposes of biblical modernism, and they did more than simply protest. In the name of the fundamentals, they fought for control of the churches, seminaries, and missions. Fundamentalism was at this stage almost exclusively a northern, urban phenomenon, and the battles between liberals and fundamentalists were generally waged by elite theologians and ministers.[4]

Despite originating with conservative theologians in the North, fundamentalism became well adapted to the southern climate. Isolation and poverty fed it. More than half of all white church members in the South belonged to one of three explicitly southern denominations: Southern Baptist, Southern Methodist, and the Presbyterian Church–South. Most others belonged to local independent congregations with no connections outside the county, let alone the region. Thus, the vast majority of southern Christians never heard about the modernist theology that was developing in Europe and the North. Fosdick and Matthews had no southern counterparts. Compounding this isolation was the grinding poverty of the post–Civil War South: little money was available for training ministers even at the rare theological seminaries that managed to survive for more than a few years, and the South in general did very little to support public education for black or white students. "Both leadership and response," notes one historian of southern religion, "carried the stamp of intellectual backwardness."[5]

One result of these weaknesses was relative quiet, at least initially. Chicago's fundamentalist Moody Bible Institute sent numerous speakers and pamphlets to the South to awaken the region but often found these services were redundant, as southerners perceived few threats to their own religious orthodoxy.[6] Evolution did little to disturb their tranquility. True, a handful of southern professors in previous decades had courted trouble by teaching about evolution. Most notably, President Woodrow Wilson's maternal uncle, the biologist James Woodrow, in 1886 had lost his position at the Presbyterian Columbia Theological Seminary in South Carolina over his public support for Darwinism.[7] But these struggles were not widely known. To a surprising extent, professors at the turn of the century did teach about evolution, but quietly, cautiously confident that only a small number of advanced students could handle the subject. Their administrators, whether motivated by intellectual sympathy or simply by fear of bad publicity, seldom raised a public protest.[8]

Their caution succeeded, at least for a while. "Left undisturbed, the rural population would have bothered itself very little over the teachings of the school or the college," wrote Joseph Wood Krutch, a Tennessee native who had become a reporter in the North.[9] Indeed, when the prosecution and defense questioned potential jurors for the Scopes trial, most of them confessed they had not heard about the controversy between evolution and the Bible until the arrest of Scopes earlier in the year. One minister in the jury pool admitted that he had previously preached on the subject of evolution—"Well, I preached against it, of course!"—but his familiarity with the issue was an exception.[10] As Krutch explained, only when "various propagandists of the Bryan school" came along did Tennesseans realize that a controversy existed.

The South was familiar territory for most of these "propagandists." Despite the North's importance in the creation of the fundamentalist movement, almost all of the early fundamentalists and antievolution leaders possessed southern connections even before they traveled south for the Scopes trial. Although William Bell Riley founded and led the World's Christian Fundamentals Association from his longtime post at First Baptist Church in Minneapolis, the "Grand Old Man of Fundamentalism" hailed from the "border South" region of southern Indiana, attended the conservative Southern Baptist Theological Seminary in Louisville, Kentucky, and served as a pastor in Kentucky for a time.[11] Likewise, while John Roach Straton's most prominent pulpit was at Calvary Baptist Church in New York City, he, too, had spent his youth in southern Indiana, and boasted a Virginia ancestry through his mother.[12] William Jennings Bryan was a Nebraskan to the core, but even before he moved to Florida in the 1920s, he had always found his strongest adulation in the South and spent much time crisscrossing the region as a politician and as a revivalist. Prior to the passage of the Butler Act, he intensified his travels through Dixie, and for good reason. Bryan placed his greatest hopes for the future on the region that "had always held to the religion of their forefathers." The South, Bryan believed, "was to be the bulwark of the defense against the attacks on Christianity by the intellectuals," and he predicted that the South was to lead "a great religious revival that would sweep the country."[13] Mississippi was the birthplace and burying ground for the activist T. T. Martin, who hawked copies of his antievolution manifesto, *Hell and the High Schools*, from a table outside the Dayton courthouse.[14] Finally, J. Franklyn Norris was thoroughly and proudly a southerner, and more responsible than any other for the "southernization" of fundamentalism.[15] Born in Alabama and reared in Texas, Norris was educated in conservative theology at Baylor University in Waco, Texas, and prepared further for the ministry at the Southern Baptist Theological Seminary, the same institution that helped form William Bell Riley's outlook, before he began his long tenure as minister of First Baptist Church in Fort Worth, Texas.[16]

Norris was not at all surprised that the threat of modernism had come down from the North. He had been warning for years that the South was not immune to the poisons of liberal theology from the outside. As he explained in his journal, *The Searchlight* (later renamed *The Fundamentalist*), "OUR PEOPLE READ, AND THE DAILY PRESS AND THE PERIODICALS ARE LOADED WITH MODERNISTIC PROPAGANDA."[17] Nor were southern institutions safe. Norris asserted that almost every instructor in the leading southern universities and seminaries "did his university work in the North in a University in the pervasive atmosphere of Modernism."[18] "Our brightest young people," he complained, "are going to these great universities for their advanced training."[19] When they returned to the South, they carried

FIGURE 2.1 The southern fundamentalist J. Franklyn Norris in a typically understated promotional flyer. He poses with the radio towers that helped him build a religious empire. Image courtesy of the Heritage Collection at Arlington Baptist College.

the northern contagion with them. Already they had infected southern institutions with their modernist thought. "There is more of it than we realize," he maintained, listing offending ministers in Atlanta, Birmingham, St. Louis, and numerous other cities.[20] He had good reason for sounding the alarm loudly and insistently. "This battle will be fought out in the South," Norris explained in 1924. "Five years from now it will be too late. We have already waited too long."[21]

For better or for worse, according to Norris's biographer, the minister was more responsible than anyone else for bringing northern fundamentalist ideas down to the South, spreading the word through his ministry, his weekly periodicals, and the radio station he founded at First Baptist—the first fundamentalist station in the nation.[22] As the leading figure of southern fundamentalism, Norris was partly responsible for cementing one of the central conclusions that many observers derived from the Scopes trial: antievolutionism and fundamentalism were the products of a bizarre southern culture characterized by militant intolerance and a crusading ignorance; its leadership, embodied by Norris, dwelt beyond the pale of reason in a parochial enclave below the Mason-Dixon Line.[23] Norris's crusade was a shaky foundation for Bryan's dream.

Another common feature that reinforced these men's identification with southern culture against the incursion of northerners was that they all considered themselves to be antielitist democrats. Bryan's record as a general in the struggle of the "little people" against the elites—the bankers, the corporate titans, entrenched privilege—is well established.[24] But Straton, Norris, and Riley each had his own strong populist streak. They had ministered to large, wealthy congregations early in their careers, but their commitments to social justice led them to break with their elite patrons. In each case, most of the well-to-do congregants, tired of being reminded of their duty to the poor and downtrodden, fled the church and left the pulpit and the building to the fundamentalists.[25] It was easy to transfer the fundamentalists' populist attitude to the Scopes trial, as it bolstered the prosecution's attempts to portray the trial as a struggle between the God-fearing majority in Tennessee and the small band of elite scientists from the North.

With their southern ties, these men were distressed when they found themselves unable to control the ways in which their region was portrayed. The Scopes trial lured more than two hundred reporters to Dayton, primarily from outside the South. Most notorious among them was H. L. Mencken, the famously acerbic journalist from Baltimore. Fresh from having founded *The Smart Set*, a self-consciously "modern" magazine of arts and opinion, Mencken allied himself firmly with the Scopes defense. While none of the other reporters could match Mencken's biliousness, they worked with him to fasten upon the South the image of a religion-obsessed backwater.[26]

In his first report from Dayton, Mencken admitted a certain admiration for the place, although Dayton's charms stood out primarily because Mencken's expectations had been lowered by decades of reading "traincar sociology" written by northerners hurrying through the region. "I expected to find a squalid Southern village, with darkies snoozing on the horse-blocks, pigs rooting under the houses and the inhabitants full of hookworm and malaria," he confessed. "What I found was a country town full of charm and even beauty."[27] Mencken noted that Rhea County had rejected the Ku Klux Klan's attempts to organize the county, and the inhabitants instead had embraced the Freemasons, whose dominance lent a certain air of tolerance and decorum to the area. In the end, though, the "Sage of Baltimore" was unwilling to generalize Dayton's attractions to the rest of the region. "We are not in the South here, but hanging on to the North. Very little cotton is grown in the valley. . . . The fences are in good repair. The roads are smooth and hard."[28] Dayton's positive attributes, by definition, removed the town from its geographical context, and for Mencken this could only be a good thing.

Mencken soon recovered his equilibrium as the trial commenced and he contemplated the religious unity of the town's inhabitants. "This is far worse than anything you could imagine," he wrote his friend Raymond Pearl. "Every last scoundrel in sight is a Christian, including the town Jew. I begin to realize what life must have been in Judea 1925 years ago. No wonder the Romans finally bumped off the son of Joseph."[29] Mencken watched in amazement as visiting preachers engaged scores of willing disputants among the Daytonians, and he noted that all agreed on the fundamental premise that the Bible itself was utterly infallible. Although a Christian in Dayton could interpret Holy Writ in a number of ways, the truth of the Bible itself was not to be questioned. "One accused of heresy among them is like one accused of boiling his grandmother to make soap in Maryland," Mencken wrote.[30] Such piety soon turned the writer against the town, as Mencken traded his initial admiration of Dayton for cultural disdain, condemning the prevalence of Coca-Cola, the *Saturday Evening Post*, and cheap literature. Although Mencken's list of Dayton's cultural offenses at this point suggests that he had not yet left the confines of Robinson's drugstore, the reporter was to find much more to appall him during his time in Dayton. "The thing is genuinely fabulous," he wrote Pearl. "I have stored up enough material to last me 20 years."[31]

Mencken was not the only writer to identify the dominance of religion in the area. "The whole region is saturated with religion," marveled the reporter Frank Kent in the *New Republic*. "Religion takes the place of golf, bridge, music art, literature, theatres, dancing, tennis, clubs. It is the fundamental communal factor."[32] Numerous scribes repeated the sentiment in reports telegraphed back to their home newspapers.

It was a little unfair for reporters to accuse Daytonians of being crazed for religion based on what they observed that July. A major trial focused on the Bible had dropped into Dayton's civic lap, and so conversations and arguments around the town square naturally revolved around theology. Had the civic leaders lured a championship prizefight to town, no doubt the reporters who came to witness the fisticuffs would have marveled at the Daytonians' obsession with the Marquess of Queensberry rules.

Nevertheless, Mencken and his fellows had discovered a southern religious intensity that made their own cities look like Sodom and Gomorrah in comparison. The South consistently ranked higher in such measures as church membership and church attendance, and southern Protestantism was in general shot through with an emotional fervor that set it apart from its northern counterpart.[33] Northern reporters found still greater religious oddities during their stay. One night on the weekend before the trial proper began, Mencken and a group of writers drove into the hills near Dayton to spy on a gathering of "Holy Rollers."[34] Mencken had heard that the "Church of God," as members preferred to call it, was making rapid progress among the "yokels" in the hills, and it was even beginning to collect adherents in the towns and cities of Tennessee. In the spirit of developing intelligence reports in a hostile foreign country, Mencken's party parked in the woods and sneaked along a cornfield to draw near to a torchlit gathering. The preacher—an "immensely tall and thin mountaineer" dressed in blue jeans and a collarless shirt—shouted and prayed aloud about the Day of Judgment and the salvation of the sanctified. A chaotic group prayer touched off in him a "vast impassioned jargon of apocalyptic texts," until he "threw back his head and began to speak in tongues—blub-blub-blub, gurgle-gurgle-gurgle." Somewhat shaken by the spectacle, Mencken and his group crept back to Dayton under cover of darkness. Although this variety of Pentecostalism had its varied roots in Ohio, Kansas, and even California, Mencken linked it closely with "these regions where the Bible is the beginning and end of wisdom, and the mountebank Bryan, parading the streets in his seersucker coat, is pointed out to sucklings as the greatest man since Abraham."[35] Together, the northern reporters drew strange southern features on the face of antievolutionism.

At the same time, the North-South conflict became bound up with the growing friction between urban and rural in the 1920s. The census of 1920 found that, for the first time, more Americans lived in cities than on farms and in small towns.[36] The definition of a "city" was fairly lax—anyone living in a town of more than 2,500 was considered an urban dweller—but the discovery pointed to a very real change in American demographics and culture: the cities were becoming more dynamic and prosperous than the countryside. Even in the South, the countryside was losing population to the city, adding to the fear and resentment that many rural leaders felt toward urban centers. Indeed, John Butler confessed that his proposal was motivated in part by his concern that the countryside was emptying out as rural youth left for town and came into contact with the kind of education that separated them from their rural values.[37]

The ideology surrounding these demographic developments was changing, too. Many urbanites were discarding the traditional American romanticization of rural life in favor of a self-conscious pride in urban living. The *New Yorker*, for example, in 1925 commenced publication as the magazine for the "caviar sophisticate" of the city. The less charming side of this new pride was a compulsion to mock rural and small-town life as stultifying and dull. The *New Yorker* proudly proclaimed that its contents were not intended for the "little old lady in Dubuque," while Sinclair Lewis expressed contempt for small-town living in his best-selling novel *Main Street*. The Scopes trial played an important role in tying together the images of southern intolerance and rural ignorance. Mencken, particularly, was fond of denigrating southern antievolutionists as "rustics," "yokels," and "hill-billies." A headline from his newspaper during the trial proclaimed, "Rustics, Ape-Style, Watch Monkey Show from Trees."[38] The depiction of antievolution as a rural impulse was only partly accurate: Tennessee legislators from urban districts had supported the Butler bill at the same rate as rural lawmakers. On the other hand, Mississippi passed its antievolution bill with an almost exclusively rural legislature, and the only state to pass an antievolution law by popular referendum, Arkansas in 1927, also tilted rural in its vote.[39] At any rate, the accuracy of the depiction was less important than its usefulness for developing a new self-image for the urban North. The new urban society was to be everything the rural South was not: tolerant, educated, cosmopolitan. The Scopes trial only underlined this purported difference between modern enlightenment and rural southern ignorance.

In response, many southerners drew their own caricatures of life in the North. Harking back to a long tradition of antiurbanism in America, these writers portrayed northern cities such as Chicago and New York as garbage bins for all the excesses of the Jazz Age, among them sexual immorality, liquor, and communism.[40] On top of that, Roman Catholics were in charge. And these were the people who proposed to teach Tennessee the error of her ways?

The tension over the "outside invasion" of Dayton revealed itself first through personal sniping. Early on in the trial, the aged and folksy former attorney general from Dayton, Ben G. McKenzie, repeatedly referred to Scopes's team as "foreign counsel" and harped on their origins in "the great metropolitan city of New York" and "the great white city of the Northwest [i.e., Chicago]."[41] Malone objected to McKenzie's implication that the defense team did not belong in the courtroom, but Judge Raulston reassured him that all of McKenzie's jabs were in good humor. Darrow, for his part, thanked Raulston for bestowing on him the southern honorific of "Colonel," and slyly redirected McKenzie's jests toward William Jennings Bryan and McKenzie's son, also present in the room. "So far as coming from other cities is concerned, why, your Honor, it is easy here," Darrow explained. "I came from Chicago, and my friend, [Dudley Field] Malone, and friend [Arthur Garfield] Hays came from New York, and on the other side we have a distinguished and very pleasant gentleman who came from California [Bryan junior] and another who is prosecuting this case, and who is responsible for this foolish, mischievous, and wicked act, who comes from Florida."[42] William Jennings Bryan had indeed recently relocated from Nebraska to Florida to hawk real estate for developers in the real estate boom there, and in any event he remained an honorary southerner, embraced by the region that had always given him its firmest support. Later in the trial, McKenzie's son implied that Darrow and his team came from even more remote precincts when he suggested that they might "represent a force that is aligned with the satellites of the devil."[43]

On the fifth day of the trial, the sectional issue came to a boil when attorneys for both sides debated the question of majoritarianism versus expertise. The ostensible issue was whether to admit experts to testify about evolution and the Bible. In light of the Butler Act's invocation of a conflict between evolution and the "story of the Divine creation of man as taught in the Bible," the defense asserted, the jury needed to know just what evolution was and just what the Bible really meant. Thus Scopes should be allowed to bring in trained experts to educate the jurors about the science of evolution and about the varied ways of interpreting the Bible. Several scientists and theologians from Harvard University, Johns Hopkins University, and the University of Chicago, among other institutions, had already traveled south to Dayton and stood ready to take the stand.[44]

The prospect of expert testimony from these men put the prosecution in a bind. Bryan had failed to find any reputable scientists in the South or elsewhere willing to testify that Genesis offered a superior explanation for the age of the earth or the origins of life on it. Under cross-examination late in the trial, Bryan did cite the work of George McCready Price, who taught at a small Seventh-day Adventist college. Price had proposed that the "Genesis Flood" rearranged the geology of the earth in such a way that the true six thousand years of the earth's existence appeared to be millions of years longer. But the reference to Price underscored the weakness of Bryan's initial strategy. Price, Darrow insisted, was "a man that every scientist in this country knows is a mountebank and a pretender and not a geologist at all."[45] Price certainly did not seem imposing next to the defense's proposed lineup of scientists. At any rate, he did not make the trip to Dayton.

Faced with this quandary, the prosecution focused instead on blocking the scientists' testimony altogether. Attorney General Tom Stewart argued that expert testimony was irrelevant, as a plain reading of the law made it clear that Scopes had violated its provisions by teaching Dayton youngsters about the theory of evolution in contradiction to the biblical story of the divine creation of man. The truth or falsehood of Genesis was not at issue; rather, the legislators' intent was the key, and that was written down in black and white for everyone to see. A jury should construe these statutes "in common ordinary language," Ben McKenzie argued, "and give them an interpretation like the common people of this state can understand. You do not need experts to explain a statute that explains itself."[46] McKenzie's stress on "plain reading" was a time-honored approach that fundamentalists for a decade had been particularly emphasizing. Intervention and interpretation by a small body of experts—whether they were scientists or priests—was absolutely unnecessary, the prosecutors firmly believed. Indeed, Bryan scoffed at the idea that a so-called expert could understand the Bible better than any of the avowedly Christian men on the jury: "The man may discuss the Bible all he wants to, but he does not find out anything about the Bible until he accepts God and the Christ of whom He tells."[47] No experts were needed to explain the meaning of such a clear, straightforward work.

In arguing against the admission of expert testimony, the prosecution and its supporters found themselves pulled away from a narrow consideration of the law and toward a broader defense of majoritarianism and democracy—which they took to be synonymous with the people of Tennessee. Inevitably, this distinction became one of southern majority versus northern experts. The position was a comfortable one for Bryan, the Great Commoner. When Bryan rose on the afternoon of the trial's fifth day to deliver his much anticipated first speech, most of the main themes had already been introduced. Bryan reiterated these points, but he came to emphasize particularly the danger that these proceedings posed to rule by the people. "This is not the place to try to prove that the law ought never to have been passed," he suggested. "The place to prove that, or teach that, was to the legislature." If the defense and its experts had real affection for the people of Tennessee, and not merely the desire to put them before the nation as "ignorant people and bigoted people," then they would have come down "at a time when their testimony might have been valuable."[48] Bryan did not mention that "outside experts" had had no opportunity to address the people of Tennessee before the Butler Act sped through the state legislature, but no matter. He found an unlikely ally in the *New Republic*, a liberal weekly that could have been expected to support Scopes. Instead, the editor condemned the American Civil Liberties Union's strategy of challenging the Butler Act in the courts. The issue was not merely that liberals distrusted the judiciary, although the Supreme Court and most lower courts at the time, including Judge Raulston's, were indeed bastions of reaction; rather, the issue was one of democracy. "The Courts can no more make us wise and tolerant and eager for the truth than they can make us kind or generous," argued the editor. "No community can become enlightened by having enlightenment judicially thrust upon it." Only if the people themselves forced the "obnoxious statute" from the books would Tennessee erase its "crime against intelligence."[49]

While denying that the Butler law was a "crime against intelligence," Bryan also defended the legislature's right to pass laws that expressed the will of the people. In particular, he argued, the people of Tennessee had the right to pass laws about what was being taught in the public schools. As he had proclaimed in many speeches and articles before the trial, "The hand that writes the check rules the schools." Bryan and his allies were adamant that the strong majority of "God-fearing" Tennesseans were opposed to the teaching of evolution, and they should not be forced to subsidize it. "Has it come to a time," Bryan demanded to know, "when the minority can take charge of a state like Tennessee and compel the majority to pay their teachers while they take religion out of the heart of the children of the parents who pay the teachers?"[50]

Bryan suggested strongly that this minority interest was not even native to Tennessee but had traveled down from the North with malign intent. Attorney General Stewart fully joined Bryan in defending the Tennessee majority against the outside invasion. "What is this thing," he asked, "that comes here to strike within the bounds of this jurisdiction, and to tell the people of this commonwealth that they are doing wrong to prohibit the teaching of this theory in the public schools? Who conceived the idea that Tennessee did not know what she was doing? . . . Why, if the court please, have we not the right to interpret our Bible as we see fit?"[51]

The defense's expert witnesses fit the role of undemocratic elites very well, especially with their highfalutin academic pedigrees. "What right," Bryan asked, "has a little irresponsible oligarchy of self-styled 'intellectuals' to demand control of the schools of the United States, in which 25,000 of children are being educated at an annual expense of nearly $2,000,000,000?"[52] Bryan's animosity against the "intellectual elite" resounded throughout antievolutionist rhetoric. T. T. Martin's *Hell and the High Schools*, for example, was riddled with complaints about the "sneers" of highbrows against the simple faith of Christians. Similarly, William Bell Riley's *Menace of Modernism* was shot through with a very personal resentment toward the arrogance of the intellectuals.[53]

While the antievolutionists' attack on scientific elites made rhetorical sense, it also came perilously close to celebrating ignorance—a refrain that was to become common in criticism directed at anticvolutionists. In rejecting the testimony of biblical scholars, Bryan asserted that anyone who believed in the Bible could understand it better than all the philologists and archeologists in the world. In his argument before the court, Bryan mocked scientists for their futile investigations into the origins of life, and he made sport of their assertion that humans were mammals. Krutch opined in the *Nation* that Bryan's chief tack was "a plea for ignorance as uncorrupted as possible by any knowledge."[54]

Attorney General Stewart asserted his own willingness to embrace ignorance if the alternative was to lose his faith. "Science should continue to progress and it should be unhampered in the bounds of reason," Stewart said. "I am proud of the progress that it has made, and I should say, your honor, that when science treads upon holy ground, then science should invade no further."[55] He continued, "Why, have we not the right to bar the door to science when it comes within the four walls of God's church upon this earth? Who says we have not?" If the people of Tennessee needed ignorance in order to maintain their religious beliefs, then Stewart was willing to embrace it. Mencken scoffed, "The chief prosecuting attorney, beginning like a competent lawyer and a man of self-respect, ended like a convert at a Billy Sunday revival."[56]

Handed such ammunition, Mencken and his imitators were relentless in their attacks on southern "yokels."[57] Cartoonists and editorialists cheerfully followed their lead, portraying the antievolutionists as rural buffoons in beards and overalls. Even the International Metric Association considered petitioning the Tennessee legislature to pass a law prohibiting the teaching of the metric system on the assumption that such an action would generate a groundswell of support for the use of meters, grams, and liters.[58] "The show," Mencken wrote to a friend, "was colossal."[59]

The mockery that stung Bryan and the South was reinforced by other weapons in what one historian has called the "war against the South."[60] For almost two centuries, the South had had to reckon with abolitionist and antislavery condemnations of the region's "peculiar institution." Southern leaders were so sensitive to the criticism that they sought to create almost an ideological bunker, using their political power to gag congressional discussion of slavery and to interdict antislavery materials from the southern mails. Long after the question of slavery had been settled, many southerners still felt besieged. By the time of the Scopes trial, social scientists had already spent decades investigating the enduring poverty and educational deficits of the region; liberal northern journalists and activists had loudly condemned southern lynching, and the "race press" had vigorously publicized the wide range of southern racial outrages. Mencken's hostility was only a sardonic twist on an old story.

Thus predisposed to defensiveness, southern antievolutionists and their supporters not surprisingly chafed at the scorn they received in 1925. Daytonians, suffering particularly under Mencken's abuse, held "indignation meetings on the street corners and in the stores," according to the *New York Times*, and a handful apparently had to be dissuaded from dragging "that cheap blatherskate of a penpusher" into an alley.[61] Two days after the trial ended, Bryan told a crowd of supporters in Pikesville, Tennessee, of his indignation "toward those who have maligned you—those who have come from another State to speak of you as 'bigots' and 'yokels.' . . . I wish that I could have dragged them here and placed them face to face with a humanity they cannot imitate."[62] In the fall, after the trial, Judge Raulston gave vent to his own resentment as he stood before a congregation in Straton's Calvary Baptist Church and loudly denounced those who had branded him and other Tennesseans as "yokels, hillsters, ignoramuses."[63]

When the Scopes trial forced many southerners to declare (or to discover) their traditionalist beliefs, the fact that Scopes's allies came largely from the North hardened this southern sense of community. Tennesseans in particular and southerners in general circled the wagons. The editor of the *Nashville Tennessean*, James I. Finney, maintained, "Thousands of intelligent Tennesseans who realized the futility and unwisdom of the [Butler] law were either silenced or became its defenders when the Civil Liberties Union [soon to become the ACLU] entered the combat." As long as "outsiders" continued to equate Tennesseans' religiosity with "mental weakness," he

FIGURE 2.2 William Jennings Bryan among southern supporters who had been, he complained, slandered as "bigots" and "yokels." Image courtesy of Bryan College.

argued, "they would never repeal the Butler law."[64] In addition, the involvement of the ACLU in the trial made it much easier for southerners to feel that they were being attacked by an alien force. The ACLU's involvement in the Scopes trial prompted the Mobile (Alabama) *Register* to repeat accusations that the organization was undeniably linked to communism and pacifism and was pledged to overthrow all American institutions.[65] The chairman of Tennessee's state law examiners suggested that the ACLU "should politely be invited to go back to New York with its bag, baggage, and money."[66]

Not everyone at the time agreed that the South held a monopoly on backwardness or intolerance. The Scopes trial offered many opportunities for laying blame. W. O. McGeehan, in *Harper's Monthly*, argued that Dayton did not deserve the calumnies aimed at it. "Why pick on Dayton?" he asked. "I am ready to maintain that the percentage of moronism in Dayton, Tennessee, is no higher than it is in New York City or any other city of the first, second, or third class. . . . The center of moronism in the United States is the exact dead center of the population with a slight inclination toward Hollywood, California."[67] Indeed, in the geographic dead center of the United States, Kansas saw one school district vote to burn a textbook that included evolution, and a minister from Kansas City proclaimed that "rape fiends" were saints "in comparison with teachers of modern science."[68] George F. Milton, a Tennessee editor, traced antievolution sentiment more generally. The case "might as well have come in Kansas or Missouri, in Washington or the State of Maine. Under such circumstances, it is hardly fair for Tennessee to be crucified on the cross of public opinion as a bog of bigotry."[69]

Despite his fondness for waving the bloody shirt against the South, even Mencken felt that Bryan's legacy was national and not regional. "Heave an egg out of a Pullman window and you will hit a Fundamentalist almost anywhere in the United States today," he lamented. "They swarm in the country towns, inflamed by their pastors, and with a saint, now, to venerate. They are thick in the mean streets behind the gas-works. They are everywhere that learning is too heavy a burden for mortal mind."[70] As usual, Mencken was more pungent than others, but he was not alone in his opinion. Elsewhere in the North, many liberals and radicals also considered the issue to be national in scope. Howard K. Beale, who had been hired by the American Historical Association to investigate freedom of teaching in American schools, maintained that the majority of northerners and southern urbanites agreed with Bryan's principle that teachers were simply hired men and women whose job it was to indoctrinate pupils with ideas approved by the taxpaying majority.[71] The urban and northern majority could criticize the intolerance that spawned the Butler Act simply because they no longer cared particularly about religion; their tolerance toward teaching evolution was based on "indifference to the beliefs scientific discovery disturbs."[72] However, Beale suggested, if one tried to teach economic radicalism in the North, those same "tolerant" citizens would embrace an identical spirit of intolerance. "Fundamentalism is to the Tennessean what the profit system is to a northern middle-class businessman—the thing each believes in with all his heart."[73] The schools could not dissent from these fundamental beliefs.

Several northern radicals drew similar conclusions. The editor of *Industrial Solidarity*, a publication of the Industrial Workers of the World, pointed out that the *Chicago Tribune* and other "reactionary American newspapers" were seizing upon the trial "to show that they are liberal, and defend the rights of free thinking and free speech. Do not be fooled," he admonished. "The great trusts have their god, too, and his name is 'Profits.'"[74] The religious element of the controversy, then, was simply a sideshow. "Let labor learn from the battle of the gods, at Dayton, that both are untrustworthy. . . . The big main ring of the circus is now as in previous generations, the continual and unresisting exploitation of labor."[75] Similarly, another labor journal, the *Daily Worker*, observed that some southern newspapers were taking their cue from northern reactionaries and blaming the "Communist snake" for the unrest in Dayton. The industrial masters, such as the Louisville and Nashville Railroad and southern subsidiaries of U.S. Steel, were solicitous of religion while teaching the southern "backwoods" to be hostile to radicalism. The industrialists, suggested the *Daily Worker*, "have a far bigger stake in the fight against modern social ideas than has Bryan."[76] Despite these claims that fundamentalism of a sort was a national force, the Tennessee controversy nevertheless hardened the association between the South and fundamentalism, both in image and in reality.[77]

Some southerners took at least parts of the criticism of the South to heart. In the decades leading up to the Scopes trial, leaders of the "New South" movement had sought to modernize a region that had been held back by slavery and an overreliance on cotton. They looked to the industrialized North as a model for development. Its trains, its factories, and its varied and vigorous agriculture all generated a prosperity that the South could only envy. But even as New South proponents prodded their section to emulate the North's economic progress, they maintained that the South must follow its own distinct path. One cartoon represented the essence of their creed: the South should develop its resources, but it should never surrender its unique morality and religiosity—indeed, these characteristics could combine with a progressive approach to development to make the New South an attractive target for investment.

In many ways, the Scopes trial punctured the New South creed. While investors were certainly attracted to the region's cheap labor force, the antievolution controversy reinforced the older image of what one historian later called "the benighted South, a savage South of racial hatred and religious fanaticism."[78] As personified by the Scopes trial, this became a standard image of the region. In contrast to the portrayal of a growing, confident North, the antievolutionist South, with its overwhelming religiosity, appeared to be mired in the past. Its religiosity did not bolster development, but rather stood in the way of progress. The South's economic renaissance lay decades in the future.

The Scopes battle also provoked into action a small group of southern intellectuals—calling themselves "Fugitives" or "Agrarians"—who were less eager to pour the South into a northern mold.[79] Associated primarily with Vanderbilt University, Donald Davidson, Allen Tate, Robert Penn

Warren, and others saw part of their common mission to be a defense of southern culture against the incursions of the northern model.[80] As undergraduates in 1917, they had joined together partly in response to the sting of northern derision loosed by H. L. Mencken's famous piece "The Sahara of the Bozart."[81] Now the Scopes invasion demanded a more vigorous response.[82] The Agrarians seemed unlikely champions. "We had been devoting ourselves almost entirely to poetry and criticism without giving much attention to public affairs," Davidson later recalled. "We rubbed our eyes and looked around in astonishment and apprehension. Was it possible that nobody in the South knew how to reply to a vulgar rhetorician like H. L. Mencken?"[83] Davidson, in particular, decided "to lose no opportunity to advance the cause of the South."[84] He went from feeling ambivalent about Dayton and the New South creed to being the most committed member of the Agrarians. In the immediate aftermath of the trial, Davidson emphasized the complexity of the South; it could not be generalized about or caricatured, as so many reporters had done. "Gaudy filling stations edge their way among ancestral mansions," he observed, and he pointed out that Vanderbilt University found its counterpart in the newly founded Bryan Memorial University.[85] Davidson saw the "complicated truth" of the antievolution movement in the South as an expression of this variety as the South faced the modernity of science and industrialism.

As he developed his defense of the region, though, Davidson ultimately discarded his assertion that the South was too complex to generalize about its culture; instead, he identified "certain peculiarities of the Southern people which do not yet deserve to perish from this earth."[86] He was initially hesitant to embrace some of these "peculiarities," for he was all too conscious that the South had long been "a major target area" for northern condemnation.[87]

> We were religious bigots. We were Ku Kluxers. We were lynchers. We had hookworm, we had pellagra, we had sharecroppers, we had poll taxes. . . . We did not have enough schools, colleges, Ph.D.'s, Deans of Education, paved roads, symphony orchestras, public libraries, skyscrapers—and not near enough cotton mills, steel mills, labor unions, modern plumbing. But we had too many . . . Methodists and Baptists, too many one-horse farms, too many illiterates, too many Old Colonels. [88]

Davidson and others must have feared that any defense of the South as a region would be complicit with these attempts to define the South purely as a negative entity. In later years, Davidson also suspected that the South in the 1920s had been merely a proxy for critics who wanted to ridicule more generally "religion and religious institutions as such," to condemn "the American political and governmental system in general," and to attack "not only the shallowness of Southern achievement in literature and the arts, but the validity of the entire Western tradition of literature and the arts."[89]

Nevertheless, Davidson and his allies in the 1920s stiffened their defense of their region's vague "peculiarities." Over time, the Vanderbilt intellectuals came to extol what the historian Fred Hobson calls "Southern provincialism, fundamentalism, and supernaturalism, those very qualities that Mencken and the Northern journalists had labeled 'barbaric.'"[90] The Fugitives' defense of the South came to fruition in 1930 with the publication of *I'll Take My Stand: The South and the Agrarian Tradition*. Rather than an expression of hope that the South could catch up to the "progress" of the North, the book was a defense of "southernness" against the incursion of northerners and northern principles.[91] The "New Confederates," as their detractors dubbed them, perceived the regional clash as one between an industrialized, secular society, based on science, individualism, and the pursuit of capital gain, and its superior opposite, the more rural and natural communities of the South. Echoes of the Scopes trial rang clearly in their juxtaposition of a secular, scientific society and an organic southern culture that valued religion, stability, and communal relations. The Agrarians, as they were now more commonly known, had difficulty defining what constituted "southernness," but they agreed that southern ideals roughly meant a better grounding in history and tradition.[92] They often invoked the mythology of an organic antebellum South, a society characterized by face-to-face relationships, shared piety, and a natural relation to the land. One member of the group, the historian Frank Owsley, inadvertently revealed some of the less savory aspects of this vision when he romanticized slavery as a benign expression of antebellum hierarchy. For his part, Donald Davidson claimed, perhaps facetiously, to keep a Confederate flag in his office, along with Robert E. Lee's sword.[93] The society these items represented was threatened by the invasion of northern outsiders.

As befitted their highbrow status, the Fugitives seldom flirted with yokelism; they insisted, on the contrary, that the more leisurely pace of southern life would foster the development of a higher, more humane culture. Thus they reviled New South proponents for trying to re-create the weaknesses of the North in the South. Rather than chase after industrial

progress in search of a profit, as the secular North did, southerners were
to venerate the better parts of the past.

Northern reactions to *I'll Take My Stand* were predictably negative, but
the Fugitives' attack on northern culture was too much even for the Macon
(Georgia) *Telegraph*. "We are to listen again to the professionally Southern
oratory of the sixties," complained the editor, "and we are to believe in the
diabolical purposes of the invading North."[94] Reviewers in many southern
newspapers agreed, and they suggested that the region's salvation lay not
in the Agrarians' nostalgic vision but in the practical programs laid out by
New South progressives. As befitted a movement led by soft-handed academics, Agrarianism in the end remained more of an ideal than a program for reconstruction. Agrarianism nevertheless exemplified the reality
that the South, whether by choice or by circumstance, was out of step with
northern culture.

The region's dissonance with national or northern ideals was and continues to be partly related to its involvement in the antievolution impulse.
Popular memory has enshrined a belief that Bryan's death five days after
the trial sounded the death knell for antievolutionism altogether. But
while it is true that after Bryan's passing antievolutionism largely faded
from the national consciousness, it did not disappear entirely. Rather, antievolution maintained its vigor, but now the impulse was largely confined
to the South. Shortly after the Scopes trial, Mississippi and Arkansas, like
Tennessee, banned the teaching of evolution outright; Texas removed evolution from the state's official textbooks. While the majority of southern
states—with almost universal support from the newspapers—rejected
such antievolution measures, evolution's opponents nevertheless had
demonstrated significant political strength, or at least tenacity.[95] Countless
county and town school boards simply proceeded to remove the subject
with no fanfare. In these early years, fundamentalists could still nurse the
hope that the crusade would go national. They could still believe the *Baptist
and Reflector*'s pre-Scopes proclamation, "As Goes the South—Goes the
Nation."[96]

Their confidence was misplaced. Antievolutionism made little headway in the North after this time. All antievolution proposals there were
quickly squelched; notoriously, the Rhode Island legislature jokingly
referred an antievolution bill to the Committee on Fish and Game.[97] As the
historian Edward J. Larson observes, the antievolution movement sput-
tered out not because of the Scopes trial or the triumph of reason but
because "it became obvious that each side had reached the geographical

limit of its influence."[98] What vigor remained among southern antievolutionists was largely siphoned off in 1928 by the crusade against the presidential candidacy of Al Smith, a Catholic and an anti-Prohibitionist from New York City, and then by the catastrophe of the Great Depression.[99]

Yet the South became critical to the further development of antievolutionism in the decades after its reputed death in Dayton. As suggested by the planting of the fundamentalist Bryan University (later Bryan College) in that same town in 1930, the South became home to many of the institutions—Bible institutes, conservative seminaries and colleges, radio ministries, and evangelical churches—that tended the fundamentalist flame. Thus they joined the Southern Baptist Theological Seminary, which had been founded, coincidentally, the same year that *On the Origin of Species* was published. Together, in the decades after the Scopes trial, these institutions prepared new generations of William Bell Rileys and J. Franklyn Norrises. More broadly, as historian William R. Glass notes, the South gave fundamentalism a region "where cultural values generally sustained and nurtured conservative interpretations of Protestant doctrine."[100] Protestantism's unchallenged dominance in the region and its lack of connections to more liberal theological influences made the South a close fit theologically; socially, a strong sense of hierarchy and a belief in traditional sexual behavior and traditional sex roles, among other values, buttressed religious conservatism.

The South has maintained this position. In a nation that consistently ranks well above other industrialized countries in its level of religious identification, the South continues to lead the way in religious intensity and biblical literalism.[101] Over the last several decades, cultural geographers have invested an enormous number of hours and gigabytes in mapping religious regions in the country, with results that are visually arresting but not surprising. Geographers can represent all of Utah, for example, in a single color that signifies the dominance of Mormonism in nearly every county; the upper Midwest is divided into large patches of moderate Catholicism and mainline Protestantism; and the Northeast is mostly moderately Catholic. Farther down on the maps, the Bible Belt is easy to pick out: counties dominated by strong and moderate evangelical Protestantism show up vividly as a streak of color running in a wide swath from the Carolinas through west Texas until they bump up against counties with significant Hispanic Catholic populations.[102]

In light of the changes the South has undergone since the 1920s, the Bible Belt's persistence is remarkable. Physically and economically, the

South today resembles more the dreams of New South advocates than the Agrarian vision of Donald Davidson. As many have observed, southern farming has become "capital-intensive, large-scale agriculture," under-written by mechanization and governmental agricultural policies.[103] Fewer farmers are needed to produce vast quantities of food, and so rural dwellers continue the twentieth-century trend of migrating to the cities of the New South, such as Atlanta and Dallas—skyscraper metropolises built on concrete, not dirt. The region has also become home to millions of transplants (sunbirds) attracted by the warm weather, office workers and technocrats in search of employment, and migrants from outside the country altogether. Contrary to expectations, neither urbanization nor in-migration has significantly altered the religious pattern. Rather, it seems, migrants to the South, except for Catholics from Latin America, are more likely in advance to share the region's religious and cultural values. Similarly, southern cities have proven to be perfectly hospitable to conservative values. Nashville, for example, has been dubbed "the Protes-tant Vatican" as a tribute to its vast array of conservative religious institu-tions, including the headquarters for the Southern Baptist Association and numerous religious publishing houses. Thus, rather than converging with the rest of the nation, the South retains a level of distinctiveness, especially in religion.

Regarding evolution in particular, polls over the last two decades have consistently found the South to be unique. A majority of Americans favor biblical creationism over evolution as an explanation for the appearance of humanity, but southerners are one and a half to two times more likely than residents of the Northeast to hold that opinion.[104] It is difficult to imagine Answers in Genesis opening its recently built Creation Museum anywhere but in a southern state such as Kentucky (though the site gives the added bonus of close proximity to Cincinnati's airport and several major population centers).

The difference of opinion manifests itself in concrete ways. While an-tievolution incidents flare up all across the nation, they are more common in the South, and come closer there to achieving success on a statewide level. In recent years, state antievolution laws have found success or near success in Mississippi and Texas, among others. Perhaps the greatest achievement came in Louisiana in 2008, when the legislature and gover-nor passed a law to allow local school boards to adopt "supplemental ma-terials" for science classes when they discuss evolution, human cloning, and global warming, with the clear intent to invite the use of materials that would oppose the commonly accepted scientific treatment of those subjects.[105] Such laws have made little headway north of the Mason-Dixon Line. Although local activity is less well recorded, formal and informal pressure from local school boards, parents, and teachers themselves in the South makes for a deemphasis on evolution that is more extensive than the state-level activity suggests. Even where state standards endorse the teaching of evolution, the state agencies that would monitor the teaching of evolution are typically understaffed or disinclined to investigate localities, especially in the absence of clear direction from the legislature. At the state and local levels, the South remains the heartland of antievolutionism.

In second place to the South stands the Midwest, exemplified by the Kansas contretemps over removing evolution from the statewide curriculum standards. Although the Kansas dispute was made possible primarily by the peculiarities of that state's political structure—specifically, the election of state school board members by popular local vote—it did embody the region's inclination toward the southern pattern of antievolutionism.

Within these broad regional boundaries, the most important variable in the geography of evolution seems to be the difference between cities and small towns, and sometimes between cities and newer suburbs. Chicago, for example, has had little agitation over evolution, but rural downstate Illinois is a different story. The nation's best-known recent fight, in 2005, occurred in Pennsylvania—but not in Pittsburgh or Philadelphia. Rather, the school board that adopted an intelligent design textbook for biology classes sat in Dover, a town of fewer than two thousand inhabitants near the southern edge of the state.[106] A less publicized controversy—over a high school intersession course on intelligent design—erupted at the same time in Lebec, California, population approximately 1,285.[107] Unlike larger cities, in which numerous groups are vying for power, less-populated towns tend to be more homogeneous demographically and religiously—Dover, for example, is 96 percent white and almost entirely Christian. A number of newer suburbs around cities such as Atlanta and Kansas City replicate on a larger scale the demographics and religious outlook of these small towns—indeed, they are often settled by in-migrants from more rural areas—and are more likely than the cities to witness antievolution activity. Their location between country and city may, in fact, make them more likely to engage in socially conservative activism when their traditional values run up against more metropolitan ideals in terms of school discipline, race, sexuality and sexism, and science.[108]

Taking power in such small towns and suburbs is even easier in school board elections, which consistently generate the lowest interest and vote tallies of any political race. Recognizing this dynamic, the Christian conservative strategist Ralph Reed in 1988 advised his allies to adopt a "stealth" approach whereby candidates for local offices would say little about their conservative religious affiliations until elected, at which point they were in a position to pursue their "real" agenda of cleansing the curriculum of evolution, sex education, homosexuality, and other bugaboos of the religious right.[109] In many cases, including Kansas, newly alert voters have thrown out the conservatives in the next election. In the case of creationist takeovers, in particular, even sympathetic voters often find the burden of ridicule and the very real costs of litigation too much to bear.[110]

Even as the geography of antievolutionism has retained its southern bias, the movement's defense of majoritarianism has become more complicated. The antievolutionists' populist rhetoric, for example, has been tamed by the pretensions of creation scientists who are eager to take their place at the bench with other "elite" scientists. While creation science literature highlights polls showing that a majority of Americans adhere to a creationist view of origins, it places greater stress on creationism's scientific validity, commonly citing support from recondite studies of molecular biology or radiometric dating rather than the "will of the people." ID leaders have been even more standoffish. Invocations of popular opinion also run into a more concrete problem: the majority of Americans, who want creationism taught alongside evolution, seem to need a great deal of prodding to swing into action. Bryan had once expected that this majority of the "common people" would propel his movement to national victory, and while polls continue to find a majority of Americans in favor of teaching some form of creationism in the schools, this majority opinion seldom coalesces into action on the local level. Indeed, the necessity of the stealth strategy underlines the tenuousness of the antievolutionists' local dominance.

Despite the antievolutionist rhetoric of "local control" and "community standards" from the beginnings of the controversy to the present day, antievolution activity at the local level is generally not so much an outburst of local indignation as a product of lobbying by national antievolution groups such as the Discovery Institute and the Institute for Creation Research. The "invasion of outsiders" John Roach Straton had once decried is now coming from both sides of the evolution question. Caught in the middle—more in the South than in the North, more in small towns and suburbs than in cities—is no national or regional majority, but rather a small number of local activists and their fellow citizens, trying to weigh the claims of faith and science while hoping to avoid the tag of "rural ignoramus" that the Scopes trial affixed to the antievolution impulse.

3

Fighting for the Future of the Race

EVOLUTION FOR AFRICAN AMERICAN PEDAGOGUES
AND PREACHERS

AMONG THE MANY visitors to John Scopes's trial in Dayton, Tennessee, was a tall, formally dressed African American man named W. H. Moses. Moses, a minister, was campaign director for the National Baptist Convention, the largest African American religious organization in the nation, and he had traveled to Dayton with an elite group of African American preachers, students, professors, and physicians from the border South. As he viewed the trial and the sideshows around it, Moses explained to reporters and curious onlookers that the controversy was particularly relevant to African Americans. A lack of broader education, Moses noted, had left black ministers "proverbially hostile to science." For that reason, the "college Negro" had become prejudiced against "Negro preachers and the religion of their fathers to a very harmful degree." Moses hoped the trial would demonstrate "that Christianity is strengthened by science rather than weakened," and thus the conflict might restore the confidence of "the darker races" in Christianity.[1] For the heavily churched black community, this was not a trivial matter.

Moses and his group were not the only African Americans with a keen interest in the trial. In addition to the Moses expedition, black newspapers and black churches sent eyewitnesses to Dayton, editorialists and intellectuals commented with great acerbity on the "monkey business" in Tennessee, and African American ministers delivered hundreds of sermons on the topic of evolution and the Bible. In Kansas City, one African American couple even pulled a knife on a friend who had taken what they considered the wrong side of the dispute.[2] Clearly the Scopes trial mattered, and mattered deeply, to many African Americans.

African American responses to the trial were not merely darker reflections of the white world.[3] On the contrary, in an era of tremendous religious and cultural ferment within African America, many leaders employed the controversy over evolution in ways that were strikingly different from white approaches. In the religious world, the trial prompted numerous black ministers to proclaim themselves fundamentalists and to declare that the race's only hope for the future lay in a conservative, literal interpretation of Genesis and the Bible. At the same time, a much smaller group of secular African American intellectuals used the trial as a club against racism in the South and identified the future of the race with the progress of science, as embodied by evolutionary theory. Many of these black intellectuals found that the Scopes controversy revealed troubling strains of fundamentalism and religious dominance at a time in which they felt the race should be moving forward under modern, secular leadership. While religious conservatives praised the native fundamentalism of African Americans, members of the secular black elite employed the Scopes trial in a twin struggle against white supremacy in the South and ministerial dominance throughout African America.[4] The Reverend W. H. Moses was right about the tensions the race was facing. Within the unsettled situation brought on by the Great Migration and the increased urbanization of African America, the Scopes trial became a part of a broader contest for cultural leadership. Who was going to lead the race, the preacher or the professional?

Just as the antievolution movement provoked many white Protestants to declare publicly that they were fundamentalists, so the Scopes trial inspired many African Americans to make public professions of their faith. Whether they were part of the growing diaspora of black southerners in the North or lifetime residents of the South, a great many members of the race in the summer of 1925 identified themselves as fundamentalists and antievolutionists. While rehearsing the standard scientific and theological critiques of evolution, however, African Americans suggested that maintaining a conservative Christian faith was uniquely important for the advancement of the race.

African Americans North and South expressed opposition to the theory of evolution. Ministers delivered sermons with titles such as "Darwin's Monkey Theory Versus God's Man Theory" and "Bible Versus Evolution." The text: "Obey God." The National Baptist Convention, with five thousand delegates at its annual meeting in Baltimore in September 1925, passed resolutions against both the Ku Klux Klan and evolution.[5] African

Americans pledged their allegiance to the Bible rather than Darwin in letters and, occasionally, in poems published in the race press. Baltimore's Thelma L. Sullivan sent six quatrains to the *Afro-American* admitting that she "humbly must confess, / This evolution stuff a mess."

> For from beginning unto the end,
> We'll never know the make of man.
> So take advice, dear friends, from me,
> Let God and all of His works be.
> For had He wanted you to know,
> He would have said so long ago,
> And so helped scientists to know
> The model of your being.
> So, do not question any more,
> If we were always men or monkeys before;
> For when we leave this world below,
> To our creator we will go.[6]

Sullivan's sentiments were race-neutral, but many black antievolutionists introduced distinctive race notes into their discussions of Darwinism. Some African American ministers found a concrete message for the race in the antievolution controversy. Dr. E. W. White, pastor of Houston's powerful Tulane Avenue Baptist Church, preached a sermon titled "Plenty Monkey, but More Hog in Man" to one of that church's largest crowds ever. White began conventionally enough, informing his congregation that evolutionists were engaged in "an old scheme of the devil" to deny all of Genesis and other biblical miracles. But White also believed "the Negro is religious by nature" and thus unlikely to fall into the modernists' snare. The minister therefore took his monkey sermon in a different direction. "Man did not descend from a monkey," White said, "but from many of his actions he has descended to a monkey." Evidence was all around. "Look at the man living with no aim, like a monkey with a cocoanut, perfectly satisfied. Tanking up on 'rot gut' stuff, running wild in automobiles, endangering lives—monkey ways." Even these simian attributes, White suggested, paled next to the "hog" in man. "When man wants to get the whole world and a fence around it, that's the hog in him," the minister explained. "Why is it men and women shun places of decency and places of uplift for the dives?" he asked. "That is the hog instinct that likes filth." Although White addressed a vexing theological issue, he held on to the

African American religious tradition of exhorting righteous living in tangible terms rather than engaging in arid theological disputes.[7]

Several African American observers felt that a continued belief in biblical inerrancy was particularly important for racial progress. Noting that African Americans were "essentially fundamentalists," Kelly Miller, the longtime dean of the College of Arts and Sciences at Howard University, rejected modernism for the race despite his own distaste for fundamentalism. "It would be risky beyond justification for our Negro denomination[s] to venture upon the new and untried experiment," he warned. "It would involve their unsophisticated followers in a maze of doubt and speculation that could only end in a maze of bewilderment and confusion." In the end, Miller was prepared to let the white denominations "try all things," but he seemed to hold African Americans to a lower standard as he urged them to hold fast to the faith of the fathers.[8]

The editor of the Norfolk (Virginia) *Journal and Guide* rephrased Miller's conclusion in more positive terms. "We find that Afro-Americans are fundamentalists, for the most part," wrote the editor approvingly. History had given them good reasons to remain so. "We have seen so many radical changes to our advantage in the gradual evolution of the past half century, and we are seeing so much of the like sort from day to day that we see no good and sufficient reason to waver in the Faith or stumble in the Promise." Further, the editor suggested, a conservative belief in the Bible preserved the race's special status with God. "The Afro-American people are comprehended in the prophecy, 'I will make me a new people and a new tongue,'" he wrote.[9] African American Christians had a long tradition of belief in God's special providence for the poor and oppressed, and African American worship conventions strongly identified the fate of the race with God's plan to liberate the ancient Hebrews from Egyptian bondage. Could black Christians throw away this trust in an immanent God who cares for his people in favor of the modernists' abstract, intellectualized faith?

The best-known expression of black antievolutionism was the Reverend Charles Satchell Morris Sr.'s well-publicized attacks on Darwinism before, during, and after the Scopes trial. Although the black journalist George Schuyler labeled him "a notorious Negro rabble rouser and pulpit clown," Morris had attended Wilberforce College and Newton Theological Seminary, served as minister of New York's respectable Abyssinian Baptist Church in the pre–Adam Clayton Powell era of 1902 to 1908, and traveled for a time as a missionary in South Africa. Now the Kentucky native lectured to thousands in Norfolk, Virginia, and elsewhere about the fallacies of evolution, and published his scientific and theological case in a seem-ingly interminable eleven-part series, "Up from Monkey or Down from God," in the Norfolk *Journal and Guide*, portions of which were reprinted in other race newspapers. Throughout, Morris contrasted the hypotheses and speculative conclusions drawn by evolutionists with the Bible's clear explanation of the origin and perpetuation of species.

Morris's series did call forth a number of liberal responses from other African Americans. For example, the Pittsburgh *Courier* published "A School Girl's Answer to Dr. Charles Satchell Morris," by Alma Booker. Booker contradicted Morris's scholarly assertions by presenting the scien-tific case for human evolution, including evidence from embryology, pale-ontology, and biology. Further, as a pious Christian, she attacked the fundamentalists' insistence "that God created man at one stroke" before turning on Morris's own lack of faith. "If Dr. Morris does not believe that all present life could have originated in one single simple cell," she argued, "he is underrating the power of God, who made that cell. If God chose to write the story of creation on the fact of the whole earth instead of on the printed page, why should we disbelieve him?"[10] Booker found allies among a small number of African American modernists, including, among others, the Reverend Shelton Hale Bishop, of St. Philip's Episcopal Church in Manhattan. Contrary to Charles Satchell Morris's charge, at least some Afri-can Americans held that faith and evolution were compatible. Despite these whispers of support for modernism, the large majority of African Ameri-cans hewed closer to Morris's belief in biblical literalism, and possibly even considered themselves fundamentalists.

Their ministers were unlikely to lead them away from orthodoxy. Whereas modernism in the North had been championed generally by younger, better-educated ministers and theology students, the rising tide of education among African Americans in the twentieth century lifted few ministers of the race up to the elite colleges and seminaries where they would have come into contact with higher criticism, evolutionary science, and other products of recent European scholarship. Laments over the poor educational background of race ministers were common in the early twentieth century. As of the mid-1920s, barely 38 percent of urban black ministers and 17 percent of rural black ministers were either college or seminary graduates (compared to 80 percent and 47 percent among white ministers).[11] The tradition in the African American church that a minister needed "little or no academic preparation" if he had been "called" by God was partly ideological and partly a practical response to a historical situation in which most African Americans were barred from higher education. These were the ministers W. H. Moses had called "proverbially hostile to science."

Further, moral conservatism appealed to the majority of black leaders and ministers who ranged themselves in opposition to the same cultural changes that engaged their white counterparts. Indeed, the preoccupation with "respectability" that Evelyn Brooks Higginbotham has identified in her study of black Baptists often boiled over into a critique of public vice and the degradation of the younger generation. For example, at the international Christian Endeavor convention taking place at the same time as the Scopes trial, a great many race speakers took the floor to denounce dancing, with one "race delegate" particularly condemning the "pagan" African heritage of many contemporary dances. It was no mere coincidence that the Virginia Baptist minister Dr. B. W. Dance later that fall followed his sermon on the errors of evolution with a hostile homily on the theme of "bobbed hair and short skirts."[12] Conservative African Americans were as estranged from the culture of the Jazz Age as they were from modernism and evolutionary science.

Yet African Americans did not become militant fundamentalists dedicated to purifying church and society. The World's Christian Fundamentals Association (WCFA), the Bryan League, the Bible Crusaders—all of the major fundamentalist organizations remained lily-white during the 1920s. Nor did African Americans found their own fundamentalist associations until decades later. A handful of conservative schools for African Americans, such as the Dallas Colored Bible Institute, begun in 1928, followed by the Manhattan Bible Institute (1938), Carver (1943), and Cedine Bible Camp (1946), did tutor blacks in conservative theology, but the first clear example of an interdenominational fundamentalist movement within the African American community came only in 1963, with the black secession from the National Association of Evangelicals to form the National Negro Evangelical Association.[13]

In the 1920s and for several decades thereafter, the development of a more aggressive fundamentalism in the African American churches was halted or diverted by a massing of internal and external obstacles. Denominational allegiances and denominational machinery played a role in defusing militancy. Where the modernist controversies struck the northern Presbyterians and the northern Baptists hardest, the vast majority of African Americans belonged either to one of the various African Methodist Episcopal denominations, to a Baptist church that was nominally associated with the National Baptist Convention—approximately six of every ten black church members in the 1920s was a Baptist—or to an independent Protestant church. These affiliations did not spur militant action. African American Methodists, like their white counterparts, had a tradition of being more concerned with experiential Christianity and righteous behavior than with doctrine, and the rise of Holiness variants only intensified this reliance on religious experience.[14] Black Baptist churches, again like their white counterparts, housed some of the most theologically conservative Protestants in America, but black and white Baptists alike lacked a centralized denominational structure. Cleansing such a notoriously decentralized system would virtually have meant purging thousands of churches one by one.

A purge of modernists in the black denominations was largely unnecessary, at any rate. Only a small number of elite ministers received training at the northern seminaries and colleges that would have introduced them to modernism. The large majority of African American ministers received no higher education at all, and the rest took their degrees or certificates from southern institutions that were generally free of heretical pedagogy. Modernism thus had made few inroads among the African American clergy of the South, and so no significant modernist threat existed in the black churches to galvanize conservative ministers into a fundamentalist reaction.

Even if modernism had loomed larger as a threat in the churches, conservative African American ministers may have lacked the stomach for a purge, for they were still doing quite well within the black community. Where white fundamentalist leaders drew their bitterness at least partly from a sense of lost influence, a feeling that America was turning its back on the revivalist Protestantism that had once shaped its public and private culture, African American clergymen were still the dominant figures in their communities. Further, the African American concern with presenting a respectable public face may well have stunted the growth of militant fundamentalism in the wake of the Scopes trial. White fundamentalists leaders such as T. T. Martin reveled in their position as outsiders and reserved their strongest vituperation for "respectable" scientists and theologians. Although these fundamentalists were well aware of the ridicule they received from cosmopolitan elites, they never needed to worry that they were damaging their race's reputation by their activism. In contrast, African American ministers were supposed to be full participants in the collective effort to improve the race's status and image—they were supposed to eradicate their outsider status, not glorify it. African American ministers who were aware of the mockery that rained down on Tennessee during the Scopes trial could be forgiven if they chose not to add such calumnies to those that were already falling upon the race.

Finally, outside the denominations, the triggers for militant action were missing. In particular, the question of teaching evolution in the public schools did not become a pressing matter for the African American community, especially in the South. This lack was critical, for Darwinism in the schools was the central issue that inspired thousands of ordinary white Protestants to attach themselves to the fundamentalist crusade.

African American children, however, were in no real danger. Although school attendance for African American youth was rising along with white rates, only a quarter to a third of eligible African Americans attended the later grades of high school—the grades in which students were likeliest to encounter evolution. This was a little less than three-fourths the rate of native-born white students, and African Americans attended institutions of higher education at approximately one-fifth the white rate. The curriculum in their typically segregated high schools seldom included such an advanced biological concept as evolution. Rather, the segregated schools tended to focus more on agriculture and trades to the exclusion of "impractical" theoretical subjects. Any advance in the high school curriculum had long been thwarted by radically unequal funding (an average in the South of four times more money spent on educating white youth than on black students), dismal facilities, and untrained faculty.[15] The state of African American education in the 1920s presented numerous reasons for anger, but evolution was not one of them. The major external factor that touched off militant action by white fundamentalists was missing for African Americans.

As the doleful state of segregated educational facilities suggests, even if external events had encouraged militant fundamentalism among African Americans, the race lacked access to the levers of power, especially in the southern states, where the great majority still resided. Eventually, a few southern white fundamentalists realized that their racial caste system was preventing them from reaching out to a natural fundamentalist constituency, and they began in the late 1920s slowly to organize Bible schools for African American students. This belated philanthropy, too, underlined the relative powerlessness of conservative African American Christians.[16]

With so few public venues available for the institutional expression of militant black fundamentalism, and with several significant factors weighing against public militancy, conservative black theology remained largely confined to the churches and did not venture out into the public sphere as white fundamentalism did.[17] Just as African Americans' residence in the South predisposed them to fundamentalism, wider social conditions in the region largely prevented them from expressing their militancy politically.

Such quiescence was anathema to growing numbers of secular black intellectuals in the North who publicly criticized conditions in the South. Although he was sui generis in so many ways, W. E. B. Du Bois was perhaps the highest representative of this intellectual elite, and he was joined in this fractious and shifting network by intellectuals, rivals, and critics such as George Schuyler, the syndicated columnist William Pickens, Dean Kelly Miller of Howard University, and the Baltimore *Afro-American*'s William N. Jones. They were generally an educated group, with degrees from Fisk and Harvard (Du Bois), Talladega College and Yale (Pickens), and Howard University (Miller), though Schuyler was an extraordinarily successful autodidact. They were largely independent of the churches, deriving their living from writing, teaching, or, in McKinney's case, labor activism. Most editors in the black press, despite the occasionally religious nature of their newspapers, also functioned as members of the secular black elite, steering discussion of public matters with their editorials and their choice of news, and occasionally influencing the political process through their participation in the Republican Party and affiliated lodges. Members of this elite were dwarfed in numbers and status by the ministerial elite, but their access to the press helped make them prominent and influential in shaping black opinion.[18] Like W. H. Moses, Charles Satchell Morris, and others, they found the controversy in Dayton compelling, but they put the case at the service of their broader attack on racism in the South, and they used it to underline the problems they saw in the religious dominance of African America. In the course of the Tennessee antievolution trial, secular African American leaders proclaimed their support for John Scopes and identified the course of racial improvement not with religious growth but with scientific progress.

W. E. B. Du Bois maintained that "Dayton, Tennessee, is America: a great, ignorant, simple-minded land."[19] The laughter that rained down on Dayton, he suggested, was simply a way of pretending that Tennessee's problem was not the nation's. Many of Du Bois's fellow black intellectuals, however, sought to hang responsibility for the trial primarily around the neck of the white South. Where white editorialists lampooned the antievolution law and the Scopes prosecution as mere rural buffoonery, black editorialists viewed Tennessee's actions as part of a larger structure of white southern repression. In some cases, African American writers came to identify with John T. Scopes as a victim of southern intolerance. The *Chicago Defender* predicted before the trial that Scopes would be convicted and thrown into a cell, where he would "wear a striped suit, learn the lock-step and spend a few years reducing rocks to a more serviceable size." And why? "That is the South's way. Anything which conflicts with the South's idea of her own importance, anything which tends to break down her doctrine of white superiority she fights. If truths are introduced and these truths do not conform to what southern grandfathers believed, then [they] must be suppressed." The *Pittsburgh Courier* suggested more than once that the Tennessee anti-evolution law grew out of a general southern habit of writing the region's customs into law, reflecting what the *Courier* called "the determination of the South to be and forever remain THE SOUTH UNCHANGED." Noting that Paducah, Kentucky, had refused to employ a mathematics teacher (who happened to be John Scopes's sister) because her opinions on evolution conflicted with the superintendent's, the *Washington Tribune* immediately drew a connection to the white South's refusal to grant African Americans their rights because they might become "trouble-makers" and challenge the status quo. "In Dayton, and in thousands of similar centers over the South," wrote the editor of the *Kansas City Call*, a traveler would find "stagnation and dry rot with Hypocrisy riding a high horse."[20]

Many of these editorialists maintained that southern racism undermined the antievolutionists' claims that they were motivated by true religious sentiment. The Scopes trial underlined what the *Kansas City Call* termed the hypocrisy of "that same old brand of white Dixie Christianity." Despite the fundamentalists' professed belief in the Bible, maintained the *Washington Tribune*, everyone in the Dayton courtroom would have run out immediately to join a "lynching party" if an African American had been accused of a crime. "Lynching, to race prejudiced minds," the *Tribune* editorialist explained, "is a literal interpretation of the teaching of the Carpenter of Nazareth."[21] Where white reporters during the trial often remarked on the Daytonians' deep religious faith, African American reporters claimed that racial hypocrisy lay behind southern professions of piety.

If their piety was suspect, then what motivated southern white antievolutionists? Secular black commentators charged that the antievolution movement, from the top on down, was goaded by fear over Darwinism's racial implications. If black and white had a common ancestry, as evolutionary theory suggested, then the South's elaborate racial barriers might seem arbitrary rather than God-given. Rather than accept this conclusion, black commentators claimed, southern whites attacked evolution.[22]

The connection seemed to make sense. To begin with, members of the black secular elite felt the antievolution movement in general suffered from guilt by close association with racists. William Jennings Bryan came in for particularly harsh treatment. On the occasion of Bryan's death five days after the trial, black editorialists pointed out that he had spent his entire political career "maliciously silent on the race question."[23] "Although dubbed as a Great Commoner, his common people never seemed to embrace Negroes," noted one prominent black politician in Virginia. In his later years, Bryan had compounded his offenses against the race by moving to Florida, where, according to the *Pittsburgh Courier*, "he became a militant disciple of color-phobia, race discrimination, and religious bigotry."[24] Bryan's problem, suggested J. A. Rogers in the *Messenger*, A. Philip Randolph's radical journal, was the same hypocrisy that tainted fundamentalists throughout the South: "Bryan from the pulpit preaches the domination of Christ; in politics he practices Ku Kluxism and white domination, the bulwarks of which are lynching, murder, rape, arson, theft, and concubinage." And Bryan was one of the more racially benign antievolutionists. One of his allies in the movement, South Carolina's governor, Cole Blease, not only endorsed a rigid antievolution law but also virulently and publicly supported the extralegal lynching of black men. Blease had earned a certain amount of notoriety by planting the severed finger of a lynched African American in the gubernatorial garden. One did not need to know that William Bell Riley, head of the antievolutionist WCFA, was fond of "darky jokes" to sense that the antievolution movement was allied with many of the forces of prejudice.[25]

Most black writers discerned a more direct connection between racial prejudice and the antievolution movement. In their view white southerners opposed evolution because it implied a common heritage for the races and therefore threatened white supremacy. In the volatile racial atmosphere of the 1920s South, the logic of evolutionary thought seemed to point in the direction of racial kinship and intermarriage. Black observers interpreted antievolutionism as a white attempt to quash these implications and to preserve the campaign for racial separation that had begun in the 1880s.

Evolution did imply an uncomfortable kinship between descendents of Africans and Europeans. The *Chicago Defender* maintained that Tennessee's legislators were suppressing evolution because of the Darwinian implication "that the entire human race is supposed to have started from a common origin." "Admit that premise," the editorialist continued, "and they will have to admit that there is no fundamental difference between themselves and the race they pretend to despise" William N. Jones in his "Day by Day" column for the Baltimore *Afro-American* asserted hyperbolically that white Tennesseans believed God had "CREATED SOME HUMAN BEING[S] DIFFERENT AND DISTINCT FROM OTHERS." Evolution clearly contradicted such a belief. Nor were black critics the only ones who claimed to see a strong racial component in antievolutionism. The southern white journalist W. J. Cash, who observed the controversy at close range, recalled later, "One of the most stressed notions which went around was that evolution made a Negro as good as a white man—that is, threatened White Supremacy."[26] Although the "race question" did not arise explicitly in the Scopes trial itself, African American intellectuals believed that the white South was seriously troubled by evolution's destabilizing implications for Anglo-Saxon supremacy.

These implications seemed particularly troubling in the spring and summer of 1925, as southern legislatures considered a series of "race integrity" laws to prohibit intermarriage between blacks and whites. The original bill's author, Representative John Powell of Richmond, Virginia, confessed he was alarmed by the "enormous increase in numbers of people with Negro blood"—that is, those of mixed European and African descent—and his counterparts in Georgia and elsewhere likewise complained of an explosion in the "production of Afro-American mongrels." The Georgia bill's sponsor, Representative J. C. Davis, thought the "greatest present danger" was "unwittingly permitting a near white mulatto to marry into our families."[27]

It was left to the *Atlanta Constitution*, a bulwark of "progressive" segregationism, to connect the dots between the white South's most potent racial fears and the theory of evolution. According to scientific evolutionists, noted the *Constitution*, "the progressive evolution of the human animal demands racial miscegenation." Indeed, the *Constitution* reported that such prominent evolutionists as H. G. Wells were calling for racial intermarriage as a conscious strategy for combating prejudice and improving the human race.[28] Evolution and evolutionists threatened to transform the wall between black and white into a marital threshold. Little wonder that many white southerners would be concerned.

Were these perceptions of antievolutionism's racial component fair or accurate? On the most accessible, surface level, race appears seldom in the antievolution literature. Leading antievolutionists were almost exclusively concerned with evolution's implications for the veracity of the Bible—its story of divine miracles, the virgin birth, the salvation of humanity. Indeed, most fundamentalists were theologically committed to the belief that humanity of all races sprang from the singular creation of Adam and Eve. Although the question of racial differentiation twisted many of them into theological knots, conservative Christians had over the previous century fought public battles against scientists such as Josiah Nott, who argued the races had been created separately. William Jennings Bryan did not have a clean record on questions of race, but he and his fellow antievolution leaders spent little time discussing the matter in the context of their movement.

The antievolution movement, however, harbored racial meanings at other levels. It is possible, for example, that the antievolutionists' palpable disgust at being related to apes conveyed, at some level, a racial sentiment. In literature and iconography at the time, satirists commonly equated Africans and African Americans with apes, and radical racists from the 1890s onward had sought to tie African Americans still closer to this "bestial" image.[29] Further, looking at the words only of the leaders may be misleading. Antievolutionism was a local movement as well as a national one, and it may be that local activists did not share the national leaders' sense of discretion. To members of the secular black elite, the antievolutionists' attack on evolutionary science seemed clearly related to their more common attacks on African Americans.

Secular black intellectuals did face one significant obstacle to their attempts to embrace science as an ally. Even as African Americans claimed that science was on their side in the struggle against white supremacy, much science in the early twentieth century endorsed regressive racial ideals at least as often as it undermined them. Although Darwinism had earlier combined with the Christian tradition of monogenesis to lay to rest the polygenist interpretation of humanity's origins, from the late nineteenth century onward many scientists and laypeople began to place evolution at the service of their racial preconceptions. Most of the new scientific racists accepted that the races had not been created separately, but they argued that the races had nevertheless diverged widely from their point of common ancestry—some remaining closer to the "primitive" form of humanity, others evolving a great deal "higher."[30] Beginning with this assumption that the races of the world could be ranged on a hierarchy from least evolved to most evolved, physical and social scientists in the early twentieth century construed the results of intelligence tests, craniometry, and physical anthropology to "prove" the existence of the hierarchy, and to argue that it provided a living snapshot of the evolutionary process. Environmental forces and other factors had pushed white Europeans—especially the Anglo-Saxons at the top of the hierarchy—to evolve "higher" physical structures and greater intelligence, while the other races of the earth were still stuck on one of the lower rungs of the ladder that led upward to the Caucasian form. Men and women of African descent, in this system of thought, preserved the form, emotions, and intelligence of primitive humans.

Scientists did not hesitate to popularize these racial ideas. Racial ranking was there in the textbook John Scopes used for teaching evolution: George W. Hunter's *Civic Biology*, the official Tennessee biology text, was typical of the genre, as it listed the "five races" in what the author took to be ascending order, starting with "the Ethiopian or negro type" and going through the Malay, the American Indian, and the Mongolian before arriving at what Hunter called "the highest type of all, the Caucasians." It was there in the eugenics movement, which fought successfully to pass racially discriminatory laws to sterilize the "feebleminded," and it was there in baroque form when the 1924 National Origins Act restricted immigration according to a complex evaluation of race, ethnicity, and regional culture.[31] Finally, racial ranking was palpably present in the public pronouncements of such leading evolutionists as Henry Fairfield Osborn, the influential director of the American Museum of Natural History in New York City. As a professional paleontologist, Osborn naturally championed evolutionary theory, and he debated William Jennings Bryan in print during the years leading up to the Scopes trial. His book *The Earth Speaks to Bryan* (1925) was a compendium of speeches in support of evolution. Osborn was at the same time a committed eugenicist, and he clearly offered a scientific endorsement of racial separation and racial hierarchy with his hypothesis that racial "stocks" had separated much earlier than previously believed.[32] The scientific justifications for white supremacy and Anglo-Saxon or Nordic superiority were simply a part of many white Americans' mental furniture: comfortable, supportive, unremarkable.

It is therefore striking that the secular black elite in 1925 expressed tremendous confidence in the power of science and evolutionary theory to threaten white supremacy. While identifying with the progressive power of the scientific endeavor, members of the secular black elite chose to read scientific developments in such a way as to maintain their belief in science's usefulness. In brief, they embraced scientific developments they found congenial and discarded the rest.

In part, their confidence in science derived from the belief of Du Bois and other race leaders that many branches of science were turning away from their earlier entanglements with racist thought. At the same moment that eugenics, for example, seemed poised to become a permanent and prominent fixture on the American landscape, a new generation of scientists had already begun the job of hammering its intellectual foundations into rubble. As they discarded their belief in the older idea of "unit-character" heredity that eugenicist thinking had depended on, leading geneticists also withdrew their support from the eugenics movement and began to write public letters recommending that their eugenicist brethren get themselves back up to speed on scientific developments. Similarly, professional anthropologists, led by Franz Boas at Columbia University, were beginning a slow turn against the racialism that had earlier provided a central organizing principle for their discipline. Boas in particular maintained close ties to numerous African American intellectuals, including Du Bois, Monroe N. Work, and Carter G. Woodson.[33] While Boas continued to harbor notions about the hierarchy of races, after 1909 he and his students grew increasingly vocal about the racial misconceptions that plagued the social and physical sciences. In a celebrated series of articles for the *Nation* on the eve of the Scopes trial, Boas and several students eviscerated the Nordic hypothesis in particular and scientific racism more generally. Boas in his own article for the series went so far as to argue that "race" made very little sense as a biological category—and no sense at all as a principle for ordering peoples into "superior" and "inferior" groups. Black newspapers such as the *New York Amsterdam News* happily reprinted several of the *Nation* essays.[34] These were only the first stirrings of American science's repudiation of racism, but during the public dispute over evolution the secular black elite expressed faith that science was becoming a reliable ally.

Scientific progress and the evolutionary hypothesis held particular meanings for the African American elite. Black leaders embraced the racial implications of evolution—the common origins of humanity and the importance of environment as well as heredity—and they believed that evolutionary science itself embodied the spirit of progress that would lift the race higher. In a series of columns for the Baltimore *Afro-American* during the spring of 1925, William N. Jones conveyed an appreciation of evolutionary progress in several senses. First, the lessons of evolution had created greater racial sympathy in the short term. As he celebrated the hundredth anniversary of T. H. Huxley's birth, Jones claimed that few white men had done as much as Huxley to help race relations, for Huxley had followed Darwin's scientific line of reasoning to question the idea that some men "by Divine right" were born kings, while others "by Divine curse" were born slaves. "Science won," Jones asserted, "and as a result the world, in spite of hidebound and narrow dogmas, is heading towards real brotherhood." Second, looking at the long term, Jones conflated biological and social evolution to bolster his faith in the future of the race. "The Negro race is passing through a stage of evolution the like of which this old world has never seen," the columnist observed. "The hope of mankind is in evolution and always has been. Not only have we slowly come up through animal life, though stone and iron ages, but we are still changing both our physical structures and institutions."[35] Jones's scientific understanding was not always accurate—he believed that human hair and teeth were passing away because "civilization" made them unnecessary—but his essays embodied the secular black elite's faith that evolutionary progress was going to lift the race out of its degraded condition.

Finally, science in the abstract appealed to the secular black elite as a force for change. In numerous editorials on the Scopes trial, African American writers trumpeted scientific objectivity as a threat to the white South's calcified traditions. "It will be established at Dayton, beyond doubt," predicted the *Pittsburgh Courier*, "that the South prefers its traditions to science; its Southern self exaltation to any truth science may have discovered, or may yet discover." Where white southerners often invoked "tradition" to justify their peculiar configuration of race relations, the secular black elite preferred to embrace the example of scientists such as Huxley, whose determination to carry "clear reasoning" to its logical end, according to William N. Jones, had led him to strike a blow against white supremacy even though he had not begun with any such "benevolent intent regarding black men and women." Like their white counterparts, black commentators on the Scopes trial often invoked the "martial metaphor" of warfare between science and religion, but African Americans drew clearer parallels between the church that silenced scientists such as Galileo for violating religious dogma and the white southerners who feared that the scientific spirit would violate their racial dogma. In both cases, men who placed their unthinking faith in "tradition" sought to choke the engine of human progress. Jones concluded, "Only science which seeks truth, wherever it may lead, has been able to guide mankind with unerring efficiency."[36] The hope of the race lay in scientific progress, not stale tradition.

Not surprisingly, many African American leaders during the Scopes trial identified with the scientific elite in opposition to the white southerners who were prosecuting the young science teacher. This was an era that saw scientific experts extending their cultural authority, a trend apotheosized in Sinclair Lewis's *Arrowsmith*, the Pulitzer Prize–winning novel about a heroic physician-scientist. *Arrowsmith* was published the same year as the Scopes trial, and the secular black elite in its condemnations of Tennessee sought to partake of the scientists' prestige it represented, if only rhetorically. Secular black leaders identified with the scientific elite as a way of claiming membership in a more cosmopolitan national culture.[37]

For these secular black leaders, the choice was easy. Evolutionary science by 1925 had begun to slough off its racialist assumptions, while antievolutionists were identified with some of the most racist features of the South; cosmopolitan science promised a future of progress without regard for the niceties of "tradition," while Tennessee seemed to offer only an insular protection for southern folkways. As the commentary on the Scopes trial demonstrated, scientific objectivity and a national outlook appeared very attractive to some African American leaders struggling against the southern "habit" of white supremacy.

As members of the secular black elite sought to bolster their own positions and the status of the race by identifying with science, they discovered a major obstacle in their road to racial respectability: African American religiosity. The white South was not the only center of support for antievolution. The large number of African Americans who were prompted by the Scopes trial to declare themselves publicly as fundamentalists and antievolutionists compelled many black intellectuals to criticize the conservative black ministry. African Americans could not expect reasonable leadership from such "pulpit clowns" as Charles Satchell Morris, Schuyler suggested. Indeed, the radical journalist and labor organizer Ernest Rice McKinney argued that religious orthodoxy was a clear impediment to progress. "The Fundamentalist simply sits by the brake and holds it down tight," McKinney scoffed. "All that he knows is that Change and Light are poison to him." Nor did McKinney find any African American fundamentalists by his side in the struggle for labor reform and radical social change. Indeed, the African American clergy's general social conservatism was so notorious that toward the end of his long life W. E. B. Du Bois confessed he was puzzled to find a Baptist minister named Martin Luther King Jr. taking a leading role in the civil rights movement. As his biographer notes, Du Bois "had expected to live to see anything but a militant Baptist preacher."[38] Having observed the Scopes trial and the arguments surrounding it, Du Bois was well aware of the conservative orthodoxy that prevailed among African American ministers. Some went further in their critique. Shortly after the Scopes trial, McKinney suggested that the race's religion problem was not so much fundamentalism as it was religion itself. "What most of us want is more money and less work," the author explained, "fewer half-baked preachers and more real business men, more homes actually built and fewer holes in the ground where a church might be some day." Black communities poured a great deal of commercial and human capital into their churches—far more by income than white communities—and McKinney complained that this focus on the kingdom of God seemed to leave secular matters neglected. A study of African American sermons a few years after the Scopes trial confirmed the suspicions of McKinney and other observers that most African American ministers offered a message that was "predominantly other-worldly," concentrating on rewards in the afterlife and submerging "the practical aspects of life on earth." This otherworldly orientation, in McKinney's opinion, contrasted poorly with the practicality that guided other peoples: "We get ready for Heaven while other races prepare to pay dividends." Even the late William Jennings Bryan, McKinney pointed out, had left behind an estate of about a half million dollars. "But as for us—well, we'll get ours 'early in the morning,'" he concluded, bitterly invoking the well-known spiritual.[39]

For members of the secular black elite, that metaphorical morning of freedom and equality was too vague, too far off in the future to hold any meaning. Instead of praying for deliverance during the nadir of race relations, leading intellectuals tried to identify the race's cause with what they saw as the forces of "progress" in the 1920s—northern urbanism, secularism, and science—and sought to distance themselves from the perceived stagnation and ignorance of the South, embodied, in their opinion, by the white South's racially motivated embrace of the antievolution movement. Along the way, however, secular black intellectuals stumbled over the stubborn faith of their own people. Just as the Scopes trial offered members of the secular black elite the opportunity to position themselves rhetorically alongside the forces of modernity, it also laid bare the gulf that existed between these aspiring leaders of the race and their ministerial competitors. The gulf was real, and it was not to the intellectuals' advantage. Eighty years later, African Americans are still significantly more religious—measured by church attendance, prayer, and the importance they place on religion—than the general population.[40] More than half the black population adheres to a literal interpretation of the Bible, as compared to one-third of the population as a whole, and African Americans are significantly more likely than the general population to adhere to a creationist account of origins.[41] For all the secular black elite's moral and rhetorical power, and for all the controversy stirred up by the Scopes trial, Sunday mornings after 1925 have continued to find the mass of African Americans in church.

4

Descent with Modification

IDEOLOGY AND STRATEGY IN ANTIEVOLUTIONISM

THE FIRST THING most visitors to the Sistine Chapel look for is Michelangelo's frescoes on the vaulted ceiling. Near the center, the master depicted the first episodes of Genesis—God separating light from darkness, parting the land from the sea, and creating the celestial bodies. These are extraordinary images, with a bearded, powerful Jehovah forging the universe out of primordial chaos, but they are not quite the focal point of the ceiling. Rather, at the very center of the chapel's vault, taking precedence over even the creation of the universe, lies "The Creation of Adam," in which Adam and the Lord strain their muscular arms toward each other until their fingertips touch, and God, in a vortex of angels and energy, brings the first man to life.

Besides portraying the creation, this Catholic shrine may seem disconnected from the Protestant crusade against evolution. Michelangelo's frescoes, however, display in dramatic fashion the three major components of the antievolution impulse—the primacy of Jesus, the centrality of man in the universe, and a fear of social disorder.

First, on the far wall of the chapel, "The Last Judgment" depicts Jesus in the center of a similar chaotic swirl, but this circular movement derives from the churning of the elect rising to heaven while a larger group of sinners descends to the pits of hell. "The Creation of Adam" and "The Last Judgment" are obviously tied together by Michelangelo's stylistic genius, but Michelangelo also united the frescoes through his depictions of Adam and Jesus. The two men bear an uncanny resemblance to each another; they could be the same person (see figure 4.2). This is no coincidence. The visual link suggests that the first man and the son of God are inextricably connected to each other. A Sistine Chapel with one but not the other

FIGURE 4.1 Michelangelo Buonarroti's *Creation of Adam* in the Sistine Chapel. Image from the Vatican Museums.

would still be a beautiful room, but it would lack the power it draws from its depiction of the unbreakable link between Genesis and the New Testament. This link lies at the heart of the antievolution impulse. For the vast majority of antievolutionists, the central mission has not been merely to defend "religion" or even the biblical account of the creation, but rather to safeguard the entire structure of creation, sin, and redemption that unites the Garden of Eden with the Garden of Gethsemane. The American antievolution impulse usually appears to be just about Genesis, but it is more fundamentally about Jesus.

"The Creation of Adam" embodies the second component of antievolutionism. Although in Genesis God creates plants and other animals, each of which will reproduce "after its own kind," Michelangelo largely ignores these creations and lavishes his attention on Adam as a separate, special creation in God's own image. He is the centerpiece of creation. The evolutionary alternative—that humans are animals and share a common ancestry with all other animals—is inherently repulsive to many, and it threatens mankind's sense of its own preeminence in the universe. Where "The Creation of Adam" emphasizes the dignity of man's special position, antievolutionists commonly accuse their opponents of lowering humans to the level of (other) animals. The innumerable antievolutionist cartoons that depict humans as descending directly from monkeys underline the absurdity of taking man down from his elevated status.

The broader scheme of "The Last Judgment" manifests the third antievolutionist theme of social disorder. The religious and political turmoil Michelangelo had lived through—the Reformation and Counter-Reformation, the

FIGURE 4.2 Michelangelo's *The Last Judgment* in the Sistine Chapel. Michelangelo Buonarotti via Wikimedia Commons.

sacking of Rome in 1527, and other events in the turbulent sixteenth century—had darkened the artist's vision, and his portrayal of the Apocalypse conveys well his sense that the civilization he had once known was falling apart. The threat of social decline has long fueled the antievolutionist impulse. Prior to the current century, the critical moments of growth came during the Great War and its aftermath, and during the cultural upheavals of the 1960s. The threat evolution poses to social order has been a powerful antievolutionist theme, linking Darwinism to the depredations of German aggression, communism, sexual liberation, secularism, crime, and a host of other dangers Michelangelo never could have imagined. Evolution may not always have played the causal role its opponents ascribed to it, but it did offer religious conservatives a coherent explanation for the tumult of their times, and it held out the possibility that they could set society aright if only they could reduce Darwin's pernicious influence.

Each of these three themes—the importance of Jesus, common descent, and social disorder—has waxed and waned in importance over the last century. They found their clearest expression during the period of the Scopes trial, when antievolutionists were able to proclaim their motivations openly without having to strategize around Supreme Court rulings on the separation of church and state. But they are still visible between the lines of intelligent design textbooks, and they still structure the ideology of antievolution activists from Seattle to Louisiana to Dover, Pennsylvania.

On a superficial level, the antievolution movement has seemed to revolve primarily around the threat evolution posed to the Genesis account of creation. The Tennessee controversy began, after all, with the Butler Act, which outlawed only school lessons that contradicted "the story of the Divine creation of man as taught in the Bible." Although the higher criticism of the Bible was at least as damaging to orthodox Christian faith as evolution was, it did not make significant gains outside the seminaries, liberal pulpits, and circles of "bohemian" opinion. When Bryan launched the crusade against evolution, therefore, he was sallying forth against the most visible threat to the Bible. But he was also narrowing his public defense of the Bible down to the issue of the veracity of Genesis.

From that time forward, observers have tended to accept the public pronouncements of Bryan and his allies that their major concern was safeguarding the biblical account of creation. Behind that public stance, however, lay antievolutionists' deeper fear that disbelief in Genesis would ultimately undermine the faith that Jesus had come to earth once and was to come again to redeem mankind from sin.

John Scopes's defense team was happy to go along with Bryan's public position that the struggle was between Darwinism and Genesis. Recognizing that the divinity and resurrection of Christ were, like the virgin birth, extremely sensitive subjects, evolution's defenders steered clear of the New Testament. Indeed, in his famous cross-examination of Bryan on the seventh day of the trial, Clarence Darrow questioned Bryan about Jonah and the whale (or the "big fish," as Bryan insisted it be called), about Joshua commanding the sun to stand still, and about another handful of what one historian calls "the more extravagant miracles of the Old Testament," but never did Darrow raise a question about Jesus' life.[1] Certainly, much of the New Testament defies scientific understanding. The virgin birth and bodily resurrection are only the most prominent among numerous episodes in Jesus' story that rely on a miraculous suspension of natural laws. But if Darrow found these episodes to be beyond the pale of reason, he kept his skepticism to himself for the duration of the trial. The defense of Darwinism did not need to become tangled up with any other disputes—especially those touching on the divinity of the Savior.

Nevertheless, Bryan and his allies knew that skepticism about Genesis inevitably would cause collateral damage to the New Testament, and from the beginning they saw their primary mission as defending the Bible as a record of God's plan for salvation through Jesus Christ. Although they focused their rhetoric on other issues, prosecutors repeatedly betrayed their fundamental fear that evolution sapped the Christian's belief in Jesus, not Genesis.

On the fifth day of the trial, just as Bryan was preparing to launch into a condemnation of man's kinship with monkeys, Judge Raulston interrupted him with a more urgent concern. "Let me ask you a question: Do you understand the evolution theory to involve the divine birth of divinity, or Christ's virgin birth, in any way or not?"[2] For a few minutes, Bryan plunged on with his rehearsed remarks—he was more accustomed to making speeches than answering questions—but he eventually circled back to Raulston's inquiry.

> Yes, because this principle of evolution disputes the miracle; there is no place for the miracle in this train of evolution, and the Old Testament and the New are filled with miracles, and if this doctrine is true, this logic eliminates every mystery in the Old Testament and the New, and eliminates everything supernatural, and that means they eliminate the virgin birth—that means that they eliminate the resurrection of the body—that means that they eliminate the doctrine of atonement and they believe man has been rising all the time, that man never fell, that when the Savior came there was not any reason why He should not go as soon as He could, that He was born of Joseph or some other co-respondent, and that He lies in his grave.[3]

These concerns were common among antievolutionists. James S. Hatcher, an African Methodist Episcopal minister in Richmond, Virginia, offered a more vivid account of the implications of throwing out a literal interpretation of the Bible. "Whither will this infidelity lead?" he asked. "If Jesus was not conceived by the Holy Ghost and born of the Virgin Mary, then God is a liar, Mary an harlot, Joseph a fornicator, and Jesus a bastard; and listen keenly, no bastard savior with a lying father and a harlot mother can save me." Rather than accept such a possibility, Hatcher asserted his belief that every word of the Bible was "the eternal, inerrant, infallible Word of God."[4]

Tennessee's attorney general, Tom Stewart, contemplated the worst possible fate for a society that decided to throw away Genesis in favor of letting science progress through the question of human origins. "The next thing you know," he warned, "there will be a legal battle staged within the corners of this state, that challenges even permitting anyone to believe that Jesus Christ was divinely born—that Jesus Christ was born of a virgin— challenge that, and the next step will be a battle staged denying the right to teach that there was a resurrection, until finally that precious book and its glorious teachings upon which this civilization has been built will be taken from us."[5] Clearly, the Butler Act was propping up a much more elaborate structure than simply the first verses of the Old Testament.

Bryan and Stewart were hardly alone in weighing the New Testament as more important than the Old. By definition, the belief that Jesus came to redeem mankind from the sin that Adam and Eve brought into the world is what makes a Christian a Christian. Christians over the centuries have developed varying interpretations of the books of the Old Testament, but they have generally treated it as prologue to the New Testament. Calling it the "Old Testament" instead of the "Hebrew Bible" certainly suggested that its significance was fundamentally tied to the support it gave to the New Testament.

Even as antievolutionism mutated into a variety of forms over the following decades, the primacy of Jesus over Genesis was to remain at the core of the antievolution impulse. The leader of the modern-day Institute for Creation Research, Henry Morris III, warns that without the events in Genesis—the creation, the Fall, and the Flood—"the gospel message would make little sense."[6] "Satan's strategic plan," Morris suggests, is to use evolution to make Christians "question the accuracy, the meaning, the authenticity, the historicity, or any other shade of all scripture," with the ultimate goal of dethroning Jesus.[7] The ICR's own publications illustrate the relative weight of the antievolution movement's concerns, for approximately 80 percent of the mass emails it sends do not deal with creation at all but rather focus on Jesus' mission of redemption. Occasionally the mailings merge the two, as when Morris stresses the oneness of God and Jesus in both creation and redemption. "The height of irony and the depth of foolishness, are reached," he argues, "when those whose very minds and bodies were created by Christ refuse even to admit the fact of creation."[8] Christ's participation in the creation was necessary for him to play his role in the world. "Only its Creator could ever become its Savior," Morris explains, "since no one else in all creation was both deserving and capable of such a mission."[9]

Morris and his allies thus elide the distance between Genesis and the Gospels, reassuring themselves and their followers that the public crusade against evolution is not a mere distraction from their evangelical mission to spread the word of Christ. On the contrary, Morris has scolded some of his fellow evangelicals for sometimes presenting the central message of the gospel—"the return of Christ and our hope of heaven"—while shying away from teaching "the *full* gospel," which includes the foundational doctrine of Christ's involvement in the creation.[10] Like many of his antievolutionist brethren, Morris reserves some of his strongest condemnation for theistic evolutionists, who try to bridge the gap between the concepts by suggesting that God guided the evolutionary process, or at least put into place the laws of nature that allowed evolution to unfold, until he intervened directly in the life of Jesus.

The importance of salvation in the antievolution controversy is rivaled by the question of common descent. Michelangelo's Adam does not share descent with other animals but rather is created in God's own image. In contrast, Darwin argued that every species had evolved from a long line of other species. More critically, Darwin suggested—obliquely in *On the Origin of Species* and directly in *The Descent of Man*—that humans, too, were part of this evolutionary process. Humans therefore were not a separate, special creation by God in his image but rather were products of material forces; they shared a common ancestry not only with the great apes and other primates but also with other mammals and reptiles and fish, stretching all the way back to the first single-celled bacterium. Common descent lay at the heart of Darwin's vision, and it provoked much of the antievolutionists' objection to evolution.

Common descent offended critics in two ways. First, the evolutionary hypothesis dethroned man as a special creation of God. Rather than the center of a divine plan, man was almost an accident, a product of the "struggle for survival" among animals over the course of millennia. This new vision of humanity raised the crucial but vexing question of when, in the train of evolution, the soul entered man. "There couldn't be any relation between man and monkey," noted the Reverend A. B. Callis, of Baltimore, in 1925. "A monkey has no soul, therefore has no salvation. But man has both a soul and a salvation."[11] Second, evolution's opponents complained that common descent linked every human with every other creature on earth. Many critics argued erroneously that evolution meant humans were direct descendents of monkeys, rather than products of a common ancestor millions of years ago. Although Darwin himself was comfortable with the idea that humans were descended from an apelike ancestor, others found it offensive to suggest that mankind's closest living relatives were at that very moment eating grubs in the jungle. Indeed, some of evolution's strongest supporters, such as the scientific popularizer Frances Mason and the paleontologist Henry Fairfield Osborn, recognized that equating humans with gorillas could arouse strong prejudice; in 1928 they fretted over the ill effect that a depiction of a gorilla on the cover of a new scientific periodical, *Evolution*, might have on popular sentiment toward evolution.[12]

In the context of the times, common descent carried implications that were still more dangerous. In a sermon to a Chattanooga gathering, T. T. Martin decried evolutionists "for teaching that your Mother and your sister have Negro, hog, and skunk blood running in their veins."[13] Billy Sunday simply found the whole idea preposterous. In a rhetorical question that continues today to echo among antievolutionists, he asked, "If man is evolved from a monkey, then why are there any monkeys now? You can't answer that to save your life."[14]

William Jennings Bryan voiced these complaints during the trial. He picked up George W. Hunter's *Civic Biology*, the book that John Scopes allegedly used to teach about evolution, and turned to Hunter's diagram "The Tree of Life," which depicted the branching off of different species over time. Bryan pointed out the last circle on the tree:

> And then we have mammals, 3,500, and there is a little circle and man is in the circle, find him, find man . . .
>
> Not only the evolution is possible, but the scientists possibly think of shutting man up in a little circle like that with all these animals, that have an odor, that extends beyond the circumference of this circle, my friends.

(Extended laughter.) . . .

Tell me that the parents of this day have not any right to declare that children are not to be taught this doctrine? Shall not be taken down from the high plane upon which God put man? Shall be detached from the throne of God and be compelled to link their ancestors with the jungle, tell that to these children?[15]

Although the idea of common descent provoked laughter and ridicule, it also punctured the bubble of mankind's considerable self-regard and threatened to lower humanity to the level of brutes. Even in 2005, a Harris Poll found that 49 percent of respondents believed plants and animals had evolved from earlier species, but the number dropped to 38 percent when asked specifically about human origins.[16]

Misgivings over the danger evolution posed to faith in salvation through Jesus and to humanity's separateness from the rest of creation might have remained latent for many years, a matter of interest primarily to theologians and church politicians, but for the threat of social disorder. Both in the early twentieth century and at the turn of the twenty-first, cultural upheavals triggered an antievolutionist response. Just as Jesus in "The Last Judgment" casts worldly sinners into the pits of hell, so have antievolutionists seen themselves as fighting for righteousness in a fallen, degraded culture.

William Jennings Bryan's own progress from mild dissenter to implacable enemy of evolutionary theory exemplified the process by which disorder in the secular world spurred theological conservatives to attack evolution. Early on, Bryan professed misgivings about evolution's scientific validity and its apparent irreligiousness, but his opinions were mild. "While I do not accept the Darwinian theory," Bryan told an audience in 1908, "I shall not quarrel with you about it."[17]

The Great War launched Bryan and his fellow conservative evangelicals on a crusade against evolutionary theory.[18] Bryan had long believed that Darwinism constituted an endorsement of warfare, but the danger of this endorsement seemed more pressing after Europe marched into the slaughterhouse of war. As President Woodrow Wilson's secretary of state, Bryan vigorously opposed America's growing involvement in the European conflict, and when Wilson seemed to tilt too consistently toward war, Bryan resigned. He searched for the causes of Europe's great conflagration and became convinced that Germany's militarism and "barbarism" had grown directly from the German high command's fondness for

Darwin and his late nineteenth-century interpreter, the philosopher Fried-
rich Nietzsche.[19] Drawing such connections between Darwinism, German
militarism, and Nietzsche was not entirely accurate, but Bryan's opinions
were crystallized by his reading of Vernon Kellogg's *Headquarters Nights*
(1917) and Benjamin Kidd's *The Science of Power* (1918).[20] Kellogg was a
native Kansan who had lived among the German military leaders while
serving with the Commission for the Relief of Belgium. From his conversations with the high command, Kellogg concluded that Germans at every
social level were motivated by the Darwinian creed of "a natural selection
based on violent and fatal competitive struggle." In Germany, Kellogg
explained, "the pale ascetic intellectual and the burly, red-faced butcher"
found common ground in their belief that the struggle for survival applied
not only to individuals but also to the nations of the world.[21] In another
book that enjoyed wide popularity in the United States, Benjamin Kidd, an
Englishman, seconded Kellogg's thesis. In continental Europe, Kidd
argued, "Darwin's theories came to be openly set out in political and military textbooks as the full justification for war and highly organized
schemes of national policy in which the doctrine of Force became the doctrine of Right."[22] The imperialistic land grab of the late nineteenth century
was one result of this doctrine; the Great War was another. Bryan saw the
"law of hate" reaping a mighty European harvest.

Bryan also became convinced that Darwinism was an immediate threat
at home. As he explained as early as 1904, "The Darwinian theory represents man as reaching his present perfection by the operation of the law
of hate—the merciless law by which the strong crowd out and kill off the
weak."[23] Bryan had heard far too many conservatives justify their opposition to reform by an appeal to Herbert Spencer's vaguely Darwinian doctrine of "survival of the fittest," with its claim that charity, social uplift, and
other forms of mutual aid interfered with the "laws of nature."[24] With the
end of the Great War, the United States seemed to be withdrawing even
further from the reform impulse.

In addition, fundamentalists could attack evolution as a cause of or at
least an accessory to a revolution in morals and manners that seemed to
threaten the traditional order. Flappers and the New Woman were only a
part of a larger cultural problem. The *Nashville Tennessean*, generally a
sober periodical, lumped evolutionists together with "the liberals, the feminists, the radicals of all degrees and shades, the birth controlists, the psy-
cho-analysts, the agnostics . . . the Socialists, social service workers,
professional 'causers.'"[25] Before this specter of radical social change, the

fundamentalists and antievolutionists took their place alongside the second Ku Klux Klan and other groups dedicated to slowing America's descent into immorality.

In the end, though, the energy behind these groups dissipated, and many of the social changes that had galvanized their discontent during the 1920s became more or less routine elements of American culture. Legal alcohol returned, young men and women continued to dance, park, and "pet," adult women achieved relatively greater emancipation, and even Catholicism no longer seemed to be a threat to the Republic. Conservative evangelicals reviled these trends, but for three and a half decades they remained largely detached from public engagement. Their hibernation was not to last.

It was perhaps only serendipity that the first salvo in the modern antievolution battle—the publication of Henry Morris and John C. Whitcomb's *The Genesis Flood*—was fired in 1961, the dawn of a decade that was to witness a transformation of American culture so dizzying that the "revolution" of the 1920s seemed comparatively tame. *The Genesis Flood* itself was the product of relatively insular debates among antievolutionists over previous decades. In the years after the Scopes trial, fundamentalists disputed among themselves whether they should continue to adhere to older ways of reconciling Genesis with the geological record, such as the "gap theory," which held that a "gap" of thousands or even millions of years could have intervened between the first days of creation and the appearance of life recorded in Genesis, or the "day-age" theory, the older orthodoxy embraced by Bryan and popularized by the 1909 *Scofield Reference Bible*, which held that the "days" of creation in Genesis might correspond to epochs of thousands of years.[26] Ranged against these theorists was a generally younger generation of "young-earth" creationists who believed the words of Genesis meant exactly what they said, so that God had created the universe in six days of twenty-four hours, and the age of the earth was indeed about six thousand years, a figure Archbishop James Ussher had calculated in the seventeenth century from the ages of figures in the Old Testament.[27] *The Genesis Flood* was the most scientific expression of this more aggressively literalist young-earth belief, employing flood hydrology (Morris had been trained as a hydrologist) to explain that the Flood had so scrambled the geological and fossil record that hapless geologists and paleontologists mistakenly believe they are looking at evidence of millions of years of evolved life rather than a true record of the earth's six thousand or so years. Ironically, at the same time as creationists began to emphasize the scientific character of their mission, they also narrowed their reading of Genesis to the strictest literal interpretation.

The young-earthers' triumph among their compatriots in the American Scientific Affiliation and other organizations would have meant little if the social unrest of the 1960s had not triggered a broader movement of social conservatives who adopted antievolutionism as one of their tenets. Christian conservatives experienced the 1960s as a series of shocks to the traditional moral order, beginning with God and the public schools. The first shock came when the U.S. Supreme Court in its 1962 *Engel v. Vitale* decision declared that mandatory prayers in the public schools violated the establishment clause of the Constitution. *Engel* was followed in short order by *Abington v. Schempp* (1963), in which the Court held that the mandatory reading of Bible verses in the public schools likewise violated the separation of church and state. After those two decisions conservatives watched as the Court tentatively built a higher wall of separation between church and state.

Outside the courtroom, conservatives found confirmation for their worst fears about the effects of "banishing" religion from the schools. In the years after *Engel* and *Abington*, *Newsweek* and *Time* both declared that American youth were in the throes of a sexual revolution, one that would eventually reach beyond New York and California to Kansas, Wisconsin, and other unlikely venues.[28] In matters of sex, clothing, living arrangements, and a host of other behaviors, a small but well-publicized counterculture raised similar challenges to traditional social structures in ways that paralleled and often intersected with the militant resistance to American military involvement in Vietnam and other Cold War hotspots. By 1968, these and other shocks had awakened a conservative counteroffensive by a new grassroots movement of "suburban warriors" who organized not simply around anticommunism at home and abroad or government intrusion but also around social issues, especially matters of sex, such as obscenity, promiscuity, and sex education.[29] Evolution fit well in this array of offenses against traditional order.

As in the 1920s, the educational system became the prime mechanism by which these disagreements over American culture became political. For antievolutionism, the seeds of the school fight were planted in 1957, when the Soviet Union launched Sputnik 1, the first artificial space satellite. Although Sputnik did little more than emit a maddening radio beep and measure atmospheric density, it shocked American policy makers into approving a crash program to improve American science education.

Among the initiatives was the federally funded Biological Sciences Curriculum Study (BSCS) at the University of Colorado, which in 1963 rolled out a series of sophisticated biology textbooks and instructional materials that thoroughly integrated evolution into their lessons.[30] With nearly half of the nation's high schools adopting BSCS material, Henry Morris and his allies found their concerns over evolution to be increasingly relevant. Now that God had been "banished" from the classroom, the public schools were free to teach about the subject that Morris called the "foundation of communism, Fascism, Freudianism, social Darwinism, behaviorism, Kinseyism, materialism, atheism and, in the religious world, modernism and Neo-Orthodoxy."[31]

As the suburban warriors' concerns over social disorder began in the 1970s to move from the margins to the mainstream of American politics, antievolution leaders seized the opportunity to make alliances with prominent conservatives who shared so much of their worldview.[32] Although they were fixated more on sexual offenses in the new culture, Jerry Falwell, Tim and Beverly LaHaye, and the leaders of numerous Christian conservative organizations found evolution to be a worthy addition to their constellation of concerns, as it reinforced their central belief that America's cultural degradation sprang directly from the spread of irreligion. Thus, the Christian Right adopted creationism as a cause, while antievolutionists readily embraced the Right's concerns as their own. The ICR's radio programming, for example, regularly features speakers from Concerned Women for America and other far-right groups addressing such topics as "Creation and the Feminist Movement," in which the president of CWA, Wendy Wright, explains that feminism "has turned into a tool that has catapulted society into an evolutionary mind-set that devalues life and, ironically, diminishes the importance of women."[33] Similarly, the August 16, 2008, ICR broadcast invoked the Right's common complaint that in "today's world just about any 'lifestyle' is accepted, condoned, and even propagated!" As the ICR noted, such latitudinarianism violated God's special creation of each person "for specific functions within the family unit"—his framework was not to be experimented with.[34] Antievolution organizations such as the Creation-Science Research Center had long echoed the Right's complaints about "special privileges for homosexuals" and other attacks on "family unity."[35] These concerns resonated at the local level as well. In Merriam, Kansas, for example, the obscure Mid-America League for Constitutional Government proclaimed it was opposed primarily to evolution, though it was also concerned about "humanism," "one-worldism" as conveyed by the United Nations, and sexual deviance.[36] It had unaffiliated counterparts throughout the nation. A fear of disruption in the traditional moral order laid the common ground between antievolutionists and their political allies.

Leading antievolutionists have followed Morris in asserting that evolution is not simply one component among many in America's cultural crisis but is nearly the central part of the threat to America. This emphasis on evolution as a primary cause of disorder has grown increasingly prominent from the 1990s to the present, and it remains at the heart of even the most "scientific" versions of modern creation science for good reason.

Lauding Louisianans' successful drive for an antievolution law in 2008, Morris explained, "They know that our morals come ultimately from a higher source, and not from animal behavior applied to humans. They suspect that teaching children they are only higher animals has a negative impact on their morals and worldview."[37] Bryan could not have said it better.

Although the antievolutionists have retained strong consistencies in their ideology over the last century, they have shown greater flexibility in developing strategies to implement this ideology, although here, too, continuities persist. Nowhere is this tactical "descent with modification" clearer than in the case of the antievolution movement's approach to science. Contrary to their opponents' charges, antievolutionists have never seen themselves as antiscience. Even if they sometimes have used their versions of science primarily to muddy the waters of the conflict, antievolutionists and scientific creationists have generally sought to wash themselves with the cleansing respectability of modern science. Perhaps it goes without saying that a demand for scientific rigor has not been the mainspring of antievolutionism, but such an assertion obscures the affirmative role that science has played for antievolutionism. Antievolutionists typically prefaced their attacks on Darwinism's social and moral consequences with brief excursions into scientific criticism of the theory. Those of Bryan's generation could still rely on a respected definition of science as "observable facts," or empiricism, which stood in opposition to Darwin's unfamiliar hypothetico-deduction method. A substantial number of people could still deny that fossils were not the equivalent of a laboratory experiment. Today such rigid empiricism seems more than a little clumsy. Antievolution activists such as the Australian Ken Ham instruct their followers to pose a simple question to evolutionists and believers in the Big Bang: "Were you there?" In empiricist terms, this failure to observe directly either evolutionary change or the origin of the universe disqualifies most modern evolutionists and cosmologists from attaining the respectability of science. It has proved a durable argument.

Bryan and his allies' second means of deploying science against evolution consisted of citing criticisms from prominent but often long-deceased scientists. A particular favorite was Harvard's Louis Agassiz. The celebrated naturalist had strongly denied the truth of evolution after the publication of *On the Origin of Species*, but at the time of his death, in 1873, he was virtually the last prominent American scientist who still dissented from the evolutionary hypothesis. Recent antievolution organizations have generated lists of living scientists who support their biblical mission, or at least doubt Darwinian evolution. A widely repeated figure of seven hundred scientific doubters was reported most prominently in *Newsweek* in 1987.[38] Perhaps surprisingly, creationists found these numbers encouraging. The antievolutionist Center for Science and Culture (CSC), which is a wing of the conservative Discovery Institute think tank, reused the figure in 2007, and attempted more specificily in 2010 with a list of scientists worldwide who were skeptical of Darwinian natural selection (without reference to the validity of evolution in general). The list gave the scientists' current institutions or the institutions from which they received their doctorates. The nature of this list resulted in such oddities as a psychiatrist specializing in obsessive-compulsive disorders at the UCLA School of Medicine finding himself listed below a Discovery Institute affiliate at the University of Idaho and above a Jehovah's Witness professor of astrophysics at the Ukrainian Academy of Sciences, as well as numerous signatories from Turkey, Nigeria, and Eastern Europe.[39] Testimonies from the much smaller number of committed creation scientists tend to undermine the Discovery Institute's claim that scientific curiosity drives much of the creationist impulse. Almost all of the fifty scientists who contributed to a 2001 volume on why they choose to believe in creationism invoked their faith as the foremost factor in their conviction, with several freely admitting that they would continue holding to their literalist interpretation of Genesis even if new evidence fully answered the scientific questions they pose about evolution.[40]

When creationists cite the support of men and women with doctorates, engineers figure prominently on the lists, for a variety of possible reasons. Their training does not involve coursework in biology, so one could argue that they are simply untethered from evolutionary scholarship. A more cultural explanation comes from the anthropologist

Christopher P. Toumey, who spent a significant period of time among scientific creationists in the North Carolina Research Triangle.[41] Toumey notes that engineers' work, because it is more technical and applied, seldom engages with the controversies over biological evolution. They are not forced to choose sides. But Toumey's particular engineers were affirmatively involved in creationism, although those with academic positions usually downplayed their beliefs among their colleagues. Toumey ventures that their engineering training actually fit well with their commitment to creationism, since they maintained that evolution contradicts the second law of thermodynamics, which holds that closed systems have a tendency toward entropy, or increasing disorder. Evolution, by contrast, seems to imply that a system, all by itself, can become increasingly ordered and complex.[42] Engineers find this principle of self-organization prima facie absurd on scientific grounds, and simply wrong on theological grounds. Indeed, Toumey's engineers willingly conflated the scientific and the religious, suggesting that entropy and sin are equivalent causes of disorder. Both suggest that the universe needs engineers: physical engineers for entropy, and what Toumey calls "God's moral maintenance engineers"—that is, conservative Christians—for sin. "In the eyes of creationist engineers," Toumey writes, "maintaining moral order against the threat of wickedness is a religious duty equivalent to a professional responsibility."[43] Because it violates the second law of thermodynamics, and fosters moral disorder by undermining religious belief, evolution presents an urgent problem for God's engineers to fix. Finally, some have suggested, tongue partially in cheek, that engineers embrace creationism because, as professional designers, they are predisposed to see design in nature, if not to claim God outright as an engineer.[44]

Despite creationism's relative popularity with engineers, the number of creationist scientists is dwarfed by the number of scientists who subscribe to evolution. To underscore the scale of this support, the most prominent anticreationist organization, the National Center for Science Education (NCSE), in 2003 launched Project Steve, a listing of only evolutionary scientists named Steve or some variant thereof, in honor of the paleontologist Stephen Jay Gould.[45] By September 2008, the "Steve-O-Meter" stood at 900-plus names, and 2009 witnessed the 1,000th Steve—fittingly, a botanist and evolutionary biologist at Tulane University named Steven P. Darwin. Presumably, the Steves are joined by many multiples of Bruces, Paulines, and other sympathetic scientists with a wide diversity of given names

This is not to say that these scientists are a united group. Mainstream scientists disagree, often vigorously, about the mechanisms and details of evolution, and these disagreements occasionally provide an opening for the antievolutionists' third scientific strategy. Antievolutionists often cite these debates as evidence that scientists do not agree that evolution is an established fact. Whatever their differences in explaining the mechanisms of evolution, modern scientists who work in biology and geology have confounded this element of the antievolutionist strategy by remaining virtually unanimous in their position that the earth is more than four billion years old and the evolution of species is a fact. Far from experiencing what the Discovery Institute claims is a "crisis" in evolutionary theory, the vast majority of scientists remain committed to the evolutionary hypothesis, while the small group of reputable scientists who once opposed this conclusion has largely gone extinct.

The antievolutionists' claim that they are engaged in science serves a strategic purpose that goes beyond clinging to intellectual respectability and settling internecine disputes; it is also a legal maneuver, albeit not a very successful one so far. In a series of decisions starting in the 1960s, the U.S. Supreme Court badly damaged the antievolution movement by progressively raising the wall of separation between church and state. First and foremost, the *Epperson v. Arkansas* decision of 1968 struck down the 1928 Arkansas antievolution statute that had been heavily influenced by Tennessee's Butler Act. The Arkansas law against teaching evolution, held the Court, was clearly an endorsement of a particular religious view, and so it violated the establishment clause's prohibition against government support for religion. Bans on evolution in other states and school districts were, by extension, also unconstitutional.[46]

It was at that point that creationists really began to emphasize the scientific side of their approach, drawing particularly on Henry Morris's scientific creationism, but the courts have consistently rejected this approach as well. In response to *Epperson*, a second wave of creationist legislators in Arkansas passed Act 590, which mandated that the teaching of "evolution-science" be balanced by giving equal time in the classroom for the acceptably secular alternative to evolution dubbed "creation-science." However, in *McLean v. Arkansas*, an influential 1982 district court ruling on the matter, Judge William Overton concluded that creation science was not a science at all but rather a simple repackaging of religious creationism. More important, in 1987 the Supreme Court also found, in *Edwards v. Aguillard*, that Louisiana legislators who had passed a similar law mandating equal treatment for evolution and creation science were guided primarily by a desire to advance religion, and this motivation, combined with *McLean's* findings, rendered Louisiana's creation science laws unconstitutional.[47]

Undaunted, antievolutionists renewed their search for an alternative to evolution that was at least ostensibly less religious than the rejected creation science. The *Edwards* decision left open the possibility that a similar law, passed with a more purely secular purpose and appearing, at least, to be more scientific than creation science, might withstand Court scrutiny. But how could creation science shed its religious trappings?

One answer came from the unlikely precinct of Berkeley, California. In 1991, Phillip Johnson, a professor at the University of California's Boalt Hall School of Law and a self-proclaimed conservative evangelical Protestant, published *Darwin on Trial*.[48] Promising a lawyer's brief, Johnson devoted most of the book to casting doubt on evolution by poking smaller holes in the theory and its history. He cited areas in *On the Origin of Species* in which Darwin confessed he was stumped, as in the evolution of the eyeball; he noted topics in evolution over which modern scientists disagreed; he cited earlier errors in evolutionary science, as when scientists were beguiled into believing in such frauds as "Nebraska Man" and "Piltdown Man"; he referred to what he considered numerous omissions and errors in contemporary evolutionary science, such as unexplained gaps in the fossil record; and he resurrected the empiricist argument against a science that does not engage in laboratory experimentation.

The popularity of Johnson's book compelled Stephen Jay Gould to pen a scabrous review of what he called

> at best, a long magazine article promoted to hard covers—a clumsy, repetitious abstract argument with no weighing of evidence, no careful reading of literature on all sides, no full citation of sources (the book does not even contain a bibliography) and occasional use of scientific literature only to score rhetorical points. I see no evidence that Johnson has ever visited a scientist's laboratory, has any concept of quotidian work in the field or has read widely beyond writing for nonspecialists and the most "newsworthy" of professional claims.[49]

Gould allowed that it would be difficult for a nonscientist such as Johnson to be fully familiar with the most current scholarship, but he added that "the density of simple error is so high that I must question wider competence when attempts at extension yield such poor results."[50]

Gould claimed to be offended most by Johnson's accusation, increasingly popular among creationists, that Darwinism explicitly denied the possibility of design and purpose in the universe and was therefore intrinsically antireligious. For the "umpteenth millionth time," the paleontologist pleaded, "science simply cannot (by its legitimate methods) adjudicate the issue of God's possible superintendence of nature. We neither affirm nor deny it; we simply can't comment on it as scientists."[51]

Unsurprisingly, Gould's critique did little harm to creationism, and ultimately it even benefited the movement. Johnson quickly became frustrated with *Scientific American*'s refusal to publish his rebuttal to Gould's charges, and the rejection spurred a "committee" of Johnson's supporters to draft a letter of protest signed by thirty-nine sympathizers. The organizers sent copies of this letter, along with Johnson's rebuttal, to thousands of scientists.[52] Their actions did not persuade any considerable number of recipients, but the simple process of putting the protest together led a number of like-minded academics to find each other. Nine of these original signatories were to become fellows of the CSC.[53]

In the year after *Darwin on Trial* was published, Johnson and a number of sympathetic scholars gathered for a conference at Southern Methodist University. Over the next few years, under Johnson's leadership and the intellectual influence of a biochemist named Michael Behe, the mathematician William Dembski, and a handful of others, the group developed a critical refinement of Johnson's critique—the philosophy of intelligent design.

ID essentially had its coming-out party at the "Mere Creation" conference, hosted by Biola University, in November 1996.[54] As more than 160 academics gathered together under the sponsorship of Christian Leadership Ministries, Johnson and his core group of activists were able to observe what Johnson called "a loose coalition of scholars from a wide variety of disciplines" coalesce into a self-conscious movement in support of Intelligent Design and its challenge to evolutionary naturalism.[55]

In its essential content, ID resurrects the "argument from design" championed by Cicero and then William Paley, by asserting that nature reveals the existence of a superintending intelligence, a designer whose works cannot be explained by purely scientific means. ID's refinement of this argument came primarily from Behe, who contributed the idea of "irreducible complexity." That is, various bodily structures, such as eyes, the flagella of certain microscopic organisms, and even the machinery of cells, were "irreducibly complex"; like a watch or a mousetrap, they could not function if all the parts were not in place, and therefore they could not have evolved in bits and pieces. Rather, the existence of irreducibly complex structures testifies to the presence of an "intelligent designer," a supernatural entity who sounds at least a little like the God of the Judeo-Christian tradition. ID proponents argue that this philosophy represents at least a validly scientific, if not entirely secular, approach to natural history, and it therefore calls into question evolution's monopoly on the science curriculum.

For all the intellectual excitement that it generated in those early years, ID was, like its creation science predecessors, less a science than a strategy. Unlike earlier creation science, which sought to prove the truth of the biblical account, ID has the luxury of making essentially a negative argument: if evolution cannot explain the origin or structure of an organism or a phenomenon, if there are "gaps" in our understanding, then an intelligent designer must be responsible. As an expert in criminal law, Johnson clearly appreciated that this approach lightens the burden of proof. "Get the Bible and the Book of Genesis out of the debate," suggests Johnson, "because you do not want to raise the so-called Bible-science dichotomy. Phrase the argument in such a way that you can get it heard in the secular academy and in a way that tends to unify the religious dissenters."[56] ID could help proponents to avoid some of the tactical mistakes that seemed to have doomed William Jennings Bryan so many years before. Johnson warned his followers to focus narrowly on the question of whether a supernatural Creator of some sort is necessary, or else they would leave themselves open to all the inconvenient questions skeptics have been asking Christians for centuries. "They'll ask, 'What do you think of Noah's flood?' or something like that," he explained. "Never bite on such questions because they'll lead you into a trackless wasteland and you'll never get out of it."[57] In accord with this advice, ID leaders have diverged from creation scientists in allowing that the earth might be much older than six thousand years. Johnson, for one, quietly avoids that central claim made by his young-earth acquaintances.

Johnson's recommendations and the ID philosophy took more formal shape in 1998, when activists at the Center for the Renewal of Science and Culture (which became the CSC) produced an internal memorandum that came to be known as the "Wedge Document." This paper identified evolution as a key component of philosophical materialism, a conception of reality that rules out supernatural forces and thus ignores or disallows the special relationship that exists between human beings and God. In some versions, philosophical materialism explicitly denies the existence of God. According to the document, Charles Darwin thus stood with Karl Marx and Sigmund Freud in portraying humans "not as moral and spiritual beings, but as animals or machines who inhabited a universe ruled by purely impersonal forces and whose behavior and very thoughts were dictated by the unbending forces of biology, chemistry, and environment."[58] This disenchanted worldview, the authors argued, had "infected virtually every area of our culture, from politics and economics to literature and art." Most dangerously, by removing God as a source of moral absolutes, materialism had bred a "moral relativism" that undermined the sense of personal responsibility in society and led to unacceptably liberal approaches to crime, welfare, and all forms of social deviancy. Perhaps in a nod of appreciation toward their wealthy sponsors behind the Discovery Institute, the document's writers cited a recent surge of product liability lawsuits as further evidence of the decline in personal morality.[59]

Johnson came to speak of philosophical materialism or metaphysical naturalism as a "log" with a number of "cracks" in it. "Our strategy," he explains, "is to drive the thin edge of our Wedge into the log of naturalism."[60] Evolution's relationship to this metaphorical log varies. Sometimes Johnson and his allies focus on evolution because they see evolutionary theory as the weakest point in the log, for evolution to them presents the clearest case of the materialist philosophy outrunning its empirical basis—drive the "wedge of truth" into that fissure, and eventually the mighty trunk of philosophical materialism will split. At other times, Wedge proponents sound more like their creationist brethren in identifying biological evolution itself as the main cause of philosophical materialism and its resulting social disorders. In either case, ID activists see themselves as the vanguard for creating a scientific and social philosophy very different from the dominant naturalist paradigm. For this difficult mission, Johnson proposed that he would serve as the leading edge of the wedge himself, or he would play the role of an "offensive lineman" who clears room for his teammates "by legitimating the issue, by exhausting the other side, by using up all their ridicule."[61]

The strategy outlined in the Wedge Document was ambitious, but it also exposed some of the ID campaign's weaknesses. In the service of ID's long-term goal of "defeating scientific materialism" and replacing it with the "theistic understanding that nature and human beings are created by

God," the authors proposed short- and long-term plans. In envisioning activity for the first five years, in particular, the Wedge Document focused as much on public relations and political maneuvering as on the science of intelligent design. In addition to calling for the publication of at least one hundred "scientific, academic, and technical articles" in peer-reviewed journals by 2003, the document dwelled on goals for press coverage in *Time*, *Newsweek*, and major newspapers, as well as public debates, television coverage, and at least the beginning of legislation friendly to ID.

The sticking point for a group with aspirations toward solid intellectual respectability was the research program. ID researchers fell woefully short of the objective to publish at least one hundred peer-reviewed articles—the coin of the realm in academic science. Depending on the definition, the number of such articles was between zero and two. This lack of scholarly production limited the amount of favorable publicity ID could expect to receive.[62]

Nevertheless, activists at the Discovery Institute were heartened by the possibility that they had found an acceptably secular alternative to evolutionary theory. Recognizing that ID was not simply going to replace evolution in the public school curriculum—at least not anytime soon—they instead lobbied for schools to "teach the controversy" between evolution and what they called the equally valid science of intelligent design. However, mainstream scientists and defenders of evolution such as NCSE vigorously asserted that no valid scientific controversy exists between evolutionary science and ID, as the latter simply does not rise to the level at which it could be called a science. Not only has ID generated almost no peer-reviewed publications, it is difficult to conceive of what, exactly, an ID research program would look like beyond a search for as yet unexplained phenomena. Opponents claim that ID is not science but rather a Trojan horse for creationism, or at least a squirt of black squid ink creationists have discharged to obscure their religious mission.[63] By 2010, the Discovery Institute had recalibrated its approach downward by calling for biology classes to teach the "strengths and weaknesses" of evolution, in the hope that this might indirectly lead to greater interest in ID.

This revision has gained traction in Texas, Louisiana, and several other states.[64] To many Americans, all of these have seemed like fair approaches. While recent polls on the topic differ greatly depending on their wording, they have generally found that a majority of Americans believe that schools should teach both Darwinism and creationism, or evolution as well as "scientific evidence that goes against Darwin's theory." Even when the polls do not specify ID as part of this "scientific evidence," they still find respondents hewing to what seems to be a "fair" balancing of opinion on a controversial subject.[65] ID activists have happily employed these figures in their arguments for inclusion.

As of 2011, the U.S. Supreme Court has not yet taken any ID cases, but the state school board of Kansas staged contentious public hearings on the subject, and various school boards have likewise dabbled with the idea of introducing ID into the curriculum. So far, the only significant court action arising out of ID has been the 2005 case in Pennsylvania of *Kitzmiller v. Dover Area School District*, which is worth treating at length, as it embodied the central issues at stake in the ID struggle.[66] A creationist majority on the Dover school board developed a statement that science teachers were required to read to their biology classes. The statement questioned the accuracy of evolutionary theory and steered students toward an intelligent-design textbook the board adopted, *Of Pandas and People*, to answer some of the questions the statement raised. Taking their language and inspiration from the Discovery Institute, the Dover majority argued publicly that intelligent design was a secular approach to biology and therefore not in violation of *Edwards v. Aguillard*. At the very least, they suggested in the Discovery Institute's strategic language, the public schools should "teach the controversy" between evolution and intelligent design.

The board's decision quickly aroused opposition in Dover. Tammy Kitzmiller, whose daughter was in the ninth grade, contacted the ACLU for help, and was joined by ten other plaintiffs—a collection of concerned parents and teachers, including science teachers at Dover Senior High School. Kitzmiller and her allies filed suit against the school board, charging that ID was merely a repackaging of creation science and therefore unconstitutional under the standards established by the *Epperson* and *Edwards* decisions. The federal district judge in the case was John E. Jones III, appointed to the bench by President George W. Bush, who had expressed sympathy with the idea that evolution and creationism should be taught side by side in science classes.

In contrast to the Scopes trial, where the judge ultimately barred Scopes's experts from testifying, Jones chose to open his court to expert testimony on both sides of the case. The plaintiffs presented a lineup of scientists and scholars, while the school board, with the aid of the conservative Thomas More Law Center, enlisted some of the leaders of the ID movement, most prominently the biochemist Michael Behe, who claimed in his work that the molecular sequence of the blood-clotting cascade was a clear example of an irreducibly complex biological process that Darwinian processes could not explain. At the trial, Behe asserted that the immune system was similarly irreducible. Upon questioning, though, Behe confessed he was unfamiliar with the peer-reviewed scientific articles on the subject that the plaintiffs' attorney heaped into a tall stack in front of him. Behe also ended up in an awkward position when he repeated ID's standard charge that the naturalistic standard of truth peremptorily excluded valid approaches that invoked the supernatural. Behe's assertion opened him up to a pointed cross-examination in which the plaintiffs' attorney successfully pressed him into admitting that ID's rejection of naturalistic explanations would leave science no way to dispute even the legitimacy of astrology, although the "science of the stars" is particularly offensive to conservative evangelicals. Behe should have known such questions were coming. In the year before the Dover controversy, a playful group of anti-evolutionists had already underlined the absurdity of this position when they posited the existence of the "Flying Spaghetti Monster" (see figure 4.3), a pasta-based demiurge whose reality, they claimed, was equally impossible to disprove under ID's proposed standard.[67] But ID's biochemist still had not developed an answer for this line of questioning. Compared to the biologist Kenneth Miller and Kitzmiller's other scientific witnesses, Behe did not fare well.

FIGURE 4.3   Conceived by Bobby Henderson in 1985, the "Flying Spaghetti Monster" lampooned Intelligent Design's inability to prove or disprove the existence of any particular supernatural "designer." Image courtesy of Niklas Jansson.

In addition to the intellectual issue of ID's validity as a science, the plaintiffs pointed to the Dover school board's religious motivation, noting that in meetings with the teachers, in public hearings, and even in a newsletter sent out to every household in the district, the majority leaders had attacked the "atheism" of Darwinian evolution and presented their actions as a defense of Christianity.[68] "Two thousand years ago, someone died on a cross," said one board member. "Can't someone take a stand now?"[69] Finally, the plaintiffs' related argument that *Of Pandas and People* was merely a rehashing of creationism was bolstered by a significant discovery: the book was virtually a word-for-word copy of an earlier, overtly creationist draft, except that after the 1987 *Edwards* decision, the authors had hastily gone through the text and replaced almost all references to "creation science" with the phrase "intelligent design" and all references to a "creator" with the word "designer."[70] The history of the book suggested overwhelmingly that, in this case at least, ID represented not an intellectual shift toward a more acceptable secular theory but merely a strategic swapping of terms.

After days of testimony, Jones issued an unusually long (139-page) judgment in the overly optimistic hope that he could lay to rest the legal controversy over ID, at least for a little while. Jones ruled that ID's scientific assertions did not rise to the level of presenting a legitimate controversy between ID and evolution. Beyond noting the overwhelming support among scientists for Darwinian evolution, Jones cited Behe's own admission that, in Jones's paraphrase, "there are no peer reviewed articles by anyone advocating for intelligent design supported by pertinent experiments or calculations which provide detailed rigorous accounts of how intelligent design of any biological system occurred."[71] In response to ID supporters' assertion that they wanted only to "teach the controversy" and foster "critical thought" among students, Jones scoffed, "This tactic is at best disingenuous, and at worst a canard."[72] He cited not only the creationist history behind *Of Pandas and People* but also the general religious impulses behind ID, particularly the Wedge Document.[73] In light of the testimony, Jones maintained, any "reasonable and objective observer" would have to conclude "that ID is an interesting theological argument, but that it is not science."[74]

Jones's conclusions came as little surprise—least of all to scientific creationists. As in Bryan's time, most antievolutionists eagerly testify (off the stand) that their work is primarily inspired not by the scientific impulse but by their religious convictions.[75] Even as Johnson publicly led the drive to develop a secular face for antievolutionism, he was suggesting in other venues that cracking the log of philosophical materialism would open us to other questions beyond those science can answer. "When we have reached that point in our questioning," Johnson wrote in 2000, "we will inevitably encounter the person of Jesus Christ, the one who has been declared the incarnate Word of God and through whom all things came into existence."[76]

While Johnson has never been a high-powered evangelist like Ken Ham of Answers in Genesis or Kent "Dr. Dino" Hovind, he aims to end up in the same place. Behind the doors of conservative churches, in the newsletters, journals, and websites aimed at supporters, and in the bleachers at evangelical pep rallies, antievolutionists speak to one another in their primary language of Christian faith and not in the foreign tongue of science—not even creation science. Rather, among the faithful, biblical literalism, the conversion of souls to Jesus, and the "battle between God and Satan" are the watchwords of creationism.[77] True believers do not confuse a strategy with a commitment.

The battle continues inside the courtroom and out of it, but modern warfare over teaching evolution in the public schools reveals strange asymmetries. At first glance, antievolutionists appear to be in a stronger political position than evolutionists. While only a small number of national and international organizations, such as the ICR, CSC, and AIG, devote themselves primarily to opposing the teaching of evolution in the public schools, these groups are very well funded, with AIG taking in approximately $10 million annually in revenue, the ICR more than $3 million, and Discovery some $3.5 million.[78] Each figure is several times larger than NCSE's budget. Further, hundreds of sympathetic churches provide additional infrastructure for antievolution activity, effectively multiplying the creationist impact. While it is true that the federal government, universities, and private firms and foundations provide tens of millions of dollars to scientists whose work draws on evolutionary facts and concepts, almost none of that money goes toward the political struggle against antievolution.

Further, polls find that a majority of Americans believe humans were created directly by God. Depending on the wording of the question, about 45 percent say they believe God created the earth in six days, and likewise stocked it with plants and animals in their present form, with another 40 percent claiming that God at least guided some form of evolutionary process. Although young-earth creationists particularly revile theistic evolution of the latter sort, the figures as a whole suggest widespread acceptance of supernatural involvement in the creation of the earth and its flora and fauna.[79]

These beliefs translate into extensive popular support for admitting some form of creationism into the public school curriculum. In a Republican primary debate for the 2008 presidential election, three of the ten candidates disavowed belief in evolution.[80] As Kansas senator Sam Brownback explained in an editorial following the debate, "I am wary of any theory that seeks to undermine man's essential dignity and unique and intended place in the cosmos."[81] By following their hearts, Brownback and the other candidates were coincidentally following the polls. Recent surveys have found that between 23 and 40 percent of Americans want only creationism to be taught, and the numbers are surely higher for registered Republicans.[82] In contrast, a mere 12 percent of Americans believe that only evolution should be taught.[83] Most Americans hew to a more ecumenical approach, with somewhere around 60 percent supporting the inclusion of both evolution and creationism in an attempt to be fair to both sides (as of 2005, few of those polled had ever heard of ID, so its popular influence is unclear).[84] These figures suggest that antievolutionists should be able to dominate the fight. Perhaps the question should be not why antievolutionists occasionally succeed—however temporarily—in places such as Kansas, Louisiana, and Dover but why they don't succeed all the time.

Leave aside for a moment the accuracy of evolutionary theory as a reason. "The truth," Stephen Jay Gould used to say, regarding public debates between evolutionists and creationists, "is only one debating strategy among many—and it might not even be the best one." A number of other factors have hampered the antievolution impulse. Popular support, for example, may be softer than the numbers imply. Leading antievolution activists are very well funded, but general support for their mission tends to be fairly passive. While a majority of Americans feel in general that the biblical account of origins carries more weight than evolutionary theory, they tend not to feel strongly about the issue. Conversely, evolutionists are a minority in the population, but as Project Steve suggests, the evolutionary hypothesis plays a fundamental role in the training, livelihood, and intellectual commitments of thousands of geologists, geneticists, biologists, ornithologists, and others, not to mention biology teachers at the secondary school level. They have significant allies. An imperfect measure of the relative importance evolution holds for both sides comes in a 2007

USA Today/Gallup poll in which one thousand adults were asked what their response would be if a presidential candidate stated "that he or she DID NOT believe in the theory of evolution." About half the respondents were indifferent. Fifteen percent said it would make them more likely to vote for that candidate, but 28 percent said it would make them less likely. Breaking those figures down into the smaller number who felt strongly about the issue, only 8 percent of all respondents said they would be "much more likely" to vote for the candidate, but twice that number said the candidate's antievolution views would make them much less likely to support him or her (see figures 4.4–4.7).[85] Popular preferences can seem almost beside the point, though, because evolution's defenders since the 1960s consistently have found the courts to be on their side. The ACLU and Americans United for the Separation of Church and State remain vigilant in policing possible violations of the establishment clause, and NCSE and other groups have proven adept at recruiting courtroom testimony from some of the best-known scientists in the country. The evolutionists' legal victories have done more than overturn antievolution laws and policies; they have chilled some of the ID movement's ardor for direct action. In the *Kitzmiller* decision, for example, Judge Jones ordered the Dover school board to pay the plaintiffs' legal fees and damages, which totaled well over $1 million—no trivial sum for a small local government.

The judgment taught a powerful lesson: "Any board thinking of trying to do what the Dover board did is going to have to look for a bill in excess of $2 million," observed one of Kitzmiller's supporters. "I think $2 million is a lot to explain to taxpayers for a lawsuit that should never be fought."[86] Discovery and its allied organizations might be well-heeled, but the local governments they need to implement their plans are generally less eager to part with their money.

Antievolutionist school boards also face the likelihood of driving themselves and their communities into a sea of ridicule. As modern creationists often complain, the long shadow of the Scopes trial continues to darken the perception of antievolution attempts, for newspaper reporters regularly resuscitate the image of rural ignoramuses from eight decades ago, usually filtered through the lens of the play *Inherit the Wind*. Local governments today are less eager than their ancestors in the 1920s to court this kind of notoriety. Many business leaders in Kansas, for example, in 2005 lamented the bad reputation the state had earned for its repeated flirtations with antievolutionism. "We have become a bit of a punch line," complained the president of the Lenexa Chamber of Commerce. "We just

FIGURE 4.4 The "Jesus fish" magnet initially signaled the car owner's general Christian faith, though it often was associated with more conservative Christianity.

FIGURE 4.5 During antievolution flare-ups, the "Darwin fish" appeared as a tongue-in-cheek rejoinder to the "Jesus fish."

FIGURE 4.6 Antievolution supporters likewise publically proclaimed their allegiance in the struggle. Image available at www.darwinism.org/UK.

FIGURE 4.7 The final word in the battle of the car magnets? Image reproduced with permission from Ring of Fire Enterprises.

tend to get lumped in there as the stereotypical conservative, backward-thinking area."[87] That kind of reputation, many in the business community feared, might prove a stumbling block in their efforts to recruit biotechnology companies, research scientists, and the kind of high-skill, high-wage jobs for which every state competes. Similarly, during a 2008 contretemps in Texas over whether the public schools should adopt the Discovery Institute's "Academic Freedom" policy of teaching the "strengths and weaknesses" of evolutionary theory, prominent local figures expressed serious reservations about the broader impact of the change. "Serious students will not come to study in our universities if Texas is labeled scientifically backward," said Dr. Dan Foster, who had served as chairman of the Department of Medicine at the University of Texas Southwestern Medical Center at Dallas.[88] In 2008, when Bobby Jindal, the Republican governor of Louisiana, signed into law a bill allowing local school districts to adopt "supplemental material" on evolution (implying ID publications, in particular), Arthur Landy, one of Jindal's genetics professors at his alma mater, Brown University, publicly expressed bewilderment over his former student's misunderstanding of fundamental biology; another biology professor there noted with relief that Jindal had never taken a course with him.[89] The law did little to raise Louisiana's—and Jindal's—educational reputation.

As these responses suggest, evolution highlights the differences between Americans who embrace the value of expertise over the dictates of democracy. When curricular decisions are left to mainstream scientists and educators, evolution has taken a secure, if not overly conspicuous, place in educational standards; only when curriculum decisions are left to popular vote and political chance does evolution find itself challenged in the schools' science standards. In Kansas, Texas, Louisiana, and a handful of other states, creationist policies were adopted by elected school boards and legislatures over the objections of professional advisors and committees. In every case, the policies met concerted opposition from groups of teachers, scientists, and citizens committed to First Amendment strictures and a belief in the validity of evolution.

Partly in recognition of their continued difficulty in breaking down the wall between church and state, some antievolutionists have chosen to bypass the public schools altogether. Private religious schools, home schools, and churches are unlikely to fall afoul of constitutional prohibitions, so they can teach creationism without fear. Similarly insulated from the First Amendment is the most striking manifestation of antievolutionism's new strategy:

AIG's 2007 construction of the Creation Museum in Petersburg, Kentucky. Intentionally situated within a day's drive of two-thirds of the American population, the $27 million museum presents a public repudiation of the scores of orthodox natural history museums scattered throughout the country. "All the familiar faces are here," observed one reporter who attended the museum's grand opening. "T. rex, giant skeletons of triceratops and apatosaurus, a pterosaur spreading its wings above the crowd. . . . There are also a couple of unfamiliar faces, for a natural history museum, in the tan and finely muscled bodies of Adam and Eve."[90] In the Creation Museum's young-earth presentation of natural history, Adam and Eve are actual historical figures, and animatronic models of human children play peacefully alongside prehistoric carnivores. "In any other place," the reporter noted, "this would be the setup for a massacre." But in the museum's replication of the biblical Garden of Eden before the Fall, all animals are vegetarians, and humans and dinosaurs coexist peacefully. Paleontologists would say the museum's chronology is off by at least 65 million years, but AIG defends the accuracy of its exhibits and timeline by invoking the young-earth explanation of the effects of the Flood.

Strikingly, the Creation Museum spends no time on intelligent design. This exclusion is made possible in part by the museum's private status: unlike creationists trying to infiltrate the public schools, the museum does not have to tailor its message to bear court scrutiny. Further, AIG's leaders largely reject the Discovery Institute's ID strategy.[91] While lauding some of ID's tactical successes, especially in its efforts to reveal naturalistic science as a secular religion, former AIG leader Carl Wieland scolds its supporters for being evasive about their purpose. "The IDM's [intelligent design movement's] refusal to identify the Designer with the Biblical God, and in particular with the *history* in the Bible," Wieland warns, "could just as easily lead to New-Age or Hindu-like notions of creation, as well as weird alien sci-fi notions."[92] The AIG scientist Georgia Purdom agrees, fearing that ID appeals to people who want to feel free to pick and choose among "a Great Spirit, Brahman, Allah, God, etc.," because it "focuses more on what is designed rather than who designed it."[93] Further, ID could comfortably lend itself to a variety of "old-earth" creationist ideas—anathema to the young-earthers in AIG as well as ICR. For their part, Wieland pledges, he and his AIG allies might use ID long enough to create an opening for conversation, but "when that opening comes, or when questioned, we will unhesitatingly affirm that we start our thinking based squarely on the real history in the Bible."[94] Thus, the very qualities that are supposed to make ID a valuable antievolution tool—its apparent neutrality and its reliance on scientific argumentation—are the same qualities that keep it locked outside of the Creation Museum.

Presumably, public schools will be hesitant to schedule field trips to the museum, but AIG counts on the institution's comeliness to lure millions of Americans who already believe in a general way in the Genesis account. The directors hope the museum can assist these visitors in hardening their vague faith into a solid belief in the tenets of young-earth creationism, and perhaps inspire many of them to take action against Darwinism in their home communities. The Creation Museum is just one piece of a worldwide AIG ministry that includes websites, radio programs, magazines, and a phalanx of professional lecturers. In focusing on creationism's failures in the courtroom and the classroom, reporters and commentators often overlook the other role creationism plays in American evangelicalism. Evolution lays bare the tensions between mainstream Christians and conservative evangelicals as it shores up the wall that separates biblical literalism from the mainline churches' bland and accommodating theology. Far from discouraging antievolutionists, the opposition of mainstream science and judicial elites has hardened the conservative evangelicals' sense of distinctiveness from the broader culture. Some have separated themselves as much as possible while remaining tethered to mainstream culture. Organizations such as AIG provide religiously correct science curricula for a thriving network of religious home schools— enough of them to sponsor national home-schooler sports tournaments in basketball, cheerleading, cross-country running, and other athletics. Ridiculed by comedians, ignored or scorned by scientists, and blocked at every turn by judges, creationism's sympathizers can intentionally stand apart.

Even as they sometimes claim to represent the majority of Americans, antievolutionists embrace their minority status. Antievolutionism serves to enlarge what religion scholar Martin Marty calls the "cognitive distance" between conservative evangelicals and the more secular culture that surrounds them.[95] A willingness to reject mainstream science forces evangelicals to come out of the closet and embrace publicly the primacy of faith over so-called reason. As John J. G. Kramer, a creationist biochemist, proclaims, "I have often considered belief in Genesis chapters 1 to 11 as the 'acid test' of believing in God, and in the salvation through Jesus Christ."[96]

Taking such a position inevitably calls forth strong reactions. Modern satirists such as the comedian Lewis Black have been pointed in their caricatures of creationists like Kramer: "These are people," Black jeers, "who think 'The Flintstones' is a documentary."[97] But condemnation and derision only solidify the sense of group identity among antievolutionists.[98] They are a saving remnant in a fallen world. William Jennings Bryan, risking his public reputation on the crusade against evolution, understood that the path from Genesis to Jesus left the believer dangerously exposed, but he was certain the faithful would never walk alone.

5

Creationism and the Campus

BRUCE LIEBERMAN AND Paulyn Cartwright are a married pair of scientists at the University of Kansas. Typical of the saltation of midwestern universities with scholars from the coasts, Lieberman is a paleontologist who studied under Stephen Jay Gould at Harvard University and took his Ph.D. under Niles Eldredge at Columbia University and the American Museum of Natural History in New York City, while Cartwright is a biologist of marine invertebrates who earned her undergraduate degree from UCLA and her doctorate from Yale. They arrived in Kansas the same year as I did, but as evolutionary scientists, they were affected more directly than I was by our adopted state's dalliance with antievolution in 1999 and 2005.

Like their counterparts across the nation, especially in the South and the Midwest, they have observed many of their students struggling with the implications of evolution. The University of Kansas draws undergraduates from small towns across the state and from the religiously conservative suburbs of Kansas City. For some of the students, Cartwright's Introduction to Biology is their first exposure to evolutionary theory. Off and on for several years, she has taught the course to lecture halls of six hundred students at a time. Despite the size of the course, she has been able to observe the reactions of many students from conservative religious backgrounds when they face what she refers to as, quite simply, "the facts of evolution."[1] The students put a great deal of thought into "sorting out their own paths toward reconciling the Bible and evolution," she observes. But they do so largely without her help. Despite her sympathy for their struggles, after several years and thousands of students the biologist has concluded, "It's not my job to show them that path for reconciliation. They've got to do it for themselves." Confounding creationist accusations that college professors are bent on forcing Darwin and irreligion down their students' throats, Lieberman likewise takes a gentle approach. "I get these students in my classes," he says. "You can see them ease up when you tell them that Darwin wasn't always right." Without that alarming name appended, evolution seems less threatening. Nevertheless, organic evolution is an integral part of the framework for Cartwright's and Lieberman's teaching and scholarly work, as it is for virtually everyone working in the life sciences. Despite the turbulence caused by the culture wars over evolution, and despite hints of dissent in the lecture hall, the controversies have had little or no impact on the actual practice of science in the lab or in the field.

However, as the Kansas scientists have witnessed, evolution does make a difference on campus. Most obviously, evolution forces the issue of college's impact on students' faith, even as it illuminates the apparent distance between the spiritual lives of students and those of many of their instructors. Antievolutionism also presents scientists with the quandary of whether they should confine themselves to their research or venture outside to defend their profession. In the case of scientists from evangelical Christian backgrounds, evolution even forces a scientific and theological reckoning over the question of God's role in the universe.

While recent scholars and reporters have focused, understandably, on the fight over creationism in the public schools, they have generally overlooked the complexities of the antievolution struggle in higher education. For most of the last century, the prospect that students might choose the "wrong" path that teachers such as Cartwright and Lieberman have opened for them has been the catalyst for antievolutionists' activism not just in the public schools but at the college level as well. In 1916, a Bryn Mawr psychologist, James H. Leuba, unintentionally galvanized William Jennings Bryan into his religious crusade with a study that traced declining religiosity among college students, almost all of whom had entered college as Christian believers who were orthodox, if somewhat confused—Leuba described them as "groveling in darkness."[2] By the time they graduated, however, more than 40 percent of them professed serious religious doubts or outright disbelief in the conventional Christian God or in "personal immortality," Leuba's phrase for the everlasting life promised by Jesus' sacrifice. In *The Belief in God and Immortality*, Leuba approvingly ascribed this secularization to an increasing sense of independence and self-reliance, particularly among males, as the students grew to maturity.[3] Perhaps because of this premise, Leuba never bothered to specify what coursework these students had taken. The format of his study, though, suggested that the students may have been reenacting their own professors' loss of faith.

Immediately following the section of the book on college students' growing apostasy, Leuba presented a chapter on his related inquiry into one thousand "men of science," in which he found high rates of irreligion among college science professors, with up to 70 percent of "elite" faculty professing doubt or disbelief.[4] For Bryan, the lesson was clear: "The teaching of evolution as a fact instead of theory caused the students to lose faith in the Bible."[5] If that happened at the college level, with relatively mature students, then how much worse would the results be if evolution was taught to younger and more innocent students in the public schools?

Beyond Leuba's findings, Bryan and his allies had at least anecdotal evidence that evolutionary teaching weakened the foundations of students' faith. Not only had Bryan often been approached by parents whose children had lost their faith after learning about evolution, but Bryan confessed that he, too, had once found his Christian belief deeply challenged by evolution's implications. Sister Aimee Semple McPherson likewise testified that Darwinism had shaken her belief when she was younger until she sought answers in the Bible. They were not the last to make this claim. Some seventy years later, Phillip E. Johnson made much of the ways in which his undergraduate education at Harvard had forced him and many of his contemporaries into atheism. Oddly, like Leuba, Johnson did not specify evolution as the source of this pressure, but he nevertheless portrayed American higher education as a factory for stripping young men and women of their religion.[6] A half century after Leuba, a series of sociological studies of apostasy in the 1960s through the 1980s seemed to confirm his findings, with several scholars concluding that education's "expansion" of a student's horizons often led directly to reduced faith, increased secularism, and even atheism.[7] Scholars found the link between college learning and unbelief to be so natural that few bothered to question whether it actually existed, and if so, how it had developed.

The first wave of studies in the 1960s did indeed uncover a great many college students who turned their backs on the religion of their parents. In that era, students were ripe for exploration. Nearly 80 percent of college freshmen in the mid-1960s reported that "developing a meaningful philosophy of life" was important to them. It was emblematic of the times that several studies had to be altered to include categories for Eastern religious traditions and novel spiritual practices alongside Episcopalianism and Catholicism.[8]

However, more recent studies, most notably those based on quantitative and qualitative surveys such as the General Social Survey and the National

Longitudinal Study of Adolescent Health, covering tens of thousands of college-age youth in the last three decades, have found the allegations of college's secularizing effect to be overblown. Investigators at the University of Texas note that religious fidelity is historically conditioned—the culture of 1996 was not the same as 1966—but they also concluded that an overwhelming majority of collegians, more than 80 percent—actually retain their religious affiliation as well as their conviction that religious faith is very important to them.[9] The various pulls and pressures of college life tend to curb church attendance for a few years, but seldom do they touch the core of faith.

Nevertheless, around 15 percent of students do graduate from college with their religious beliefs greatly diminished or nonexistent, and their paths to this state need to be traced. Disregarding the belief that evolutionary teaching is inherently corrosive—a belief that stretches from Bryan and McPherson all the way to modern-day creationists—sociologists who study religious adherence among youth have tended to follow Leuba's example in downplaying the influence of the intellect on unbelief. Even in the 1960s, students only occasionally pointed to classroom content as a source of their religious vacillations. More recent investigators have spent even less time on the impact that classroom teaching makes on religious belief, one team citing as justification for this omission the precipitous decline between 1966 and 1996 in the percentage of freshmen who professed interest in "developing a meaningful philosophy of life."[10] Far from seeing mass deconversion as the norm for college students, the Texas authors note that only the small number of students who are already interested in "morals and beliefs" tend to major in those "fields—the social sciences and the humanities—[which] are the most likely to diminish their religiosity."[11] In a conclusion that should resonate with many college instructors, the authors propose that most students do not see education as a threat to their faith, both because they pay so little attention to their classes and because their religious understanding might be so limited that "they would have difficulty recognizing faith-challenging material when it appears."[12]

A number of students, however, do arrive in college intellectually armed to defend their faith against what they take to be Darwinian threats.[13] The cases are legion of high school biology teachers having to defend themselves against students and parents primed to challenge the teaching of evolution—but creationist groups such as Answers in Genesis and the Institute for Creation Research also furnish literature and videos to prepare college students to confront skeptics among their faculty and fellow students.[14] Although such materials help furnish interested students with a vocabulary and a strategy for their discontent, and professors such as Cartwright and Lieberman certainly make an impact on individual students, investigations of the broader patterns in college and unbelief have generally shied away from analyzing the intellectual interactions between faculty and students. Adopting instead the dismal premise that students, whether they are in the classroom or in church, pay precious little attention to their instructors, the Texas researchers argue that diminished religiosity among young adults is more associated with behaviors and life choices. To put the matter very broadly, marriage and children in early adulthood tend to bolster both church attendance and religiosity, whereas cohabitation, drug use, and binge drinking correspond with diminished religiosity—perhaps, the investigators postulate, because such behaviors create "cognitive dissonance" with religious values. They allow that these behaviors might only predispose young adults to the secularizing influence of higher education, but the authors find that only one-third of the small number of college students who "dropped out" of religion cited intellectual skepticism as the cause.[15] In fact, the investigators find that the most influential factor in developing a secular attitude is the weakness or strength of religion in a young adult's family background. "Simply put, more religious parents tend to more effectively socialize their adolescents to be religious," they write. "Parent religiosity is typically the strongest predictor of both adolescent religious service attendance and religious salience."[16]

And yet college education does matter, but not in the way that earlier scholars postulated. Perhaps most striking, and contrary to the long-held belief that higher education leads to apostasy, the research group discovered that "it is the respondents who *did not go to college* who exhibit the highest rates of diminished religiosity," as measured by church attendance and the importance they place on religion. "Those with the highest level of education—the respondents with a least a bachelor's degree—are the least likely to curtail their church attendance," the authors observe. "The most educated are also the least likely to report a decrease in religion's importance."[17]

In a useful reminder that religiosity is not synonymous with creationism, college graduates—who have higher rates of church attendance and religiosity—are also significantly more likely than the underchurched high school graduates to believe in evolution.[18] Many of their professors, though, are surely disappointed that even college graduates do not accept evolution in particularly large percentages; indeed, when pressed directly on the topic of human evolution, college graduates are likely to favor creationism over evolution.[19] College, then, is hardly an incubator of heresy, despite the fears (and hopes) aroused by James Leuba and his heirs.

At the same time, empirical evidence bears out the charge that American scientists' religious outlook differs significantly from that of the population as a whole, and not just in their support for evolution. Leuba's original 1916 study set the standard for evaluating faculty religious belief. In the most notorious section of his book, Leuba carried out an inquiry with one thousand "men of science"—including faculty in several fields at colleges and universities across the country—and found that 58.2 percent were agnostics or atheists, by his definition. Provocatively, that percentage rose significantly for elite faculty—around 70 percent—compared to the less distinguished. Calculated by field, disbelief and doubt were highest among biologists, psychologists, and sociologists.[20]

However, contrary to Leuba's expectation that the scientific community would grow increasingly secular over the course of the century, the passage of time has done little to alter the rate of belief among American scientists. Instead of finding increasing atheism and agnosticism among scientists, a pair of researchers who replicated Leuba's study in 1996 found that the general run of present-day scientists were only a few points less likely to believe in God than their predecessors. Strikingly, though, the 1996 survey found that the "greater" scientists—in this case, members of the National Academy of Sciences—did follow Leuba's predictions and were approximately 20 percent less religious than the already low figures for Leuba's original elite grouping.[21] A smaller 2007 survey of social and natural scientists at seven elite universities found that fully 52 percent claimed no religious affiliation, with physicists and biologists ranking at the bottom of religiosity. This compares to a mere 14 percent of the general population professing no religious adherence.[22] Further, of the minority of scientists who claimed a religious affiliation, most ranged themselves on the liberal edge of the spectrum. A recent study did uncover a modest amount of "thin spirituality" among scientists—a flexible, highly individualistic sense of nonmaterial forces in their lives, including vibrations from practices such as meditation, but this was seldom associated with anything resembling adherence to established religion, liberal or otherwise.[23] Faculty members are thus significantly less religious than their students. In a sign that most science faculty hold their identities as scientists equal to or above their religious identities, among major universities only the faculty at Brigham Young University claimed to value their religious commitments above their academic ones.[24]

Creationists often cite Charles Darwin's own life as a case study in evolution's fostering of unbelief, for the biologist had been reared a devout Anglican but later descended into agnosticism. However, Darwin's father and some other members of the family were largely unbelievers to begin with, and Darwin gradually lost his own Christian faith well after he had fully formulated his evolutionary theory. His reasons for this belated apostasy were much more personal. As Darwin testified in his autobiography, his father's death in 1848 shook him badly, and the early death of his beloved daughter three years later turned him against not just the Christian doctrine of eternal damnation but also the idea of a benevolent, caring God.[25] The erosion of the naturalist's faith in the decades following *On the Origin of Species* owed more to these searing events than to the implications of biological evolution. Darwin's religious development nevertheless scores a strong rhetorical point for his opponents. "How can any teacher tell his students that evolution does not tend to destroy his religious faith?" Bryan asked during the Scopes trial. "How can an honest teacher conceal from his students the effect of evolution upon Darwin himself?"[26]

However, contrary to accusations that evolutionary research had made scientists discard their religion, the 2007 study found that these men and women were, rather, "disproportionately selected from homes where there was no religion or where religion was not important" in the first place.[27] Stephen Jay Gould exemplified this path to a scientific career. Raised in a secular Jewish family in Queens, New York, Gould at five years old had an epiphany on viewing the *Tyrannosaurus rex* at the American Museum of Natural History in Manhattan. As Gould remembered it, he decided on the spot that he would become a scientist—a paleontologist, to be precise. His irreligious upbringing placed no barriers to his choice. This is not to say that a secular background is always a requirement. The ranks of evolutionists also include numerous men and women who renounced their religious tradition because it seemed to conflict with their growing belief in evolution. Richard Dawkins, reared a conventional Anglican like Darwin, is one such case; a more wrenching break came for the biologist E. O. Wilson, whose conservative Southern Baptist background put a strain on his decision, as a biology major at the University of Alabama, to accept evolution as an alternative to the literal story of Genesis. Wilson's case notwithstanding, the surveys point more toward family background as a predisposing factor. As a corollary, the same holds true for creation scientists, who grew up overwhelmingly in actively religious families, usually with a strong bent toward conservative evangelicalism, and continued that tradition in their work. It remains an open question exactly why a secular family should make one more likely to become a scientist, but the central fact remains that scientists are significantly more secular than the general population.

Such results add fuel to creationist accusations that evolutionary scientists are at the very least blind to their own secular prejudices, and are possibly actively seeking to impose their naturalistic worldview on the rest of society. In an early essay that set the tone for the many books that were to make his reputation as ID's prophet and publicist, Phillip E. Johnson argued that evolutionary scientists were bent on a naturalistic approach that "absolutely rules out any miraculous or supernatural intervention at any point. Everything is conclusively presumed to have happened through purely material mechanisms that are in principle accessible to scientific investigation, whether they have been discovered or not."[28] Johnson lampooned what he took to be scientists' collective myopia: "Because we cannot examine God in our telescopes or under our microscopes, God is unreal."[29] For Johnson, mainstream scientists' methodological naturalism is not so much a heuristic device as it is a disguise for their much farther-reaching ambition: to convince Americans that God and the supernatural simply do not exist. The accusation scores rhetorical points, but the attorney is mistaken on historical grounds. Methodological naturalism—the doctrine that science can adduce only natural explanations for natural phenomena—is rooted in the Christian tradition. As early as the middle ages, some churchmen interested in explaining the workings of nature eschewed supernatural explanations, finding them to be, in the words of one future Bishop, "the last refuge of the weak."[30] These religiously orthodox scholars preferred naturalistic explanations, maintaining that it was impious to believe that God could not have acted through the natural laws he had first created.[31] Even as this reliance on naturalism gradually became more exclusive from the seventeenth century through the nineteenth, it remained well within the province of Christian belief. A scientific focus on secondary causes did not call into question God's role as the primary cause. Only in the latter years of the nineteenth century did militant antichurch crusaders attempt to enlist scientific naturalism in their war on organized religion. Earlier generations would not have understood the conflict, and a century later, most theologians and scientists outside of the creationist circle continue to disavow the existence of a contradiction between methodological naturalism and religious belief.

Nevertheless, Johnson's accusation gathers some of its force from the prominence of a handful of atheistic evolutionists such as Richard Dawkins. Originally trained in zoology, Dawkins rose to prominence as a sociobiologist in the 1970s, arguing that natural selection took place at the level of genes and that genetic evolution played a significant—though not determining—role in animal behavior, including in humans. From his post at Oxford University and later as a pugnacious free-lance intellectual, Dawkins has invested much of his energy in attacks on organized religion and, in particular, its creationist subvarieties. The title of his 2006 best-seller, *The God Delusion*, hints at the intensity of Dawkins's disdain for religion. Further, he sees his endeavors as a unified whole. In an oft-quoted passage from his 1986 book, *The Blind Watchmaker* (the title an allusion to William Paley's argument from design), Dawkins writes, "Although atheism might have been logically tenable before Darwin, Darwin made it possible to be an intellectually fulfilled atheist."[32] Such statements have made Dawkins the favorite scientist of creationists seeking to equate evolution with atheism. Indeed, if Dawkins had never been born, it would have been necessary for creationists to form him from the dust.

The creationist criticism that Dawkins and his fellow scientists cannot see through the blinkers of their own secularism has found unlikely support from inside the academy, where the field of science and technology studies (STS) often echoes the antievolutionists' charges that scientific inquiry is inherently value-laden; scientific "truths," STS scholars argue, are not so much revelations of objective reality as they are propositions the scientific community has agreed to hold as true.[33] "Scientific truth" is therefore demoted to the status of a social construction, and as such, it is irremediably shaped by the scientists' own habits, prejudices, and interactions, as well as by the social and political context in which they work. Typically coming from the academic left, STS scholars have tended to focus on the ways in which assumptions about gender, race, and other issues affect the practice of science, but their approach allows room for other challenges to scientific authority.

While most creationists simply charge evolutionists with being irreligious or antireligious, a small number of sophisticated critics, such as Johnson, employ STS insights to criticize the naturalistic assumptions that evolutionary scientists make, maintaining that their irreligion leads them to seek only naturalistic explanations for phenomena such as speciation or the functionality of the eyeball. One prominent STS scholar, Steve Fuller, from Warwick University in the United Kingdom, created a stir when he placed his expertise at the service of the school board in the Dover trial. Fuller testified that the scientific community used the requirement of naturalistic explanations primarily to reinforce its professional boundaries against potentially threatening competitors. The idea that science must exclude supernatural explanations in order to be considered valid, Fuller asserted, was "rubbish." Despite the many counterexamples laid before him by the opposing attorney, Fuller maintained strenuously that the scientific academy was essentially a closed shop of like-minded elitists; its monopoly over institutions and resources meant that unorthodox theories such as ID would never receive a fair hearing. Fuller's testimony did little to convince the judge that science was merely a social construction, though, and he further damaged his own cause when he casually commented that ID was strongly linked to creationism.[34] Nevertheless, Fuller's arguments embodied a hopeful, if unorthodox, flirtation between ID and STS.

If scientific naturalism is primarily a product of community agreement, as STS implies, then it may also be more fragile than commonly believed, more vulnerable to criticism and rapid change. Johnson and his fellows look particularly to a founding document of STS, Thomas Kuhn's influential *The Structure of Scientific Revolutions*, which was published one year after *The Genesis Flood*, to support their argument that social constructions in the sciences—in this case, the naturalistic methodology that underpins modern science—are open to "paradigm shifts," in Kuhnian language. As Johnson paraphrases Kuhn, a paradigm "is not a mere theory or hypothesis but a way of looking at the world that is influenced by cultural prejudice as well as by scientific observation and experience."[35] Fuller echoed the charge: "I really think methodological naturalism is just a fig leaf for metaphysical naturalism when it gets right down to it."[36]

ID leaders believe that when the weaknesses of Darwinism and the body of evidence for creationism become too great to ignore, and when the social context of religious belief becomes too powerful to resist, then a new paradigm, such as ID, could emerge that will rapidly reinterpret the "anomalies" that evolution seems unable to explain.[37] The scientific paradigm could shift rapidly from an enterprise based on the search for naturalistic explanations to one that will accept an element of the supernatural—including, most ID adherents quietly hope, evidence that may allow for a conservative interpretation of Christianity.[38] Before his death in 1996, Kuhn came to criticize some of the more radically relativistic uses of his theory, and surely he and most STS specialists did not intend their social constructionism to be placed at the service of creationism. Their ideas have nevertheless nurtured a spark of hope in the ID community. Although it is ironic for these Christian conservatives, who are committed to absolute standards of morality and truth, to dabble in postmodern relativism, the STS approach nevertheless has helpfully reinforced their attempts to demote science from its privileged position as a neutral arbiter of truth. If evolutionary science is merely a product of group consensus, then why should it take precedence over ID or other forms of creation science?

Johnson and his ID allies, however, misread Kuhn and other scholars in his tradition. The "paradigm shifts" Kuhn sees in the transition from Ptolemaic astronomy to Copernican, for example, or from Newtonian physics to Einstein's relativity, have been revolutions within the context of scientific naturalism. ID's attack on scientific naturalism, however, is of a different order, as it seeks to do away not just with the Darwinian mechanism of natural selection but also with the naturalistic context of scientific proof altogether. One could make a stretch and allow that ID proponents such as Johnson and Michael Behe may indeed find factual anomalies the modern evolutionary synthesis cannot account for (though the "anomalies" they have perceived to date have usually been more the products of their own unfamiliarity with the material than instances of evolution's failure to explain novel discoveries). If these anomalies were to pile up sufficiently, the evolutionary paradigm could indeed undergo a revolution in the same way that Darwinism eventually upended special creation, or Einstein's theories superseded Newton's. However, under ID's new scientific standard, investigators would have no way of evaluating whether the new paradigm was actually an improvement over the old. It would be analogous to asserting that your car would drive faster if it did not have a speedometer. The assertion may be true, but within your new system of reference, you no longer have a way to measure that. The creationist attempt to discard the naturalistic evaluation of proof altogether is not quite the paradigm shift Kuhn had in mind.

Contrary to Johnson's allegations, most scientists and theologians agree that scientific naturalism does not—cannot, by definition—make pronouncements about the supernatural. Gould called religion and science "non-overlapping magisteria" (NOMA), each with its own privileged place in human culture. He pleaded with his colleagues, not always consistently, to avoid using science to make pronouncements on topics better left to religion and philosophy—morality, for example, or the ultimate meaning of the universe.[39] Dawkins, however, has never listened to such timorous calls for coexistence, and neither, it is clear, have leading antievolutionists. Johnson complains that Gould and other scientists still consider science the ultimate arbiter of truth, even in the evaluation of "whether heaven is real or illusory," or "whether divine revelation can be a foundation for knowledge." The scientific magisterium would always treat the religious magisterium as a junior and much inferior partner, and so serious compromise is impossible. "If Gould's NOMA were a bus," Johnson argues, "there would be no doubt about who owns and drives the bus and who is required to ride only in the back seats."[40] Partly in response to this threat of scientific imperialism, one of modern creationism's great successes has been to convince a large percentage of Americans that evolution and the Bible are wholly incompatible, even if science and religion are not, and that they must make a decisive choice between these interpretations of origins.[41]

Nevertheless, a substantial percentage of scientists reject the either/or that creationists have tried to fasten on the subject. Indeed, some of the greatest evolutionary scientists have been able to reconcile their religion with their evolutionary commitment, from the time of Darwin's great and pious American ally Asa Gray until the present. Surveys from Leuba onward indicate that of the nearly 100 percent of American scientists who accept evolution, close to half remain willing to allow that God may have played some role in the process. A recent Gallup Poll on attitudes toward evolution found far more scientists clustered around the position that God played no role in evolution (55 percent) than Americans in general (9 percent), but for the middle position that allows for some sort of supernatural involvement in evolution, scientists actually mirror the broader population, with 40 percent of each group accepting the "overlap" position.[42] "Either half my colleagues are enormously stupid," wrote Stephen Jay Gould, "or else the science of Darwinism is fully compatible with conventional religious belief—and equally compatible with atheism, thus proving that the two great realms of nature's factuality and the source of human morality do not overlap."[43]

While working scientists seem largely unconcerned with the epistemological struggles over naturalism, and entirely untroubled by the possibility that the scientific paradigm of naturalistic inquiry might suddenly shift under their feet, some suggest that the antievolution movement has influenced their scholarly activities, if only a little. "There's a certain amount of circling of the wagons," Lieberman confides. "Until you're of a certain level of status in the field, you feel hesitant to criticize Darwin . . . Even Gould caught flak for his criticisms." Lieberman refers to a period in the 1970s and 1980s in which several rivals attacked Gould and Niles Eldredge's theory of "punctuated equilibrium" in the evolution of species for straying too far from Darwin's model of slow, uniform development and for resembling, ever so faintly, the creationists' catastrophism—a supremely damning charge among evolutionary scientists, and a baffling accusation to level against two of the most prominent evolutionists of the late twentieth century.[44] "As scientists," Lieberman concludes, "we're constrained not to give aid and comfort to the creationists, but most of us aren't comfortable joining up with Richard Dawkins, either."

This caution, however, does not mean that scientists are locked into an unquestioning acceptance of Darwinian evolution. On the contrary, the scientific world is fundamentally patricidal. As one prominent biologist remarks, "If I or any other scientist thought that we really could upset the ideas of Charles Darwin and replace them with a new or superior theory, boy, there would be no better way to make your reputation, to ensure scientific immortality, and to get the best possible grant funding. It is that very sort of self-promotion that makes science work."[45] In the end, the disputes that make evolution look like "a field in crisis" to creationists are simply the give-and-take of normal science, as researchers argue over evidence and mechanisms within the broader context of evolution. On the bench, they spend little to no time speculating about the philosophical foundations of their work, because methodological naturalism has become the only practical approach to investigating and evaluating natural phenomena. God may be out there somewhere, but that is a matter better left to philosophers, theologians, and political activists. Scientists at secular universities and most religiously affiliated colleges are free to pursue their evolutionary scholarship without giving much thought to its philosophical or political ramifications.

Their freedom from doubt finds its mirror image among the much smaller number of avowedly creationist scientists, who are perfectly comfortable with valuing their religious identities above their scientific self-image. In addition to the usual roster of ID adherents, in 2001 fifty men and women with doctorates in various scientific fields (including, as expected, a great many engineers) offered their testimony in the collection *In Six Days: Why Fifty Scientists Choose to Believe in Creation*.[46]

True to their self-presentation as scientists, most of the contributors adduce some form of scientific proof for a young-earth creation, but most also echo a biochemist, John P. Marcus, who proclaims in his first sentence, "My belief in a literal six-day creation of the universe is based primarily on the teaching of the Bible and my understanding that this is God's Word and is true."[47] Most of the contributors hark back to their upbringing in a conservative Christian faith, and several of the "confessions" also follow the traditional Christian testimonial pattern: unmoored by Darwinism from religious belief, a lost soul wanders through the fields of skepticism. These spiritual travails continue until the doubter faces the crucial moment of crisis, the "hour of decision," in which all doubts are resolved by a new consecration in Jesus Christ.[48] Phillip Johnson had faced this crisis, and so, too, had John Calvert at the Intelligent Design Network; the creationist leader of the Dover, Pennsylvania, school board; and countless other born-again Christians who make up the rank and file of the creationist movement.

Not all evangelicals share this sense of certainty. Even as the Discovery Institute and the ACLU clash prominently in the courtroom and the media, a vigorous dialogue over evolution has taken place among conservative evangelicals, far from the media attention that descended upon Dayton, Topeka, and Dover, and far from the mutual incomprehension that characterizes so many interactions between creationists and evolutionists. For these Christians, the question of evolution brings into the open their more fundamental differences over the nature of God and the role of the scientist. Naturally, Phillip E. Johnson looms large in these conversations, often physically present for debate and always intellectually near at hand. But a number of pious scholars do not cede to him sole possession of the conservative religious position on origins. The best known of these is Francis Collins, the geneticist who headed the Human Genome Project and was elevated to the directorship of the National Institutes of Health in 2009. Collins is a lapsed atheist turned evangelical Protestant, and he has widely proclaimed, through books, articles, and public talks, that evolution and the Big Bang theory of the creation of the universe are fully compatible with Christianity if one does not take the position of reading Genesis literally. In staking out this middle ground, he has also engaged in public discussions—*debate* is too strong a word—with Richard Dawkins as well as with his fellow evangelicals.[49] Along with his religious allies, Collins rejects the claims of ID without jettisoning his own faith. "Because I do believe in God's creative power in having brought it all into being in the first place," he told Dawkins, "I find that studying the natural world is an opportunity to observe the majesty, the elegance, the intricacy of God's creation."[50] To some extent, one can hear the faint echoes of Paley's natural theology. Indeed, in his book *The Language of God*, Collins testifies that his work on DNA, while certainly supporting the reality of evolution and common descent, also reinforced his belief in God. Similarly, he finds the Big Bang to be fully consistent with Genesis, and maintains that other elements of the universe may point the way to God's existence. For example, Collins invokes C. S. Lewis's influential argument that the existence of a moral sense among humans is powerful evidence for the existence of a deity—for him in particular, a Christian deity who set the parameters for the evolution of his creation.[51] As a theistic evolutionist, Collins stakes out a broad middle ground.

Collins has chosen intentionally to step outside his scientific box in order to touch on matters of belief, but for some scientists, talking about their faith is not simply a matter of choice. Researchers and teachers called to serve at upper-tier conservative Christian colleges cannot avoid wrestling with the tension between evolution and biblical revelation. As evangelicals, they cannot simply ignore evolution's implications for faith, as their counterparts at secular universities may easily do; but as scientists at colleges with high academic aspirations, they cannot reflexively place their religious commitments above their scholarly identities, as many creation scientists do. Evangelical scholars such as the Pentecostal Denis O. Lamoureux at St. Joseph's College, University of Alberta; Howard J. Van Till, a physicist now retired from Calvin College (and more recently estranged from his evangelical heritage); and Van Till's erstwhile colleague Davis A. Young, a geologist, share a number of principles with Johnson and his closest allies. It goes without saying that all believe (or at least believed) God exists and has played a role in the existence of the universe. All have rejected deism, the theology that a supreme being created the universe and then simply left it alone, without further intervention or guidance, for this belief would rule out miraculous interventions such as the resurrection of Jesus. All reject the materialist vision of a spiritless cosmos. Even those who accept the reality of evolution by natural selection reject the idea of dysteleological evolution—that is, evolution as a completely random process, with no organizing principle toward a better end. At least some of their arguments with ID revolve around the question of whose position actually comes closest to these rejected doctrines. They are not biblical literalists, but Christian faith shapes their identity as scientists in a way that it does not for more secular "mainstream" scientists.

This common ground creates at least a foundation for amity with ID adherents. Despite the differences between himself and Johnson, Lamoureux testifies, "I know well of his commitment to our Lord and Saviour Jesus Christ, and I would be the first to pass and receive the communion cup to and from him on a Sunday morning."[52] From the late 1990s into the twenty-first century, Lamoureux and Johnson have carried on a running debate over their differences, joined by seconds from each camp.

Lamoureux maintains, perhaps overoptimistically, "There has been a quiet revolution among many North American evangelicals as they have come to accept with little resistance the standard cosmological and geo-logical dating of the universe and earth in the billions of years."[53] But Lamoureux cautions that many of these evangelicals have nevertheless fallen into other fallacies, such as Johnson's theory of intelligent design. With its invocation of the supernatural to explain certain phenomena for which scientists are alleged to have no explanation, such as the "irreduc-ible complexity" of the blood-clotting cascade, ID runs into both practical and theological difficulties. Lamoureux's criticism of Johnson is wide-ranging, including condemnations of Johnson's slippery rhetoric and his ad hominem attacks on scientists, but he asserts that the most obvious practical problem with Johnson's position may be the lawyer's shaky grasp of evolutionary science. Echoing Gould's attack on *Darwin on Trial*, Lamoureux points out many areas in which Johnson misinterprets or misses altogether the most up-to-date scientific scholarship, taking partic-ular issue with Johnson's treatment of whale evolution, which featured prominently in *Darwin on Trial*. Citing numerous instances in which Johnson, like many ID supporters, points to nonexistent scientific gaps as evidence of God's work, Lamoureux bluntly concludes, "Johnson has not done his homework."[54] Skipping his homework has created potentially dangerous theological consequences as well. "According to Johnson the only God worthy of praise and worship would be one who actively inter-venes in his creation throughout time," Lamoureux argues.[55] The new "science" of ID, then, is simply a God-of-the-gaps argument—God inter-venes regularly in his creation, creating the "gaps" that are inexplicable without the existence of a divine designer. "But as history records," Lamoureux warns, "the God-of-the-gaps approach is vulnerable to the advance of science and has led to disastrous pastoral consequences. The closure of alleged gaps results in the retreat of this type of God into nar-rower recesses of human ignorance."[56] Johnson's misunderstanding of the "gaps" in scientific knowledge exacerbates this problem.

Lamoureux sadly observes that Johnson's approach has rocketed to success in evangelical circles and bids fair to become a major element in the Christian home-school science curriculum. Lamoureux denies that this development will help secure the Christian faith. Quite the contrary. "What happens to the child who is taught young earth creationism or progressive creationism in a Christian school or a church Sunday school," Lamoureux asks, "and then sees the scientific data for evolution first-hand in the university or paleontological museum?" His answer is not encouraging: "Those who have seen such a scenario unfold often report disastrous spiritual consequences." Further, when Christians such as Johnson "weld their antievolution to the Cross of Christ and their faith," they prompt nonbelievers to "disregard the Cross as they angrily mock scientific understanding of the antievolutionists," especially in the university environment.[57] As the historian Mark A. Noll wrote in his influential 1994 book, *The Scandal of the Evangelical Mind*, "My cri de coeur is to proclaim that the only 'wedge' Johnson is introducing into our society is a wedge between the evangelical church and the modern university."[58] Far from defending the word of God, antievolutionism only makes it more vulnerable. Keith B. Miller, a research assistant professor of geology at Kansas State University, accuses Johnson of weakening evangelicalism, ironically, by ceding too much ground to his opponents. "By accepting that evolution and metaphysical naturalism are inseparable," Miller argues, "Johnson allows the atheists to define the terms and set the agenda of the debate. Evolution becomes an alternative to Christian theism, and the debate is reduced to a choice between undirected, purposeless change and a personal, creatively active God."[59] Not only do a great many practicing scientists reject these "false dichotomies," but evangelicals, too, should resist the temptation to equate evolution with metaphysical naturalism.

Entering these discussions does not require evangelical scientists to radically retool their intellectual commitments. Like most of his peers, Van Till recounts an upbringing saturated with theological discussion: "My parents have little education, but they read and talked theology between themselves and with friends all the time. Theology was part of the atmosphere in which I grew up."[60] Van Till's rigorous Dutch Reformed engagement with Christian doctrine continued into his faculty position. "At Calvin College," he notes, "theological discussion is fair game in *any* course."[61]

Hardened by these intellectual challenges, Van Till's colleagues are likewise prepared to engage in doctrinal disputes. Beyond their assertion that creationism and ID are empirically wrong as science, Lamoureux and his allies also aver that creationism, especially of the ID variety, misrepresents the essence of the deity and his creation. Where ID focuses on the gaps in scientific explanations for natural phenomena as evidence that God has designed or intervened in the natural order, scientists such as Collins and Lamoureux maintain that it is precisely the regularity and perspicuity of natural phenomena that supports their Christian faith. "God can certainly do whatever he wants," allows Lamoureux. "And it is logically possible that there are gaps in nature attributable to God's direct action. But the question arises, 'Does God routinely intervene to "violate" the laws he established?'"[62]

Some evangelical evolutionists go further than Lamoureux to reject the distinction many on both sides of the argument make between God and his physical creation. Loren Wilkinson, a professor of interdisciplinary studies and philosophy at Regent College, loosely affiliated with the University of British Columbia in Canada, denies that God is in the habit of occasionally intervening in his creation, as ID seems to suggest. Rather, he argues, "the upholding energies of the Creator are necessary *at every instant* for each thing to be. There is no question of God intervening in such a creation, because each thing depends on God for its very existence. If God were not in some way upholding the creature's existence, the creature would cease to exist."[63] No "gaps" or punctuated interventions could exist in this theological framework. Nor would it help theologically if they did. As Wilkinson quotes one of Darwin's nineteenth-century defenders, "A theory of occasional intervention implies as its correlative a theory of ordinary absence."[64] Wilkinson's approach is particularly attractive in that it sidesteps the problem of deism as well as design. Karl Giberson, an evangelical physicist and scientific popularizer, maintains the conventional dualism between Creator and creation but argues that ID "turns God into a kind of conjurer, one who comes in every now and then to do a trick in nature." "How," he asks, "is this a helpful model for God?"[65]

Although he later was to move significantly farther away from his evangelical commitment, in his initial entry into the debate Van Till sought to combine Wilkinson's rejection of dualism with Lamoureux and Giberson's emphasis on the gapless regularity of the universe. In an essay published in 1999, Van Till maintained the entire universe is a "creation that has being only as an expression of God's effective will."[66] Rather than having been created all at once and then left alone, as deism would suggest, the universe is "radically dependent" upon God at all times. But rather than stepping in sporadically to fine-tune his creation, as ID suggests, God has given the universe the gift of a "formational economy," "a vast array of creaturely capabilities for action and interaction, including capabilities for self-organization and transformation."[67] Whereas ID is in thrall to a naturalistic outlook, in which "'purposeless, unintelligent, naturalistic processes' are only occasionally punctuated by episodes of special creation or intelligent design," Van Till saw the hand of God as ever-present in the formational economy.[68] Surely, he concluded, we should not be "tempted to search for empirical evidence of gifts withheld, as if God's creative work would best be known not by the gifts of being that are present but by those that are absent."[69] Evangelical Christians need not appeal to the jerry-rigged mechanism of ID to reconcile their faith with science.

His fellow evangelicals' arguments in favor of theistic evolution have been a bit much for Phillip Johnson. Indeed, Van Till, who has debated with Johnson several times, characterizes the attorney as "very touchy" when challenged, especially by his coreligionists. Beyond rebutting specific charges about his scientific ignorance and theological shallowness, Johnson has occasionally called into question these opponents' motives. "The main point of theistic evolution is to preserve peace with the mainstream scientific community," he told a 1992 symposium at Michigan's conservative Hillsdale College. "The theistic evolutionists therefore unwittingly serve the purposes of the scientific naturalists, by helping to persuade the religious community to lower its guard against the incursion of naturalism."[70] Five years later, in a radio interview with the conservative Christian activist James C. Dobson, Johnson hinted that these theistic evolutionists might not be so unwitting after all. Citing the occasionally strong resistance he meets, ironically, at Christian colleges, such as Calvin and Wheaton, Johnson suggested that many of those institutions have developed a "faculty culture" in which professors embrace theistic evolution primarily to enhance their "respect and prestige" in the secular academy. Their professional ambitions, in other words, have come to outweigh their religious identities.[71] Within the conservative Christian community, these were harsh words. Van Till rejects the claim. "What's behind Phil's talk about how biologists at Christian schools are just interested in prestige from the secular academy," he says, "is the fact that he is always wondering why biologists at Christian colleges believe in evolution and don't listen to him."[72] Johnson could have leveled his accusations at any number of professors at Christian colleges who for decades have been quietly teaching evolutionary biology and Big Bang cosmology as dictated by the professional standards of their discipline. They teach at institutions ranging from

Calvin and Wheaton to unlikelier outposts such as the Seventh-day Adventist Loma Linda University and La Sierra University.

One obvious target for Johnson may have been Van Till himself, whose experiences at Calvin College illustrate well the tension faculty at elite evangelical institutions can face when their scientific identities seem to conflict with their religious institutional context (see figure 5.1). The conflict is almost imperceptible at a militantly fundamentalist institution with lower academic aspirations such as Bob Jones University, but at a college like Calvin, it can flare up in a very public manner. As Van Till recalls, "I went merrily along for ten or fifteen years teaching as I thought best according to my discipline. Although I taught freely, I did try to be sensitive to the students, and I chose my words carefully."[73] But in the mid-1980s Van Till and two colleagues decided to push their coreligionists a little further and ended up inciting a controversy that the college's chronicler calls "one of the most severe conflicts between college and Church" in Calvin's history.[74] In the early 1980s, at the same time as the Supreme Court was considering antievolution cases such as *Edwards v. Aguilard*, one of Van Till's colleagues, geologist Davis Young, published *Christianity and the Age of the Earth*, in which he came out as an old-earth creationist, cautioning evangelicals who held to a young-earth view—the recognized orthodoxy for Calvin College and the Christian Reformed Church—to accept that the earth and the universe were millions of years old.[75] In a 1984 interview, the chair of Young's department, Clarence Menninga, echoed that conclusion and added the more inflammatory assertion that humanity was tens of thousands of years old. Meanwhile, Van Till was preparing to throw himself squarely into the controversy. "I was becoming increasingly frustrated with the debate over the 'war' between science and religion, and I was especially upset at the caricature of my discipline," he remembers. "So in the 1980s, it became time either to do something or quit my bitching."[76] One of the products of his decision was *The Fourth Day: What the Bible and the Heavens Are Telling Us About the Creation*.[77] As an introduction to astronomy, the book recapitulated much of what Van Till had been teaching in the classroom. But Van Till went farther than his colleagues in rejecting both old-earth and young-earth creationism in favor of a less literal reading of the Bible that allowed for different forms of theistic evolution.

For many members of the Christian Reformed Church—Calvin College's denominational sponsor—these challenges to Genesis were the definitive signs of Calvin's lapse from orthodoxy. Protests from congregations, which

FIGURE 5.1 Howard Van Till. Photo by Steve Van Till, courtesy of Howard Van Till.

had begun in 1982 with Young's geological pronouncements, began to pour into the synod, the college, and its board of trustees. A local businessman in Grand Rapids paid for what one Calvin seminary student publication called "the most hideous, slanderous and unchristian advertisements" in the *Grand Rapids Press*. [78] The conservative Christian Reformed journal *Christian Renewal* launched more high-minded but equally intemperate attacks on all three scientists. Much was at stake. The church was already riven by the issues of women's ordination, homosexuality, and biblical literalism.[79] As was the case in American culture at large, the more conservative members of the church lumped evolution together with all of these issues as a dark, indivisible threat to moral order. "I expected to arouse some *useful* controversy," Van Till explains, "but I was not prepared for the intensity of fear and distrust I met."[80]

In response to these pressures, the board of trustees of Calvin College appointed an ad hoc committee to investigate the professors' orthodoxy, in particular whether their teachings called into question the "event-character" status of biblical history—that is, whether they considered Genesis to be a record of actual events or merely an allegory or a symbolic story.

After a full three and a half years of conversation and interrogation, the committee concluded that Young's and Menninga's teachings were "in accord with Christian Reformed Doctrine."[81] Van Till presented more of a problem. Unlike Young and Menninga, he had suggested that Genesis 1–11 was not intended to be a scientific history of creation but rather is "primeval history," part of a genre used to explain the establishment of a "covenant" between Creator and creation.[82] The committee feared that Van Till's use of literary categories such as "genre" was a method of biblical interpretation that "could lead to conclusions which would call into question the event character of the history in these early chapters."[83] Unlike Young and Menninga, Van Till was to continue to be subject to the committee's examination for some of his "ambiguous or incomplete" statements.[84]

Much of the dispute surely escaped Calvin College's undergraduates, most of whom were involved—albeit in a context of purity—with the ordinary challenges and temptations of early adulthood and college life. Not so the students at the Calvin Theological Seminary, eight of whom submitted a report that argued Young, Menninga, and Van Till were "*not* in accordance with our denomination's guidelines."[85] For the seminarians, the men's ambiguous or unclear positions had "far-reaching and potentially dangerous implications for several areas in the life and doctrine of the Christian Reformed Church."[86] Other seminarians were more charitable. The editor of *Kerux*, the seminarians' newsletter, suggested that a world of difference existed between the atheistic evolution proposed by scientists such as Carl Sagan and the theistic evolution that Van Till seemed to support, even if it was not obviously orthodox. While allowing that it was legitimate to question whether such views should be represented among the faculty of a denominational college, the editor nevertheless cautioned some of his more militant fellow Calvinists against the rigidity of believing "that only those who are free from error—not sin, but doctrinal error—will enter heaven."[87] A spirited debate over evolution continued in the pages of the paper for months; even the three controversial professors contributed articles and letters to answer questions and accusations from students.[88]

Meanwhile, Van Till was still under examination over "ambiguities" in his beliefs, and he was growing tired of a process that included nearly monthly meetings for three years. "Eventually, I stopped going to all their meetings to answer their uninformed questions," he says. "Finally, I just told them, 'Let me know when you're done.'"[89] He left the committee with a memorandum answering most of its questions, and left matters at that. The memorandum's personal pledge to "teach nothing that is contrary to the doctrinal positions adopted by the Christian Reformed Church" was ultimately enough to mollify the committee while preserving Van Till's conviction that these doctrines had always been sufficiently elastic to allow for his position on origins, evolution, and biblical interpretation.

However, Van Till was not finished fulfilling his old vow to "do something" about the public discussion on science and faith. "When the dust of turmoil settled," he told an audience in 2006, "I discovered that I had been irreversibly changed by what I had experienced. I also came to realize that it was essential for me to reexamine my personal world-view."[90] Part of that reexamination launched Van Till into his running debate with Phillip Johnson over intelligent design, and in the following years they appeared together on stage and in the pages of books and journals such as *First Things*.[91] The other part consisted of Van Till seriously questioning the Calvinist tradition in which he had been raised. While he accepts that it is possible to teach about evolution at some church institutions, in 1997 the physicist took early retirement from Calvin College, liberating himself from an institution and a tradition that seemed increasingly constrictive. Within a decade, Van Till was speaking with excitement of "my journey out of traditional Christianity into new religious territory—progressive Christianity, respectful agnosticism, reverent naturalism . . . all options now open to a recovering Calvinist."[92]

The drama of the Van Till affair will not often be replicated in the labs of working scientists at other universities. While everyone has assumed for more than a century that natural scientists endorse evolution, recent polls have supplemented the analyses of public opinion on evolution with surveys that finally quantify scientists' own attitudes on the subject. The results have been overwhelming. During the 2002 intelligent design controversy in Ohio, for example, political scientists at Case Western Reserve University and the University of Cincinnati surveyed 460 Ohio academic scientists and found that 91 percent of them believed ID was only a religious belief, and an even higher percentage—93 percent—recognized no "scientifically valid evidence or an alternate scientific theory that challenges the fundamental principles of the theory of evolution."[93] This reinforced a larger 1998 study of natural and physical scientists that found more than 95 percent identifying themselves as evolutionists.[94] Other surveys have found even higher rates of scientists believing in evolution's validity. Perhaps they are simply being realistic. In a 1973 essay, one of the fathers of the evolutionary synthesis, the biologist Theodosius Dobzhansky, famously proclaimed, "Nothing in biology makes sense except in the light of evolution."[95]

Why, then, aren't more scientists actively involved in fighting creationism? "Most scientists are busy people," Cartwright observes. "There's also a self-selection of scientists—they're not public people, or even social people." Lieberman also notes a systemic barrier: "There aren't any rewards for participating in the controversies. It's considered time away from the research you're doing, and research universities aren't really in the business of that kind of public service."

Kenneth Miller knows better than most the difficulty of balancing research and public activism. A professor of cell biology at Brown University and coauthor with Joseph S. Levine of one of the most popular high school biology textbooks, Miller is one of the few prominent scientists actively involved in the fight against creationism.[96] Indeed, with the deaths of Stephen Jay Gould and Carl Sagan, Miller might be the best-known American evolution controversialist, and unlike those two men, Miller has the advantage, as a practicing Catholic, of being free from the "taint" of atheism. After letting a group of undergraduates inveigle him into a public debate at Brown with Henry Morris ("I won the debate convincingly, and Morris admitted it," Miller fondly recalls), Miller has lent his scientific expertise and rhetorical skill to the anticreationists off and on for more than two decades, testifying before judges and school boards, and presenting his case in such venues as William F. Buckley's conservative *Firing Line*. His testimony in the Dover, Pennsylvania, ID case was considered particularly helpful in undermining ID's claims to scientific legitimacy.[97] In addition to his intellectual and professional commitment to the cause, Miller good-naturedly admits that his interest in the issue is partly self-defense—his biology textbook regularly comes under fire from antievolution activists. He concedes that this public activity and his textbook work have slowed his research slightly, but he readily cites his long list of publications, along with honors from Brown and numerous national organizations, as evidence that activism need not always impede scholarship.

Despite his success, Miller has misgivings about participating in the fight for evolution and has not engaged in debates for several years. "It doesn't help to say you'll debate anyone, anywhere, anytime," he maintains. "A one-on-one debate always gives the false impression that these are somehow two equal sides."[98] Miller notes that the media tend to reinforce this impression. "They feel obliged to balance the scientist's comment with someone from 'the other side.' And the 'other side' is one group of about eight people at the Discovery Institute," he explains. "So you have this very curious thing where the entire scientific community is being balanced against seven or eight outspoken advocates at the Discovery Institute. It gives people a very false impression."[99] He is "absolutely, positively" concerned about giving such a platform to the antievolutionists. Moreover, Miller fears that his fellow scientists tend to come up short in debates against creationists. When he first agreed to debate Morris at Brown, Miller recalls, he took a quick look at the creationist's debating record, which revealed many episodes in which Morris made his evolutionist opponent look unprepared and foolish. "I got scared, so I prepared," says Miller.[100] Only by studying Morris's particular arguments and strategies was Miller able to counter the creationist's sometimes obscure attacks. Miller worries that his allies will not take the task as seriously. "Most of us in science would approach a creationist with over-self-confidence," he says.

At any rate, Miller observes, scientists are not overly eager to enter the fray. "Doing science is so fun and so absorbing that we're already consumed," he says. Further, Miller ventures, many scientists can afford to feel well insulated from the controversies. "Most active researchers see the fight more as an annoying curiosity," he says. The geography of higher education reinforces their confidence. "They regard this as a problem that doesn't occur in the Northeast. It's just in 'flyover country.'"[101] Nevertheless, Miller remains convinced that scientists must become involved in these controversies. Despite his misgivings, the veteran of the science wars concludes, "It would be a terrible mistake to let ID and the creationists have the public square all to themselves."[102]

In contrast to the large number of creationist ministries and institutes, only one national organization is dedicated solely to keeping evolution wedged into that public square. Headquartered in Oakland, California, the National Center for Science Education pursues a two-track strategy of political action and public education, and it serves to coordinate resistance to creationist activities. In the decades after the Scopes trial, when the antievolution movement operated largely out of the sight of northern and urban observers, such an organization seemed unnecessary. The ACLU team at the Scopes trial split up immediately afterward, and their allies in the Science Service, whose reporters collaborated with the Scopes defense, likewise dropped away from focusing on the evolution controversy; Maynard Shipley's Science League of America also disbanded by 1932.[103] Except for a handful of cases that compelled ACLU involvement, both sides in the fight seemed to have retreated from confrontation.

In the 1970s, however, as the creationist movement revived, its resurrection also called forth a new generation of anticreationists.[104] At first, grassroots anticreationists were entirely uncoordinated—individual groups fighting local battles with little awareness of each other's efforts. In the early 1980s, however, a number of these activists created state "Committees of Correspondence" with initial backing from the National Association of Biology Teachers (NABT). One early leader, a retired New York biology teacher named Stanley Weinberg, complained that professional scientists were of no use in such contests, as they refused to "descend from their ivory tower," and contented themselves with writing indignant letters to one another.[105] The Committees of Correspondence, in contrast, were almost entirely involved in local trench warfare against creationists. They lobbied state and local school boards, wrote letters to editors and politicians, educated teachers and parents, and occasionally picketed creationist talks. In Iowa and Georgia, in particular, they succeeded in turning back powerful creationist initiatives. But while Weinberg believed deeply in the power of grassroots organizing, the committees were still handicapped by their localistic orientations and their essentially reactive strategy. Further, Weinberg and other leaders fought over whether anticreationism should devote itself primarily to political activity or to education. These issues were partly resolved in 1983 when the extant Committees of Correspondence united to become the National Center for Science Education. Despite his personal devotion to grassroots political action, Weinberg, as the first NCSE leader, ironically shepherded the organization into becoming a more centralized institution with a strong educational focus. In 1986, funding from a number of sources—including a grant for $150,000 that the Carnegie Corporation nearly had to force upon Weinberg—allowed the organization to hire an executive director and set up a permanent office.[106] With a doctorate in physical anthropology, extensive experience with the Committees of Correspondence, and deep reserves of energy, Eugenie Scott became the NCSE's first (and so far only) executive director (see figure 5.2). The NCSE eventually grew out of its first headquarters, in Scott's basement in Berkeley, California, and though the organization's funding lags significantly behind that of its creationist counterparts, the NCSE has lent stability and direction to the anticreationist cause.

The NCSE's directors echo Miller's opinion that scientists need help in the task of defending evolutionary teaching. "They may think that all that they have to do to resolve a controversy over teaching evolution is

FIGURE 5.2   Eugenie Scott of the National Center for Science Education. Photo courtesy of National Center for Science Education.

to explain the science," observes Glenn Branch, Eugenie Scott's deputy director, "and that's simply not so."[107] The problem is more political. Branch notes, "It's essential to have a broad base of support for teaching evolution properly, including not only scientists but also teachers, parents, clergy, businesspeople, and citizens in general. Creationism isn't a problem that can be dispelled just by throwing science at it, we've learned."[108]

As NCSE's experience in the Dover, Pennsylvania, ID case suggests, anticreationists have done well to throw lawyers at the problem. The organization often coordinates legal action with state chapters of the American Civil Liberties Union, and it also participates in legal strategies with Americans United for the Separation of Church and State. NCSE's legal allies vary from state to state in their devotion to anticreationism, though. Some state ACLUs are more interested in capital punishment, for example, others in free speech. "It was lucky for us that *Kitzmiller* was in Pennsylvania!" Branch exclaims.

The NCSE now pursues both the grassroots fight against "flare-ups"— the office's term for local evolution disputes—and a positive education program about evolution. Rather than rely solely on university faculty for its educational mission, the NCSE publishes books and pamphlets, coordinates speakers and symposia, and lends extensive support to local teachers and parents who find themselves embroiled in anti-Darwin brushfires. Scott is a ubiquitous figure at scientific meetings across the country, maintaining the strong ties between her organization and the academic community.

Major organizations such as the NCSE, ACLU, and Americans United for Separation of Church and State are not alone in the fight. Harking back in some ways to Stanley Weinberg's uncoordinated local activism, since the mid-1980s hundreds of people have joined the evolution controversies online. Beginning with the precursors to the World Wide Web, such as newsgroups, listservs, and Usenet groups, evolution supporters and anticreationist activists have been meeting online to exchange scientific ideas, research interests, and tactical information about combating creationism (see figure 5.3). Most prominent among these early entities was the talk.origins Usenet group, started in 1986, which initially included postings from creationists as well as a larger collection of evolutionists. Eventually, the majority proevolutionists grew tired of writing what one participant called "the same old rebuttal to the same old creationist arguments," so they created the TalkOrigins Archive as a repository for collectively vetted answers to common creationist objections.[109] The archive has gone on to spawn several related websites, including creationist doppelgangers such as the TrueOrigins Archive.[110] Although the TalkOrigins Archive became a much-used resource, some of the participants have gone beyond mere intellectual involvement, and their broadened activity is consistent with research that shows that people who participate in Internet activity of this sort are also more engaged in real-world social networks and political engagement.[111] Several TalkOrigins alumni, along with affiliates at the related site Panda's Thumb and other online proevolutionists, put their expertise at the service of the plaintiffs in the 2005 *Kitzmiller* trial. They aided Barbara Forrest's testimony about the direct connection between a creationist textbook and ID's *Of Pandas and People*, and Michael Behe's disastrous testimony on the stand owed a great deal to their involvement. "Much of the scientific takedown of Behe had been tried out ahead of time in the preceding years on the forums and blogs," recalls Nick Matzke, a prominent Internet participant who went on to pursue a doctorate in integrative biology at the University of California, Berkeley. "We knew what Behe's answers were, what his backup answers were, and what his backup-backup answers were." [112] Indeed, two years prior to the Dover trial, Matzke had contributed to the TalkOrigins Archive a "massive" essay debunking Behe's pet example of irreducible complexity, the bacterial flagellum. As Wesley Elsberry, an early and leading participant in online anticreationism, concludes, "This online work absolutely fits in well with NCSE's approach."[113]

FIGURE 5.3 "Duty Calls." Unaffiliated (and generally uncompensated) Internet activists have played a role in the national debate over evolution. Cartoon courtesy of "xkcd: a webcomic of Romance, Sarcasm, Math, and Language," at xkcd.com/386/.

In light of many scientists' observation that there are no rewards for participating in this sort of public outreach, the enthusiasm that Elsberry, Matzke, and their allies have brought to the antievolution conversation is striking. The Panda's Thumb weblog involves about twenty-five contributors, with a "backstage" email list of another fifty to seventy-five correspondents. Like their creationist counterparts, many of them have a conversion story, albeit usually a less dramatic one. Matzke was already puzzled by the creationist literature his grandmother sent to his family when he was young, and he decided to look more deeply into the subject when he ended up in college with friends who were, as he recalls, "straight-up young-earthers."[114] He was already interested in evolution, and their arguments prodded him into becoming what he calls a "serious reader" of the TalkOrigins Archive. By 2000 he was, in his own words, "obsessed" with the fallacies of irreducible complexity, and he became deeply immersed in the online discussions of it. "In one sense, asking why people debate creationists on the Internet is asking like why alcoholics drink," Matzke explains. "Some people try it, some people dislike it, other people get hooked."[115] Wesley Elsberry's narrative is only slightly less quotidian. In February 1986 he attended a lecture by a young-earth geologist who seemed, to Elsberry's young and untutored eye, quite convincing. The lecturer made the mistake of handing Elsberry a copy of Henry Morris's *The Scientific Case for Creationism.* "As I read that book, I started highlighting things that were pretty obviously contrafactual," Elsberry told an online audience in 1997. " I think that there are perhaps five pages total without highlighter in the book now."[116] As he recalls today, "I was just appalled at what I was reading. I came to believe that to stand by and not say anything about what he was doing to science and to religion would have made me complicit in that."[117] The moment was important enough that more than fifteen years later, Elsberry still has the notes he took down at the lecture. With his background in both biology and computer science, Elsberry became very involved in online discussions, and in 2001 he took over responsibility for the TalkOrigins Archive, which he ran until stepping down because of a lack of time for his unpaid efforts. Like Matzke, he sees his involvement as a personal mission. "It comes down to an individual who can't let it go. You have to see it as something too important to drop."[118] Matzke himself sums up their involvement in a way that appropriately mixes the fervor of the activist and the science nerd: "I would say that the serious 'creationism watchers' consider themselves to be a bit like the Rangers in *The Lord of the Rings*," he explains.

> It is indeed important that someone, somewhere, corrects misinformation on the Internet. You can't get it all, and you can't address the same argument a million times individually, but you can put up a website or blog and at least have it there for the search engines to find. If you're a science fan, you just like science for its own sake, but it's even better if reading and writing about science helps you save Western civilization while you're at it.[119]

Anticreationists, though, are not the only people busy saving Western civilization through their desktop computers. Creationist groups have their own websites, led by AIG's slick promotional pages, and creationist websites and blogs are just as plentiful as the proevolution sites. TalkOrigins offers links to more than two hundred anticreationist websites and blogs, but similar numbers show up for creationist or antievolutionist

URLs. A direct fight for online dominance also continues on Wikipedia, where the background "View history" for entries related to evolution reveals a byzantine struggle over definitions in by far the most prominent source, for better or worse, of easily accessed information.[120]

As the anticreationist sites repeatedly emphasize, by all objective measures evolution has won the scientific side of the battle. More broadly, mainstream scientists such as Cartwright, Lieberman, Miller, and Van Till are united in their conviction that the scientific enterprise depends on methodological naturalism, and based on that foundation, the vast majority of scientists evince few qualms, if any, about identifying themselves as evolutionists. Indeed, for biologists, paleontologists, zoologists, and their many colleagues, that is their central academic identity. But while evolution maintains the upper hand in the academic realm, in the political arena creationists and evolutionists are more evenly matched. They are locked together in a struggle for the schools and popular opinion in this most religious land. One hundred and fifty years after the publication of *Origin of Species*, more than eight decades after the Scopes trial, indications are that the controversy is far from over.

How could it be otherwise? Antievolutionism is not simply a cultural aberration or the last gasp of social reactionaries. Rather, it is an impulse deeply enmeshed in other features of the social landscape, including religious passion and creativity, to be sure, but also a vigorous democratic ethos, social and sexual anxiety, regional identity, racial barriers, and numerous other elements. From the Scopes trial through the modern incarnations of scientific creationism such as flood geology and intelligent design, the antievolution controversies have exposed fault lines that already ran through the culture, and in many cases the fights over Darwin have deepened and reinforced these rifts. At its core, though, antievolutionism is also intensely personal. A few years after the Scopes trial, the journalist and philosopher Walter Lippmann wrote an inquiry into the Dayton proceedings, and though his personal sentiments rested squarely with Scopes, he found he could not fully condemn the antievolutionists' position, for they were defending not so much specific stories in the Bible as the possibility that God could communicate at all with humans through the Bible or other means of revelation. "It is of no consequence in itself whether the earth is flat or round," Lippmann wrote. "But it is of transcendent importance whether man can commune with God and obey His directions, or whether he must trust his own conscience and reason to find his way through the jungle of life." In such a conflict, Lippmann recognized, accepting evolution meant a rejection of revelation and the sacrifice of an "eternal plan of salvation." Little wonder that antievolutionists in 1925 and for the following century have chosen not "to smile and to commit suicide."[121]

The evolution fight conjures up a final emblematic image. As part of its strategy of positive education, the NCSE annually hosts a rafting expedition through the Grand Canyon to explore the awe-inspiring stratigraphic record of the earth's age. Coincidentally, the Institute for Creation Research also sponsors trips through the canyon to analyze the same formations as evidence of the earth's youth and the Flood's destructive power. It has not happened yet, but I like to imagine the two excursions running into each other on the Colorado River. I picture one boat shooting downstream first, leaving the other expedition to paddle furiously to maintain contact. Just whose boat takes the lead depends on the ever-changing configuration of the river's rapids, rocks, swirls, and eddies. And so they both beat on, gesturing ceaselessly at the record of the past while borne upon unpredictable currents into the future.

Notes

PREFACE

1. The most prominent expression of this thesis—one that has proved hard for historians to shake—appeared in Frederick Lewis Allen, *Only Yesterday: An Informal History of the 1920's* (New York, 1931), 163–71.
2. Howard Odum, "Editorial Notes," *Social Forces* 4 (September 1925): 190.
3. The most influential exposition of this view came in the *Scofield Reference Bible*, first published in 1909; see also Ronald L. Numbers, *The Creationists: From Scientific Creationism to Intelligent Design*, expanded ed. (Cambridge, MA, 2006), 7, 10–11; and Alexander Winchell, *Preadamites; or, A Demonstration of the Existence of Men Before Adam; Together with a Study of Their Condition, Antiquity, Racial Affinities, and Progressive Dispersion over the Earth* (Chicago, 1880).

INTRODUCTION: DARWIN COMES TO AMERICA

1. John William Draper, *History of the Conflict Between Religion and Science*, 3rd ed. (New York, 1875), vi.
2. As was pointed out during the Scopes inquiry, it is possible to conclude that Genesis records two stories of the divine creation of man: first, in Genesis 1:26, God creates humans in his own image, both male and female at the same time, and commands them to "be fruitful and multiply" and to "have dominion" over the earth and every living thing thereon. Then, after six days of exertion, he rests. The second "history of the heavens and the earth" seems to begin with Genesis 2:4b, with the fuller story of God forming Eve from Adam's rib and then expelling the two of them from the Garden of Eden. It may be worth noting that, contrary to some folk beliefs, human males have the same number of ribs as human females, and it is an even number. For a provocative and probably tongue-in-cheek speculation that Adam's missing "rib" in Genesis

actually refers to the absence of a baculum, or penis bone, among humans (an absence rare in the mammalian world—only humans and spider monkeys lack a baculum), see Scott F. Gilbert and Ziony Zevit, "Congenital Human Baculum Deficiency: The Generative Bone of Genesis 2:21–23," *American Journal of Medical Genetics* 101 (2001): 284–85.

3. *Kalevala, the Land of the Heroes*, trans. W. F. Kirby (London, 1907), 1:5–7, quoted in Barbara C. Sproul, *Primal Myths: Creation Myths Around the World* (San Francisco, 1979), 176–78.

4. Hesiod, *Theogony*, ll. 96–496.

5. For an overview of creation stories, see Sproul, *Primal Myths*.

6. David C. Lindberg, *The Beginnings of Western Science: The European Scientific Tradition in Philosophical, Religious, and Institutional Context, 600 B.C. to A.D. 1450* (Chicago, 1992), 11.

7. Ibid., 25–26.

8. Ibid., 39–40. Plato's best-known expression of the world of forms comes in his allegory of the cave in Book VII of *The Republic*.

9. Lindberg, *Beginnings of Western Science*, 54–55. Aristotle's assertion about the eternal nature of the universe later gave rise to theological gymnastics among medieval scholastics as they attempted to reconcile their orthodox Christian interpretation of creation with their strong commitment to Aristotelianism.

10. David Keck, *Angels and Angelology in the Middle Ages* (New York, 1998), 76.

11. Ibid., 74.

12. Richard J. Blackwell, *Galileo, Bellarmine, and the Bible: Including a Translation of Foscarini's Letter on the Motion of the Earth* (Notre Dame, IN, 1991), 66.

13. On the myth of Galileo's persecution, see Maurice A. Finocchiaro, "That Galileo Was Imprisoned and Tortured for Advocating Copernicanism," in Ronald L. Numbers, ed., *Galileo Goes to Jail and Other Myths About Science and Religion* (Cambridge, MA, 2009), 68–78.

14. Although Paley made a significant impact as a scholar and activist, he was not a compelling figure. Information of sorts on his strikingly uneventful personal life may be found in M. L. Clarke, *Paley: Evidences for the Man* (London, 1974); and Edmund Paley, *An Account of the Life and Writings of William Paley* (Farnborough, Hants, UK, 1970 [1825]).

15. Marcus Tullius Cicero, *On the Nature of the Gods*, trans. Francis Brooks (London, 1896).

16. William Paley, *Natural Theology: or, Evidences of the Existence and Attributes of the Deity, Collected from the Appearances of Nature* (London, 1802), 1–9.

17. Ibid., 2.

18. Ibid., 3–4.

19. Ibid., 19.

20. See Cotton Mather, *The Christian Philosopher: A Collection of the Best Discoveries in Nature, with Religious Improvements* (Gainesville, FL, 1968).

21. Paley, *Natural Theology*, 578–79.

22. George M. Marsden, *Understanding Fundamentalism and Evangelicalism* (Grand Rapids, 1991), 130–31.

23. Jon H. Roberts notes, however, that theological arguments against natural theology were at least as important as biological considerations; he further cautions against the myth that natural theology did not outlive the nineteenth century. Jon H. Roberts, "That Darwin Destroyed Natural Theology," in Ronald L. Numbers, ed., *Galileo Goes to Jail and Other Myths About Science and Religion* (Cambridge, MA, 2009), 161–69.

24. Charles Darwin, *The Autobiography of Charles Darwin, 1809–1882*, ed. Nora Barlow (New York, 1958), 56–57.

25. Ibid., 58–59.

26. Ibid., 71.

27. Ibid., 85.

28. Ibid., 118.

29. Ibid., 118–24.

30. B. S. Lieberman and R. A. Kaesler, *Prehistoric Life: Evolution and the Fossil Record* (Oxford, 2010), 279–83.

31. Charles Darwin, *On the Origin of Species by Means of Natural Selection, or the Preservation of Favoured Races in the Struggle for Life* (Cambridge, MA, 1964 [1859])]; Ernst Mayr, *The Growth of Biological Thought: Diversity, Evolution, and Inheritance* (Cambridge, MA, 1982), 405.

32. Mayr, *Growth of Biological Thought*, 505–9.

33. Ronald L. Numbers, *Darwinism Comes to America* (Cambridge, MA, 1998), 47.

34. Darwin, *On the Origin of Species*, 486.

35. Mayr, *Growth of Biological Thought*, 513–25. Excellent histories of evolutionary ideas include Edward J. Larson, *Evolution: The Remarkable History of a Scientific Theory* (New York, 2004), and Peter J. Bowler, *Evolution: The History of an Idea*, 3rd ed. (Berkeley, 2009).

36. Mayr, *Growth of Biological Thought*, 510.

37. Darwin, *Autobiography*, 87.

38. Paul Conkin, *When All the Gods Trembled: Darwinism, Scopes, and American Intellectuals* (New York, 1998), 37.

39. Darwin, *Autobiography*, 76.

40. Charles Darwin, *The Descent of Man* (London, 1871).

41. Numbers, *Darwinism Comes to America*, 48.

42. The best examination of the alleged donnybrook and the falsity of its mythology is David N. Livingstone, "That Huxley Defeated Wilberforce in Their Debate over Evolution and Religion," in Ronald L. Numbers, ed., *Galileo Goes to Jail and Other Myths About Science and Religion* (Cambridge, MA, 2009), 152–60.

43. Isabella Sidgwick, "A Grandmother's Tales," *Macmillan's Magazine* LXXVIII, no. 468 (October 1898): 433–34, quoted in J. R. Lucas, "Wilberforce and Huxley: A Legendary Encounter," *Historical Journal* 32 (1979): 314.

44. Lucas, "Wilberforce and Huxley," 324.

45. Ibid.

46. Ibid., 326.

47. Alveros Giron, "The Moral Economy of Nature: Darwinism and the Struggle for Life in Spanish Anarchism (1882–1914)," in Thomas F. Glick, Rosaura Ruiz, and Miguel Angel Puig-Samper, eds., *The Reception of Darwinism in the Iberian World* (Boston, 2001), 189–203; Marta Irurozqui, "'Desvio al Paraiso': Citizenship and Social Darwinism in Bolivia, 1880–1920," in Glick, Ruiz, and Puig-Samper, eds., *Reception of Darwinism* (quotation on 207).

48. The best studies of the diversity of the American reception are in Ronald L. Numbers and John Stenhouse, eds., *Disseminating Darwinism: The Role of Place, Race, Religion, and Gender* (New York, 1999).

49. Shailer Mathews, *The Faith of Modernism* (New York, 1924), 36.

50. Jon H. Roberts, *Darwinism and the Divine in America: Protestant Intellectuals and Organic Evolution, 1859–1900* (Madison, 1988); Marsden, *Understanding Fundamentalism and Evangelicalism*, 130–31.

51. Conkin, *When All the Gods Trembled*, 25–26.

52. James R. Moore, *The Post-Darwinian Controversies: A Study of the Protestant Struggle to Come to Terms with Darwin in Great Britain and America, 1870–1900* (New York, 1979), 216–51.

53. Edward J. Larson, "Before the Crusade: Evolution in American Secondary Education Before 1920," *Journal of the History of Biology* 20 (Spring 1987): 89–114; Edward J. Larson, *Trial and Error: The American Controversy over Creation and Evolution* (New York, 1985), 7–18.

54. Judith V. Grabiner and Peter D. Miller, "Effects of the Scopes Trial: Was It a Victory for Evolutionists?" *Science* 185 (September 6, 1974): 832–37. See also George W. Hunter, *A Civic Biology* (New York, 1907); J. Peabody and A. Hunt, *Biology and Human Welfare* (New York, 1912); Gerald Skoog, "Topic of Evolution in Secondary School Biology Textbooks: 1900–1977," *Science Education* 63 (1979): 624–27. The textbook at issue in the Scopes trial, George William Hunter, *A Civic Biology* (New York, 1914), included marginally more evolutionary information than most of its competitors. On *A Civic Biology*, see Adam R. Shapiro, "Civic Biology and the Origin of the School Antievolution Movement," *Journal of the History of Biology* 41 (Fall 2008): 409–33.

55. See Ronald L. Numbers, *The Creationists: From Scientific Creationism to Intelligent Design*, expanded ed. (Cambridge, MA, 2006), 162–64; also George M. Marsden, "Fundamentalism as an American Phenomenon: A Comparison with English Evangelicalism," *Church History* 46 (June 1977): 225–28. See also Adam Laats, *Fundamentalism and Education in the Scopes Era: God, Darwin, and the Roots of America's Culture Wars* (New York, 2010).

56. Benson Y. Landis, "Trends in Church Membership in the United States," in "Religion in American Society," special issue of *Annals of the American Academy of Political and Social Science* 332 (November 1960): 4.

57. "U.S. Religious Landscape Survey," Pew Forum on Religion and Public Life, Report 1: Religious Affiliation (2008), http://religions.pewforum.org/reports (accessed November 28, 2008).

58. For a lively set of examinations of these trends, see the essays in William R. Hutchison, ed., *Between the Times: The Travail of the Protestant Establishment in America, 1900–1960* (Cambridge, UK, 1989).

59. A handful of Catholics and Jews at the Discovery Institute are among the rare exceptions.

60. Walter Lippmann, *A Preface to Morals* (New York, 1929), 34–35; for an argument that intense theological disputes within and among Protestant denominations paradoxically intensified dependence on the Bible as the true foundation of faith, see Jeanette Keith, *Country People in the New South: Tennessee's Upper Cumberland* (Chapel Hill, NC, 1995), 46–47.

61. Marsden, *Understanding Fundamentalism and Evangelicalism*, 141–53.

62. Jonathan Zimmerman, *Whose America? Culture Wars in the Public Schools* (Cambridge MA, 2005); Jeffrey P. Moran, *Teaching Sex: The Shaping of Adolescence in the 20th Century* (Cambridge MA, 2000).

63. John T. Scopes and James Presley, *Center of the Storm: Memoirs of John T. Scopes* (New York, 1967), 70; Edward J. Larson, *Summer for the Gods: The Scopes Trial and America's Continuing Debate over Science and Religion* (New York, 2006), 98–103.

64. "*Foreign Amazement* at Tennessee," *Literary Digest* 86 (July 25, 1925): 18–19.

65. "British View of Our 'Land of Liberty,'" *Literary Digest* 86 (August 22, 1925): 17–18.

66. *New York World News*, July 22, 1925.

67. *The World's Most Famous Court Trial: Tennessee Evolution Case* (Dayton, TN, 1978 [1925]), 322.

68. Ibid., 299.

69. Peter Tuney Hiett, letter to the editor, *Nashville Tennessean*, August 1, 1925, 4; Paolo E. Coletta, *William Jennings Bryan* (Lincoln, NE, 1969), 3:271–77.

70. "The End of the Scopes Case," *Literary Digest* 88 (February 5, 1927): 14.

71. "Europe and Tennessee," *Outlook* 140 (July 22, 1925): 416–17.

CHAPTER 1: MONKEYS AND MOTHERS

1. *Philadelphia Inquirer*, July 5, 1925; on John W. Butler, see Jeanette Keith, *Country People in the New South: Tennessee's Upper Cumberland* (Chapel Hill, NC, 1995), 201–5.

2. W. B. Marr to William Jennings Bryan, July 6, 1925, in William Jennings Bryan, *The Memoirs of William Jennings Bryan by Himself and His Wife Mary Baird Bryan* (Philadelphia, 1925), 481; *Nashville Tennessean*, March 14, 1925, 8.

3. Kenneth K. Bailey, "The Enactment of Tennessee's Antievolution Law," *Journal of Southern History* 16 (November 1950): 478; Royce Jordan, "Tennessee Goes Fundamentalist," *New Republic* 42 (April 29, 1925): 259.

4. Mrs. E. P. Blair, "The Battle Hymn of Tennessee," *Nashville Tennessean*, June 29, 1925, 2.

5. Rollin Lynde Hartt, "What Lies Beyond Dayton," *Nation* 121 (July 22, 1925): 111. From the publication of *On the Origin of Species* onward, women were the objects of evolutionary speculation that primarily sought to explain their inferiority, but some feminists not only argued against these ideas but also employed Darwinian theory to support their own claims to equality. See Sally Gregory Kohlstedt and Mark R. Jorgensen, "'The Irrepressible Woman Question': Women's Responses to Evolutionary Ideology," in Ronald L. Numbers and John Stenhouse, eds., *Disseminating Darwinism: The Role of Place, Race, Religion, and Gender* (Cambridge, UK, 1999): 267–93.

6. Gail Bederman, "'The Women Have Had Charge of the Church Work Long Enough': The Men and Religion Forward Movement of 1911–1912 and the Masculinization of Middle-Class Protestantism," *American Quarterly* 41 (September 1989): 432–65.

7. The classic analysis of separate-spheres ideology is Barbara Welter, "The Cult of True Womanhood, 1820–1860," *American Quarterly* 18 (Summer 1966): 151–74. For a caution about Welter's terminology, see Tracy Fessenden, "Gendering Religion," *Journal of Women's History* 14 (2002): 163–69. On women's missionary work, see Barbara Welter, "She Hath Done What She Could: Protestant Women's Missionary Careers in Nineteenth-Century America," *American Quarterly* 30 (Winter 1978): 624–38. On women's participation in party politics in the early nineteenth century, see Elizabeth R. Varon, "Tippecanoe and the Ladies, Too: White Women and Party Politics in Antebellum Virginia," *Journal of American History* 82 (September 1995): 494–521.

8. Ella Seass Stewart, "Woman Suffrage and the Liquor Traffic," in "Women in Public Life," special issue of *Annals of the American Academy of Political and Social Science* 56 (November 1914): 150.

9. Ibid., 144.

10. David Kyvig, "Women Against Temperance," *American Quarterly* 27 (Fall 1976): 465–82.

11. Discounting the theory that women voted for Warren Harding's pulchritude is Sara Alpern and Dale Baum, "Female Ballots: The Impact of the Nineteenth Amendment," *Journal of Interdisciplinary History* 16 (Summer 1985): 52–53. Alpern and Baum also maintain that the "woman vote" had more to do with party lines than with women voting as a bloc—especially as a moral bloc.

"Citizen mothers" phrase from Stewart, "Woman Suffrage," 146; on the initial disappointment over women's suffrage, see "Woman Suffrage Declared a Failure," *Literary Digest* 81 (April 12, 1924): 12–13; for a female reporter's evaluation of women's general lack of interest in public affairs, see George Madden Martin, "American Women and Public Affairs," *Atlantic Monthly* 133 (February 1924): 169–71; a more positive assessment appears in "What Have Women Done With the Vote?" *Literary Digest* 78 (September 22, 1923): 50–52. For a different emphasis by a modern historian, see Nancy Cott, "Feminist Politics in the 1920s: The National Women's Party," *Journal of American History* 71 (1984): 43–68.

12. J. Stanley Lemons, "The Sheppard-Towner Act: Progressivism in the 1920s," *Journal of American History* 55 (March 1969): 776–86.

13. Ann Douglas illustrates that this was hardly a new impulse at the turn of the century; she suggests that nonevangelical ministers in the mid-nineteenth century were in many ways ahead of their time in reacting against the potential irrelevance of their profession in the face of feminine competition and masculine disdain; Ann Douglas, *The Feminization of American Culture* (New York, 1988), 36–45. Although Gail Bederman claims the evidence for a "gender crisis" at this time is not fully convincing, her work is nevertheless part of an extensive literature on a cultural crisis in the 1890s that included an important gender component; Gail Bederman, *Manliness and Civilization: A Cultural History of Gender and Race in the United States, 1880–1917* (Chicago, 1995), 10–11. See also John Higham, "The Reorientation of American Culture in the 1890s," in John Higham, ed., *Writing American History: Essays on Modern Scholarship* (Bloomington, IN, 1978); Peter G. Filene, *Him/Her/Self: Sex Roles in Modern America* (Baltimore, 1988). The central work in the history of neurasthenia was George Miller Beard, *American Nervousness: Its Causes and Consequences* (New York, 1881). The diagnosis of neurasthenia has become for historians what it once was for doctors, a catchall term embodying the observer's preexisting notions. For a useful corrective, see Barbara Sicherman, "The Uses of a Diagnosis: Doctors, Patients, and Neurasthenia," *Journal of the History of Medicine* 32 (January 1977): 33–55. The best recent interpretation of the era is Jackson Lears, *Rebirth of a Nation: The Making of Modern America, 1877–1920* (New York, 2009).

14. Bederman, *Manliness and Civilization*, 15; Elliot J. Gorn, *The Manly Art: Bare-Knuckle Prizefighting in America* (Ithaca, NY, 1986).

15. On Roosevelt's intertwining interests in masculinity and race, see Bederman, *Manliness and Civilization*, 170–215. Bederman's emphasis, like Roosevelt's, is on racialized imperialism rather than religion.

16. William James, "The Moral Equivalent of War," *McClure's Magazine* 35 (1910): 463–68.

17. On an interesting related struggle over manhood in this era, including Teddy Roosevelt's involvement, see Adam Rome, "'Political Hermaphrodites': Gender and Environmental Reform in Progressive America," *Environmental History* 11 (July 2006): 440–63.

18. On the prominence of women in the congregations of Muncie, Indiana, in the 1920s, see Robert S. and Helen Merrell Lynd, *Middletown: A Study in American*

Culture (New York, 1929), 359. The Lynds, too, assessed the ratio of women to men in the Protestant churches as nearly 70 percent. See also Welter, "'She Hath Done What She Could,'" 624–38. Recent data continue to show stronger religious adherence among American women. See, for example, figures from the Pew Forum U.S. Religious Landscape Survey in 2008, distilled in "The Stronger Sex—Spiritually Speaking," Pew Forum on Religion and Public Life: Publications, February 26, 2009, http://pewforum.org/docs/?DocID=403 (accessed July 10, 2009). Some researchers have found women's greater religious participation to be close to a transhistorical truism, as in Rodney Stark, "Physiology and Faith: Addressing the 'Universal' Gender Difference in Religious Commitment," *Journal for the Scientific Study of Religion* 41 (September 2002): 495–507.

19. R. W. Conant, *The Manly Christ: A New View* (Chicago, 1904), 7.
20. Ibid., 8.
21. Clifford Putney, *Muscular Christianity: Manhood and Sports in Protestant America, 1880–1920* (Cambridge, MA, 2001).
22. Bederman, "'Women Have Had Charge,'" 432–65.
23. In addition to Conant's work, see, for example, the Ohio minister Jason Noble Pierce's *The Masculine Power of Christ, or Christ Measured as a Man* (Boston, 1912).
24. Harry Emerson Fosdick, *The Manhood of the Master* (New York, 1913), 18.
25. Ibid., 37.
26. All following quotations from Bruce Barton, *The Man Nobody Knows: A Discovery of the Real Jesus* (New York, 1925), preface.
27. R. Laurence Moore, *Touchdown Jesus: The Mixing of Sacred and Secular in American History* (Louisville, KY, 2003), 64.
28. Bederman, "'Women Have Had Charge,'" 441.
29. Susie Cunningham Stanley, *Feminist Pillar of Fire: The Life of Alma White* (Cleveland, OH, 1993).
30. By far the best work on Ellen G. White is Ronald L. Numbers, *Prophetess of Health: A Study of Ellen G. White* (Grand Rapids, MI, 2000).
31. Sarah Comstock, "Aimee Semple McPherson: Prima Donna of Revivalism," *Harper's Monthly Magazine* 156 (December 1927): 12. The Aimee Semple McPherson Papers are in the Billy Graham Center Archives at Wheaton College in Wheaton, Illinois, and at the International Church of the Foursquare Gospel, Los Angeles, California.
32. Comstock, "Aimee Semple McPherson," quotations from 17; Matthew Avery Sutton, *Aimee Semple McPherson and the Resurrection of Christian America* (Cambridge, MA, 2009).
33. On the tension between McPherson's embrace of traditional notions of women's subordinate role and her personal flouting of these rules as her more direct access to God allowed her to build an ambitious empire, see Sutton, *Aimee Semple McPherson*, esp. 85.

34. For a slightly different approach to the role of women in the origins and course of early fundamentalism, see Margaret Lamberts Bendroth, "Fundamentalism and Femininity: Points of Encounter Between Religious Conservatives and Women, 1919–1935," *Church History* 61 (June 1992): 221–33. Running roughly parallel to my interpretation is Betty A. DeBerg, *Ungodly Women: Gender and the First Wave of American Fundamentalism* (Minneapolis, MN, 1990). On the need to separate fundamentalist pronouncements on the role of women from fundamentalist practice, see Michael S. Hamilton, "Women, Public Ministry, and American Fundamentalism, 1920–1940," *Religion and American Culture* 3 (Summer 1993): 182–85.

35. Barry Hankins, *God's Rascal: J. Frank Norris and the Beginnings of Southern Fundamentalism* (Lexington, KY, 1996), 25.

36. Ibid., 26.

37. John Clover Monsma, "To the Former Subscribers of the New Reformation," *The Searchlight*, October 9, 1925, 2. While some fundamentalists developed a particular obsession with the absence of forthright manliness in the popular paintings of Jesus, none complained about the absence of Semitic features in most portrayals of the Jewish Messiah.

38. "Dictator" quotation in Barry Hankins, "The Strange Career of J. Frank Norris, or, Can a Baptist Democrat Be a Fundamentalist Republican?" *Church History* 61 (September 1992): 383.

39. A. Cyrus Hayat, "Billy Sunday and the Masculinization of American Protestantism: 1896–1935," M.A. thesis, Department of History, Indiana University, 2008. Margaret Bendroth cautions that the complexity of women's reactions to Sunday's hypermasculine performance suggests that the popularity of his revivals cannot be reduced simply to a crusade for masculine vigor; Margaret Bendroth, "Why Women Loved Billy Sunday: Urban Revivalism and Popular Entertainment in Early Twentieth-Century American Culture," *Religion and American Culture: A Journal of Interpretation* 14 (Summer 2004): 251–71.

40. Grover C. Loud, quoted in Robert J. Higgs, *God in the Stadium: Sports and Religion in America* (Lexington, KY, 1995), 256.

41. William G. McLoughlin Jr., *Billy Sunday Was His Real Name* (Chicago, 1955), 46–47.

42. Ibid., 123, cited in Martin E. Marty, *A Nation of Behavors* (Chicago, 1976), 202.

43. Michael Kazin, *Godly Hero: The Life of William Jennings Bryan* (New York, 2006), 177.

44. Ibid.

45. DeBerg, *Ungodly Women*, 5–11, 40–58.

46. The literature on the broader aspects of the "new culture" of the 1920s began multiplying when the curtain had just barely come down on the decade, with the most influential interpretation coming from Frederick Lewis Allen, *Only Yesterday: An Informal History of the Nineteen-Twenties* (New York, 1931).

47. A. R. Funderbark, *Can a Bobbed Haired Woman Go to Heaven?* [pamphlet] (Kansas City, MO, n.d.), n.p.; "Is the Younger Generation in Peril?" *Literary Digest* 69 (May 14, 1921): 9–12.

48. For the secular search for the causes of new female behaviors, see Freda Kirchwey, ed., *Our Changing Morality: A Symposium* (New York, 1972 [1930]); Florence Guy Woolston, "Girls, and Then Some," *New Republic* 30 (March 15, 1922): 79; "The Case Against the Younger Generation," *Literary Digest* 73 (June 17, 1922): 38.

49. Quoted in Hayat, "Billy Sunday and the Masculinization of American Protestantism," 60.

50. T. T. Martin, *Hell and the High Schools: Christ or Evolution: Which?* (Kansas City, MO, 1923).

51. Edward J. Larson, "Before the Crusade: Evolution in American Secondary Education Before 1920," *Journal of the History of Biology* 20 (Spring 1987): 112–13.

52. For Tennessee in particular, see Charles A. Israel, *Before Scopes: Evangelicalism, Education, and Evolution in Tennessee, 1870–1925* (Athens, GA, 2004). Also Jeffrey P. Moran, "'Modernism Gone Mad': Sex Education Comes to Chicago, 1913," *Journal of American History* 83 (September 1996): 481–513; Jonathan Zimmerman, "'Each "Race" Could Have Its Heroes Sung': Ethnicity and the History Wars in the 1920s," *Journal of American History* 87 (June 2000): 92–111; American Civil Liberties Union Committee on Academic Freedom, *The Gag on Teaching* (New York, 1931).

53. *Nashville Tennessean*, July 3, 1925, 4.

54. Mrs. E. P. Blair, letter to the editor, *Nashville Tennessean*, March 16, 1925, 4.

55. Jonathan Zimmerman, *Distilling Democracy: Alcohol Education in America's Public Schools, 1880–1925* (Lawrence, KS, 1999); Jeanette Keith, *Country People in the New South: Tennessee's Upper Cumberland* (Chapel Hill, NC, 1995), 98–99, 208.

56. Rollin Lynde Hartt, "What Lies Beyond Dayton?" *Nation* 3133 (July 22, 1925): 111; on the tepid support and shadowy pressure for the bill, see Royce Jordan, "Tennessee Goes Fundamentalist," *New Republic* 42 (April 19, 1925): 259.

57. Hartt, "What Lies Beyond Dayton?" 111.

58. For the argument that evolution was not the only offense in *A Civic Biology*, see Adam Shapiro, "Civic Biology and the Origin of the School Antievolution Movement," *Journal of the History of Biology* 41 (September 2008): 409–33.

59. Mrs. Jesse Sparks, letter to the editor, *Nashville Tennessean*, July 3, 1925, 4.

60. Letter to the editor, New York *World*, July 13, 1925, n.p., American Civil Liberties Union Papers, vol. 278, Seeley G. Mudd Manuscript Library, Princeton University.

61. Ann Douglas, *Terrible Honesty: Mongrel Manhattan in the 1920s* (New York, 1995), 8.

62. This was a theme Malone tried out shortly before the trial, as reported in the *Nashville Tennessean*, June 28, 1925, 2.

63. Ibid.
64. Regina Malone, "The Fabulous Monster," *Forum*, July 1926, 26–30.
65. Sutton, *Aimee Semple McPherson*, 121; information on Proposition 17 found in untitled document on the history of the initiative process in California from the California Secretary of State's Office (2001), www.sos.ca.gov/elections/init_history.pdf (accessed October 28, 2010), 18.
66. Sutton, *Aimee Semple McPherson*, 8–10.
67. Ronald L. Numbers, "Creation, Evolution, and Holy Ghost Religion: Holiness and Pentecostal Responses to Darwinism," *Religion and American Culture* 2 (Summer 1992): 134.
68. McPherson Papers, Reel 1, covering Box 2, Folder 1. I have filled out parts of McPherson's debate outlines in order to make her arguments more intelligible.
69. Michael S. Hamilton, "Women, Public Ministry, and American Fundamentalism, 1920–1940," *Religion and American Culture* 3 (Summer 1993): 182–85. Hamilton cautions against looking solely at prescriptive literature from conservatives, and suggests instead paying closer attention to fundamentalist practice.
70. The Pulse Research survey of 800 Kansans had a margin for error of 3.5 percent. Survey reported in "Can God, Evolution Coexist?" *Lawrence* (KS) *Journal-World*, ctober 9, 2005, www2.ljworld.com/news/2005/oct/09/can_god_evolution_coexist/?evolution (accessed July 10, 2009). In other surveys on evolution, the opinions of Kansans as a whole mirror the national responses, so it seems likely that the gendered responses in the Sunflower State may be generalized to the rest of the nation, though all such polls should be used with caution depending on their wording.
71. On Segraves and Sumrall, see Ronald L. Numbers, *The Creationists: From Scientific Creationism to Intelligent Design* (Cambridge, MA, 2006), 270–71; on conservative activism in southern California, see Lisa McGirr, *Suburban Warriors: The Origins of the New American Right* (Princeton, 2002); on sex education and the New Right, see Jeffrey P. Moran, *Teaching Sex: The Shaping of Adolescence in the 20th Century* (Cambridge, MA, 2000), 156–93; on women as activists in the New Right, see Rebecca Klatch, *Women of the New Right* (Philadelphia, 1988).
72. Numbers, *The Creationists*, 243.
73. Ibid., 244–45, 284–85.
74. Guyla Mills, "The Creation/Evolution Debate: Education v. Indoctrination," February 1, 2002, Concerned Women for America website, www.cwfa.org/articledisplay.asp?id=921&;department=CWA&;categoryid=education (accessed July 22, 2009), manuscript in author's possession; thanks to Guyla Mills for sending me a copy of the original. On CWA's involvement in one local antievolution case, see Karen O'Connor and Gregg Ivers, "Creationism, Evolution and the Courts," *PS: Political Science and Politics* 21 (Winter 1988): 15.

75. Michael Lienesch, *In the Beginning: Fundamentalism, The Scopes Trial, and the Making of the Evolution Movement* (Chapel Hill, NC, 2007), 214–19.

76. "Dr. Margaret Helder: Creationist Botanist," Answers in Genesis website, www. answersingenesis.org/docs/1336 (accessed July 22, 2009).

77. Eugenie Scott, telephone interview with the author, August 19, 2008.

CHAPTER 2: REGIONALISM AND THE ANTIEVOLUTION IMPULSE

1. John Roach Straton, "The Most Sinister Movement in the United States," *American Fundamentalist,* December 26, 1925, 8–9, reprinted in Willard B. Gatewood Jr., *Preachers, Pedagogues, and Politicians: The Evolution Controversy in North Carolina* (Chapel Hill, NC, 1966), 355–57.

2. Ibid.

3. On the importance of local conditions in the reception of Darwinism, see, for example, Ronald L. Numbers and John Stenhouse, eds., *Disseminating Darwinism: The Role of Place, Race, Religion, and Gender* (Cambridge, UK, 1999); and David N. Livingstone, *Putting Science in Its Place: Geographies of Scientific Knowledge* (Chicago, 2003).

4. George Marsden, "Fundamentalism as an American Phenomenon: A Comparison with English Evangelicalism," *Church History* 46 (June 1977): 225–28.

5. Kenneth K. Bailey, "Southern White Protestantism at the Turn of the Century," *American Historical Review* 68 (April 1963): 618, 622.

6. William R. Glass, *Strangers in Zion: Fundamentalists in the South, 1900–1950* (Macon, GA, 2001), 34, 58–59; more directly, see Adam Laats, "The Quiet Crusade: The Moody Bible Institute's Outreach to Public Schools and the Mainstreaming of Appalachia, 1921–1966," *Church History* 75 (September 2006): 565–93, and Adam Laats, *Fundamentalism and Education in the Scopes Era* (New York, 2010).

7. Clement Eaton, "Professor James Woodrow and the Freedom of Teaching in the South," *Journal of Southern History* 28 (February 1962): 3–17; Ronald L. Numbers, *Darwinism Comes to America* (Cambridge, MA, 1998), 67–70.

8. Ronald L. Numbers and Lester D. Stephens, "Darwinism in the American South," in Numbers and Stenhouse, eds., *Disseminating Darwinism,* 123–43.

9. Joseph Wood Krutch, "Tennessee: Where Cowards Rule," *Nation* 121 (July 15, 1925): 88–89.

10. *The World's Most Famous Court Trial: Tennessee Evolution Case* (Dayton, TN, 1978 [1925]), 14; examination of potential jurors is 11–44.

11. William Vance Trollinger Jr., *God's Empire: William Bell Riley and Midwestern Fundamentalism* (Madison, WI, 1990). The inimitable T. T. Martin seems to await scholarly treatment, but the careers of others in the group are traced in Ferenc M. Szasz, "Three Fundamentalist Leaders: The Roles of William Bell Riley, John Roach Straton, and William Jennings Bryan in the Fundamentalist-Modernist

Controversy," Ph.D. dissertation, University of Rochester, 1969. On the importance of the Southern Baptist Theological Seminary, see Gregory A. Wills, *Southern Baptist Theological Seminary, 1859–2009* (New York, 2009).

12. Straton's son, Hillyer H. Straton, published several works about his father, including "John Roach Straton: Prophet of Social Righteousness," *Foundations* 5 (January 1962): 17–38.

13. *New York Times*, July 9, 1925, 1.

14. T. T. Martin, *Hell and the High Schools: Christ or Evolution, Which?* (Kansas City, MO, 1923).

15. Barry Hankins, *God's Rascal: J. Frank Norris and the Beginnings of Southern Fundamentalism* (Lexington, KY, 1996).

16. Ibid., 25–26.

17. *Searchlight*, March 14, 1924, 4.

18. Ibid.

19. Ibid.

20. *Searchlight*, April 18, 1924, 7.

21. Ibid.

22. Hankins, *God's Rascal*, 176.

23. Ibid., 174.

24. Michael Kazin, *A Godly Hero: The Life of William Jennings Bryan* (New York, 2006).

25. Edward J. Larson, *Trial and Error: The American Controversy over Creation and Evolution* (New York, 2003), 32–34.

26. Donald F. Brod, "The Scopes Trial: A Look at Press Coverage After Thirty Years," *Journalism Quarterly* 42 (1965): 219–26. On Mencken and the South, see Fred C. Hobson Jr., *Serpent in Eden: H. L. Mencken and the South* (Chapel Hill, NC, 1974).

27. Baltimore *Evening Sun*, July 9, 1925, 1.

28. Ibid., 2.

29. Mencken to Raymond Pearl, July 14, 1925, in Carl Bode, ed., *The New Mencken Letters* (New York, 1977), 187–88.

30. Baltimore *Evening Sun*, July 11, 1925, 2.

31. Mencken to Raymond Pearl, July 14, 1925, in Bode, ed., *New Mencken Letters*, 187–88.

32. Frank R. Kent, "On the Dayton Firing Line," *New Republic*, July 29, 1925, 259.

33. John B. Boles, "Evangelical Protestantism in the Old South: From Religious Dissent to Cultural Dominance," in Charles Reagan Wilson, ed., *Religion in the South* (Oxford, MS, 1985), 13–34; Roger W. Stump, "Regional Divergence in Religious Affiliation in the United States," *Sociological Analysis* 45 (1986): 283–99; Donald G. Mathews, Samuel S. Hill, Beth Barton Schweiger, and John B. Boles, "Forum: Southern Religion," *Religion and American Culture* 8 (Summer 1998): 147.

34. Mencken's account of the evening was published in the Baltimore *Evening Sun*, July 13, 1925, 2.

35. Ibid.

36. United States Bureau of the Census, 1920 Census, vol. 1, *Number and Distribution of Inhabitants*, 43.

37. Jeanette Keith, *Country People in the New South: Tennessee's Upper Cumberland* (Chapel Hill, NC, 1995), 203–4.

38. Baltimore *Evening Sun*, July 21, 1925, 6.

39. Larson, *Trial and Error*, 81; Virginia Gray, "Anti-Evolution Sentiment and Behavior: The Case of Arkansas," *Journal of American History* 57 (September 1970): 352–56.

40. Southern newspapers were rife with negative portrayals of Jazz Age cities; for two examples among many, see Nashville *Tennessean*, June 19, 1925, 4; *Nashville Tennessean*, June 21, 1925, 11.

41. *World's Most Famous Court Trial*, 58.

42. Ibid., 74.

43. Ibid., 281.

44. Their testimony, read into the trial record but not delivered to the jury, is recorded in Ibid., 27–280.

45. Ibid., 297; on Price, see Ronald L. Numbers, *The Creationists: From Scientific Creationism to Intelligent Design* (Cambridge, MA, 2006), 88–119.

46. *World's Most Famous Court Trial*, 58.

47. Ibid., 181.

48. Ibid., 171.

49. "Tennessee and the Constitution," *New Republic*, July 8, 1925, 167–68.

50. *World's Most Famous Court Trial*, 172.

51. Ibid., 196–97.

52. "Text of Bryan's Proposed Address in Scopes Case," bound in *World's Most Famous Court Trial*, 322. Bryan's figures were not quite accurate (or else the court stenographer mistyped): by the 1920s, the high school population was approximately two million, as noted in Edward J. Larson, "Before the Crusade: Evolution in American Secondary Education Before 1920," *Journal of the History of Biology* 20 (Spring 1987): 112–13.

53. Trollinger, *God's Empire*, 35–36.

54. Joseph Wood Krutch, "Darrow vs. Bryan," *Nation*, July 29, 1925, 136–37.

55. *World's Most Famous Court Trial*, 197.

56. H. L. Mencken, "Battle Now Over, Mencken Sees; Genesis Triumphant and Ready for New Jousts," *Baltimore Evening Sun*, July 18, 1925, 1.

57. As was apparent to everyone, the metropolitan reporters were strongly on Scopes's side, as noted in *Nation*, July 22, 1925, 103.

58. *New York Times*, July 12, 1925, 2.

59. H. L. Mencken to Gamaliel Bradford, July 28, 1925, in Bode, ed., *The New Mencken Letters*, 189.

60. Fred C. Hobson, *Tell About the South: The Southern Rage to Explain* (Baton Rouge, 1983), 184.
61. *New York Times*, July 17, 1925, 3.
62. Baltimore *Evening Sun*, July 10, 1925, 1.
63. *New York Times*, November 9, 1925, 18.
64. "Why the 'Monkey Law' Still Stands," *Literary Digest*, August 29, 1931, 18.
65. *Mobile* (AL) *Register*, July 22, 1925, 10.
66. *Nashville Tennessean*, June 17, 1925, 1.
67. W. O. McGeehan, "Why Pick on Dayton?" *Harper's Monthly* 151 (October 1925): 623.
68. Harbor Allen, "The Anti-Evolution Campaign in America," *Current History* 24 (September 1926): 894.
69. George F. Milton, "A Dayton Postscript," *Outlook* 140 (August 19, 1925): 250.
70. H.L. Mencken, "Editorial," *American Mercury* 6 (1925): 158–60.
71. Howard K. Beale, *Are American Teachers Free? An Analysis of Restraints upon the Freedom of Teaching in American Schools* (New York, 1936), 257–58.
72. Ibid., 258.
73. Ibid., 259.
74. "The 'Bloody Duel' at Dayton," *Industrial Solidarity*, n.d., Series 1—Academic Freedom—Clippings, 1925, vols. 275–78, Reel 39, American Civil Liberties Union Papers, Mudd Library, Princeton University.
75. Ibid.
76. "South Blames Scopes 'Heresy' on Communists," *Daily Worker*, July 16, 1925, Series 1—Academic Freedom—Clippings, 1925, vols. 275–78, Reel 39, American Civil Liberties Union Papers, Mudd Library, Princeton University.
77. See Mary Beth Sweetnam Mathews, *Rethinking Zion: How the Print Media Placed Fundamentalism in the South* (Knoxville, TN, 2006), 115.
78. George B. Tindall quoted in Hobson, *Tell About the South*, 183.
79. See Donald Davidson, *Southern Writers in the Modern World* (Athens, GA, 1958).
80. Thomas Daniel Young, "From Fugitives to Agrarians," *Mississippi Quarterly* 33 (1980): 420–24; Edward S. Shapiro, "The Southern Agrarians, H. L. Mencken, and the Quest for Southern Identity," *American Studies* 23 (1972): 75–92.
81. H. L. Mencken, "The Sahara of the Bozart," *New York Evening Mail*, November 13, 1917 (much reprinted elsewhere).
82. Hobson, *Tell About the South*, 185–86; see also Paul K. Conkin, Henry Lee Swint, and Patricia S. Miletich, *Gone with the Ivy: A Biography of Vanderbilt University* (Knoxville, TN, 1985), 324.
83. Davidson, *Southern Writers*, 37.
84. Ibid., 41.
85. Donald Davidson, "First Fruits of Dayton: The Intellectual Evolution in Dixie," *Forum* 79 (June 1928): 896.
86. Ibid., 902.
87. Davidson, *Southern Writers*, 35.

88. Ibid.

89. Ibid., 36–37.

90. Hobson, *Tell About the South*, 186.

91. Twelve Southerners, *I'll Take My Stand: The South and the Agrarian Tradition* (New York, 1930). The literature on the Agrarians/Fugitives is voluminous. For one example that places the group in a biographical and academic framework, see Paul K. Conkin, *The Southern Agrarians* (Knoxville, TN, 1988); see also Paul V. Murphy, *The Rebuke of History: The Southern Agrarians and American Conservative Thought* (Chapel Hill, NC, 2001). A more political and cultural approach is taken in Alexander Karanikas, *Tillers of a Myth: Southern Agrarians as Social and Literary Critics* (Madison, WI, 1966). Following *I'll Take My Stand* came the one Agrarian work devoted entirely to religion, John Crowe Ransom's recondite *God Without Thunder: An Unorthodox Defence of Orthodoxy* (London, 1931).

92. As literary men, Davidson and Ransom ran into the problem of southernness as they attempted to pull together a collection devoted to southern literature— was it subject matter, author's heritage, or just a state of mind? Either way, was regional affiliation to have more weight than literary quality? Their difficulties are noted in a letter from Addison Hibbard to Donald Davidson and John Crowe Ransom, May 27, 1927, in Donald Davidson Papers, Box 8, Folder 7, Jean and Alexander Heard Library, Vanderbilt University.

93. Donald Davidson letter to T. H. Alexander, January 1, 1950, in Donald Davidson Papers, Box 1, Folder 14, Jean and Alexander Heard Library, Vanderbilt University.

94. *Macon* (GA) *Telegraph*, September 24, 1930, n.p.

95. Numbers and Stephens, "Darwinism in the American South," 137.

96. *Baptist and Reflector*, March 19, 1925, 7.

97. Ferenc M. Szasz, "The Scopes Trial in Perspective," *Tennessee Historical Quarterly* 30, no. 3 (Fall 1971): 290.

98. Edward J. Larson, *Summer for the Gods: The Scopes Trial and America's Continuing Debate over Science and Religion* (New York, 2006), 230.

99. Larson, *Trial and Error*, 83; Szasz, "Scopes Trial in Perspective," 293.

100. Glass, *Strangers in Zion*, 282. This is not to say that institutions outside the South did not play a role; Moody Bible Institute in Chicago, Biola in Los Angeles, and Wheaton and Calvin College all contributed significantly to modern conservative evangelicalism.

101. For a sampling of the literature on the cultural geography of American religion, see Wilbur Zelinsky, "The Uniqueness of the American Religious Landscape," *Geographical Review* 91 (2001): 565–85; James R. Shortridge, "A New Regionalization of American Religion," *Journal for the Scientific Study of Religion* 16 (June 1977): 143–53; Roger W. Stump, "Regional Variations in the Determinants of Religious Participation," *Review of Religious Research* 27 (1986): 208–24; and Roger W. Stump, *Boundaries of Faith: Geographical Perspectives on Religious*

Fundamentalism (Lanham, MD, 2000). For an interesting overview of regional religious differences, see Samuel S. Hill Jr., *The North and the South in American Religion* (Athens, GA, 1980).

102. See, for example, John Thomas Bauer, "Stability and Change in United States Religious Regions, 1980–2000," M.A. thesis, Department of Geography, University of Kansas, 2006, esp. map on 102; Wilbur Zelinsky, "The Uniqueness of the American Religious Landscape," *Geographical Review* 91 (2001): 565–85; Roger W. Stump, "Regional Migration and Religious Commitment in the United States," *Journal for the Scientific Study of Religion* 23 (1984): 292–303.

103. Pete Daniel, "The Transformation of the Rural South: 1930 to the Present," *Agricultural History* 55 (July 1981): 231–48; see also Bruce J. Schulman, *From Cotton Belt to Sunbelt: Federal Policy, Economic Development, and the Transformation of the South 1938–1980* (New York, 1991); Shane Hamilton, *Trucking Country: The Road to America's Wal-Mart Economy* (Princeton, 2008).

104. "Nearly Two-Thirds of U.S. Adults Believe Human Beings Were Created by God," Harris Poll 52, July 6, 2005. The regional variation is greater than the difference of opinion between adults over the age of fifty-five and adults between eighteen and fifty-four, and it is nearly as large as the gap between Americans with high school education or less and those with postgraduate degrees.

105. *New York Times*, June 21, 2008; New Orleans *Times-Picayune*, June 27, 2008.

106. The Dover Area School District overseen by the board is larger, with approximately 3,500 students in all grades.

107. *Hurst v. Newman*, case no. 1:06-CV-00036-OWW-SMS, U.S. District Court, E.D. California (2006).

108. On the suburban dynamic in modern Christian conservatism, see Thomas Frank, *What's the Matter with Kansas? How Conservatives Won the Heart of America* (New York, 2004).

109. Michael Lienesch, *In the Beginning: Fundamentalism, the Scopes Trial, and the Making of the Antievolution Movement* (Chapel Hill, NC, 2007), 218–19.

110. "'Intelligent Design' Costs Dover over $1,000,000," news release from National Center for Science Education, February 24, 2006, http://ncse.com/news/2006/02/intelligent-design-costs-dover-over-1000000-00899 (accessed September 8, 2011).

CHAPTER 3: FIGHTING FOR THE FUTURE OF THE RACE

1. *Pittsburgh Courier*, July 25, 1925, 9.

2. "Wife Holds Man—Husband Stabs," *Kansas City* (KS) *Call*, July 10, 1925, 1.

3. Three generations of interpretation of the trial can be observed in Frederick Lewis Allen, *Only Yesterday: An Informal History of the Nineteen-Twenties* (New York,

1931), 201–6; Ray Ginger, *Six Days or Forever? Tennessee v. John Thomas Scopes* (Boston, 1958); Edward J. Larson, *Trial and Error: The American Controversy over Creation and Evolution* (New York, 1985); Edward J. Larson, *Summer for the Gods: The Scopes Trial and America's Continuing Debate over Science and Religion* (New York, 1997); Paul K. Conkin, *When All the Gods Trembled: Darwinism, Scopes, and American Intellectuals* (Lanham, MD., 1998). An edited trial transcript and related documents from the controversy can be found in Jeffrey P. Moran, *The Scopes Trial: A Brief History with Documents* (New York, 2002).

4. On the tensions over leadership, see Kevin K. Gaines, *Uplifting the Race: Black Leadership, Politics, and Culture in the Twentieth Century* (Chapel Hill, NC, 1996); and Curtis J. Evans, *The Burden of Black Religion* (New York, 2008); see as well Paula Giddings, *When and Where I Enter: The Impact of Black Women on Race and Sex in America* (New York, 1984), 135–97. Still the best source for the Harlem Renaissance is David Levering Lewis, *When Harlem Was in Vogue* (New York, 1981).

5. *Houston* (TX) *Informer*, August 1, 1925, 4; *Kansas City* (KS) *Call*, July 17, 1925, B1. See also reports of antievolutionist sermons in the *Savannah* (GA) *Tribune*, July 24, 1925, 1; *Savannah Tribune*, August 6, 1925, 12. National Baptist Convention report in *Norfolk* (VA) *Journal and Guide*, September 19, 1925, 8.

6. *Baltimore* (MD) *Afro-American*, September 5, 1925, 10.

7. Information on White's sermon taken from Houston *Informer*, July 25, 1925, 5; Benjamin Elijah Mays and Joseph William Nicholson, *The Negro's Church* (New York, 1933), 17, 59.

8. *Baltimore Afro-American*, June 20, 1925, 11.

9. *Norfolk Journal and Guide*, June 13, 1925, 12.

10. Charles Satchell Morris, "Up from a Monkey or Down from God," was originally printed in the *Norfolk Journal and Guide*, June 27, July 4, July 11, July 25, August 1, August 8, August 15, August 29, September 5, September 12, and October 3, 1925 (on page 12 in each issue). Description of Morris's public lecture in *Norfolk Journal and Guide*, June 13, 1925, 6; and *Norfolk Journal and Guide*, June 20, 1925, 1. George Schuyler, "Thrusts and Lunges," *Pittsburgh Courier*, July 18, 1925, 16; Alma Booker, "Is Evolution Based upon a Guess?" *Pittsburgh Courier*, August 8, 1925, 5; Topeka (KS) *Plaindealer*, July 24, 1925, 3. See also reports of the Reverend Richard H. Bowling's addresses in *Norfolk Journal and Guide*, September 5, September 12, and September 26, 1925 (page 6 in each issue).

11. Figures from 1926 Government Census of Religious Bodies, reported in Mays and Nicholson, *The Negro's Church*, 40–41. See also W. A. Daniel, *The Education of Negro Ministers* (New York, 1925), 101–3.

12. Evelyn Brooks Higginbotham, *Righteous Discontent: The Women's Movement in the Black Baptist Church, 1880–1920* (Cambridge, MA, 1993), 187–209; *Pittsburgh Courier*, July 11, 1925, 14; *Norfolk Journal and Guide*, October 10, 1925, 12.

13. Jim Jones, "Still Playing Catch-up," *Christianity Today* 41 (May 19, 1997): 56.

14. On the "black Protestant establishment," see David W. Wills, "An Enduring Distance: Black Americans and the Establishment," in William R. Hutchison, ed., *Between the Times: The Travail of the Protestant Establishment in America, 1900–1960* (New York, 1989), esp. 168–92; percentage and information on the continued vitality of the black Baptist church during the "era of sects and cults" in Randall K. Burkett, "The Baptist Church in the Years of Crisis: J. C. Austin and the Pilgrim Baptist Church, 1926–1950," in Paul E. Johnson, ed., *African-American Christianity: Essays in History* (Berkeley, 1994), 134–58; reliance on experiential Christianity noted in Ronald L. Numbers, *Darwinism Comes to America* (Cambridge, MA, 1998), 112–19; and Willard B. Gatewood Jr., *Preachers, Pedagogues, and Politician: The Evolution Controversy in North Carolina 1920–1927* (Chapel Hill, NC, 1966), 76–79.

15. Attendance calculations derived from Frank Alexander Ross, *School Attendance in 1920: An Analysis of School Attendance in the United States, and in the Several States, With a Discussion of the Factors Involved* (Washington, D.C., 1924), 11. Biology does not show up as a separate subject in the curricula for county training schools for black students, and "general science," which may or may not have included the subject, was not a common offering, as reported in Jessie Carney Smith and Carrel Peterson Horton, eds., *Historical Statistics of Black America: Agriculture to Labor and Unemployment* (New York, 1995), 505. On disparities in funding, see Thomas Jesse Jones, "Trends in Negro Education (1915–1930)," in *Twenty Year Report of the Phelps-Stokes Fund 1911–1931* (New York, 1932), 35–39.

16. On the critical role that Bible schools played in the development of (white) fundamentalism, see Virginia Lieson Brereton, *Training God's Army: The American Bible School, 1880–1940* (Bloomington, IN, 1990). The Dallas Colored Bible Institute began in 1928, followed by the Manhattan Bible Institute in 1938, Carver in 1943, and Cedine Bible Camp in 1946, as noted in Albert G. Miller, "Construction of a Black Fundamentalist Worldview: The Role of Bible Schools," in Vincent L. Wimbush and Rosamond C. Rodman, eds., *African Americans and the Bible: Sacred Texts and Social Textures* (New York, 2000), 718.

17. Garry Wills, *Under God: Religion and American Politics* (New York), 106–7. On the tension between theological conservatism and social activism in Martin Luther King Jr.'s background, see Clayborne Carson, "Martin Luther King, Jr., and the African-American Social Gospel," in Johnson, ed., *African-American Christianity*, 1994.

18. On George S. Schuyler, see *Black and Conservative: The Autobiography of George S. Schuyler* (New Rochelle, NY, 1971); and Kathryn Talalay, *Composition in Black and White: The Life of Philippa Schuyler* (New York, 1995). The best source for the intriguing Pickens is his autobiography, *Bursting Bonds: Enlarged Edition* [of] *The Heir of Slaves* (Boston, 1923). On Kelly Miller, the mathematician and sociologist who was the longtime dean of Howard University's College of Arts

and Sciences, see Carter G. Woodson, "Kelly Miller," *Journal of Negro History*, January 1940, 137–38. Ernest Rice McKinney was a native West Virginian who became a communist organizer with a specialty in labor and African American issues, as noted in Peter Drucker, *Max Shachtman and His Left: A Socialist's Odyssey Through the "American Century"* (Atlantic Highlands, NJ, 1994), 75. Brief biographical facts about William N. Jones are available in Hayward Farrar, *The Baltimore Afro-American, 1892–1950* (Westport, CT, 1998), 11, 150–51. On the publishers of the *Chicago Defender* and the *Pittsburgh Courier*, the two largest and most influential race newspapers, see Roi Ottley, *The Lonely Warrior: The Life and Times of Robert S. Abbott* (Chicago, 1955), and Andrew Buni, *Robert L. Vann of the Pittsburgh Courier: Politics and Black Journalism* (Pittsburgh, 1974). Perhaps the most accomplished African American scientist of the time, biologist Ernest Everett Just, seems to have said nothing about the trial, though evolutionary theory, primarily in the cooperative version put forth by Prince Kropotkin, was obviously important in his work see Kenneth R. Manning, *Black Apollo of Science: The Life of Ernest Everett Just* (New York, 1983), 263.

19. W. E. B. Du Bois, "Scopes," *Crisis* 30 (September 1925): 218.

20. *Chicago Defender*, May 23, 1925, sec. 2, 10; *Pittsburgh Courier*, June 6, 1925, 16; *Pittsburgh Courier*, July 18, 1925, 16; *Washington Tribune*, n.d., reprinted in *Kansas City Call*, July 31, 1925, B4; *Kansas City Call*, July 31, 1925, B4.

21. *Kansas City Call*, July 31, 1925, B4; *Washington Tribune*, n.d., reprinted in *Kansas City Call*, July 31, 1925, B4.

22. For their own purposes, secular black leaders chose not to mention the central role that religion had played decades earlier in defeating the racialist doctrine of polygenism. For background, see Eric D. Anderson, "Black Responses to Darwinism, 1859–1915," in Ronald L. Numbers and John Stenhouse, eds., *Disseminating Darwinism: The Role of Place, Race, Religion, and Gender* (Cambridge, UK, 1999), 247–66.

23. *Norfolk Journal and Guide*, August 1, 1925, 1. For more on William Jennings Bryan, see *Amsterdam News*, July 15, 1925, 2; *Amsterdam News*, July 29, 1925, 16; *Norfolk Journal and Guide*, August 8, 1925, 12; *Chicago Broad Ax*, August 1, 1925, 1; and *Baltimore Afro-American*, August 8, 1925, 11.

24. *Norfolk Journal and Guide*, August 1, 1925, 1; *Pittsburgh Courier*, August 1, 1925, 16.

25. J. A. Rogers, "The Critic: Do They Tell the Truth," *Messenger* 7 (July 1925): 271; Blease support noted in *Baltimore Sun*, July 15, 1925, 2. On William Bell Riley, see William Vance Trollinger Jr., *God's Empire: William Bell Riley and Midwestern Fundamentalism* (Madison, WI, 1990); I thank William Trollinger for informally sharing information on Riley's racial views.

26. *Chicago Defender*, May 23, 1925, sec. 2, 10; *Baltimore Afro-American*, July 18, 1925, 9; W. J. Cash, *The Mind of the South* (New York, 1941), 347. The actual structure of southern white belief on this issue was less clear than these writers claimed, as the common interpretation of Genesis also compelled

Christians to accept that humans shared a common heritage; see the discussion of polygenesis below.

27. John Powell's comments in *Atlanta Constitution*, n.d., reprinted in *Atlanta Independent*, July 2, 1925, 1; J. C. Davis quoted in *Pittsburgh Courier*, July 11, 1925, 3. For the Ku Klux Klan's stance against "amalgamation," see Dr. F. L. L. [pseud.], "The Negro—His Relation to America," *Kourier Magazine* 2 (January 1926): 17–19. For background on miscegenation, see Martha Hodes, *White Women, Black Men: Illicit Sex in the Nineteenth-Century South* (New Haven, CT, 1997), and Joel Williamson, *The Crucible of Race: Black-White Relations in the American South Since Emancipation* (New York, 1984), esp. 39–42 and 306–10.

28. *Atlanta Constitution*, n.d., reprinted in *Atlanta Independent*, July 2, 1925, 1.

29. George M. Fredrickson, *The Black Image in the White Mind: The Debate on Afro-American Character and Destiny, 1817–1914* (New York, 1971), 256–82.

30. On the polygenist interpretation and its tension with biblical interpretations of race, see Josiah C. Nott, *Two Lectures on the Connection Between the Biblical and Physical History of Man: Delivered by Invitation from the Chair of Political Economy of the Louisiana University in December, 1848* (New York, 1849), 24–47. On the polygenists' response to Darwinism, see William Stanton, *The Leopard's Spots: Scientific Attitudes Toward Race in American 1815–1859* (Chicago, 1960), 185–86. On the ambiguity of Darwin's racial message and the lack of a unified or vigorous African American response in this earlier period, see Anderson, "Black Responses to Darwinism, 1859–1915," 247–66. See also Carl N. Degler, *In Search of Human Nature: The Decline and Revival of Darwinism in American Social Thought* (New York, 1991), 14–20; and Elazar Barkan, *The Retreat of Scientific Racism: Changing Concepts of Race in Britain and the United States Between the World Wars* (New York, 1992), 17–18. Probably the most influential work in the racial interpretation of history was Arthur, Comte de Gobineau, *Essai sur l'inégalité des races humaines* (Paris, 1967 [1854]); for an influential American version, see Madison Grant, *The Passing of the Great Race; or the Racial Basis of European History* (New York, 1916). For a relatively late scientific use of cephalic indexes for racial classification, see Roland B. Dixon, *The Racial History of Man* (New York, 1923). On scientific racism and racial hierarchy, see John S. Haller, *Outcasts from Evolution: Scientific Attitudes of Racial Inferiority, 1859–1900* (Urbana, 1971); Hamilton Cravens, *Triumph of Evolution: American Scientists and the Heredity-Environment Controversy 1900–1941* (Philadelphia, 1978), esp. 50–55; I. A. Newby, *Jim Crow's Defense: Anti-Negro Thought in America, 1900–1930* (Baton Rouge, 1965), 22–49; Barkan, *Retreat of Scientific Racism*, 17–23; and Williamson, *Crucible of Race*, 119–24.

31. George W. Hunter, *A Civic Biology: Presented in Problems* (New York, 1914), 195–96, 261–63. On eugenics, see the classic work by Daniel J. Kevles, *In the Name of Eugenics: Genetics and the Uses of Human Heredity* (Cambridge, MA, 1995 [1985]). On immigration restriction, see John Higham, *Strangers in the Land:*

Patterns of American Nativism, 1860–1925 (New York, 1963), and Barbara Miller Solomon, *Ancestors and Immigrants: A Changing New England Tradition* (Cambridge, MA, 1956).

32. Newby, *Jim Crow's Defense*, 22–23. For black concerns that a celebrated search for the "missing link" in Africa in 1925 might be intended to demonstrate that black people "are direct descendents of the missing link, and are not humans," see *Chicago Broad Ax*, August 8, 1925, 2, and *Amsterdam News*, August 5, 1925, 2. The responsibility of Osborn and others for conveying a distorted sense of the human evolutionary timeline is discussed in Constance Areson Clark, "Evolution for John Doe: Pictures, the Public, and the Scopes Trial Debate," *Journal of American History* 87 (March 2001): 1275–303, and in Constance Areson Clark, *God or Gorilla: Images of Evolution in the Jazz Age* (Baltimore, 2008); see also Brian Regal, *Henry Fairfield Osborn: Race and the Search for the Origins of Man* (Burlington, VT, 2002).

33. On the scientists' turn against eugenics, see Cravens, *Triumph of Evolution*, 171–75, 178; Vernon J. Williams Jr., "Franz Boas and the African American Intelligentsia," *Western Journal of Black Studies* 19 (Summer 1995): 81–89. African Americans also contributed their own research to the cause, including W. E. B. Du Bois, ed., *The Health and Physique of the Negro American: Report of a Social Study Made Under the Direction of Atlanta University; Together with the Proceedings of the Eleventh Conference for the Study of the Negro Problem, Held at Atlanta University on May the 29th, 1906* (Atlanta, 1906); Vernon J. Williams Jr., *Rethinking Race: Franz Boas and His Contemporaries* (Lexington, KY, 1996), 4–36. On Boas and his milieu, see George W. Stocking Jr., *Race, Culture, and Evolution: Essays in the History of Anthropology* (New York, 1968).

34. Franz Boas, "What Is a Race?" *Nation*, January 28, 1925, 89–91; Herbert Adolphus Miller, "Race Pride and Race Prejudice," in *Amsterdam News*, June 3, 1925. A useful caution focusing on the persistence of eugenics in the Deep South can be found in Edward J. Larson, *Race, Sex, and Science: Eugenics in the Deep South* (*Baltimore*, 1995).

35. *Baltimore Afro-American*, May 16, 1925, 11; April 4, 1925, 11.

36. *Pittsburgh Courier*, July 18, 1925, 16; Jones quotations in *Baltimore Afro-American*, May 16, 1925, 11. On the "military metaphor" of warfare between science and religion, see James R. Moore, *The Post-Darwinian Controversies: A Study of the Protestant Struggle to Come to Terms with Darwin in Great Britain and America, 1870–1900* (New York, 1979), 20–49; the influential John William Draper, *History of the Conflict Between Religion and Science* (New York, 1875); Donald Fleming, *John William Draper and the Religion of Science* (Philadelphia, 1950); and Andrew Dickson White, *A History of the Warfare of Science and Theology in Christendom* (New York, 1955).

37. On the rising prestige of science and expertise, see David A. Hollinger, "Justification by Verification: The Scientific Challenge to the Moral Authority of Christianity in Modern America," in Michael J. Lacey, ed., *Religion and Twentieth-Century*

American Intellectual Life (New York, 1989), 121–23; and Thomas L. Haskell, ed., *The Authority of Experts: Studies in History and Theory* (Bloomington, IN, 1984).

38. George Schuyler, "Thrusts and Lunges," *Pittsburgh Courier*, July 18, 1925, 16; McKinney in *Chicago Broad Ax*, August 15, 1925, 2; David Levering Lewis, *W. E. B. Du Bois: The Fight for Equality and the American Century, 1919–1963* (New York, 2000), 557. The evaluations of African American religion by Du Bois and other intellectuals are discussed in Barbara Dianne Savage, "W. E. B. Du Bois and 'The Negro Church,'" *Annals of the American Academy of Political and Social Science* 568 (March 2000): 235–49.

39. Both McKinney quotations from Ernest Rice McKinney, "This Week," *Kansas City Call*, August 21, 1925, B2. On the African American Baptist church as a "multiple site," see Evelyn Brooks Higginbotham, *Righteous Discontent: The Women's Movement in the Black Baptist Church 1880–1920* (Cambridge, MA, 1993), 7; on the higher percentage of African American church membership, see Jessie Carney Smith and Carrel Peterson Horton, eds., *Historical Statistics of Black America: Media to Vital Statistics* (New York, 1995), 1766. Updated statistics demonstrate the persistence of African American religiosity, as in "A Religious Portrait of African Americans," Pew Forum on Religion and Public Life, January 30, 2009, http://pewforum.org/docs/?DocID=389 (accessed January 30, 2009); on the "otherworldly" orientation of African American religions, see Mays and Nicholson, *The Negro's Church*, 59.

40. "A Religious Portrait of African Americans."

41. George Bishop, "The Religious Worldview and American Beliefs About Human Origins," *Public Perspective* 9 (August-September 1998): 42.

CHAPTER 4: DESCENT WITH MODIFICATION

1. Edward J. Larson, *Summer for the Gods: The Scopes Trial and America's Continuing Debate over Science and Religion* (New York, 2006), 188.

2. *World's Most Famous Court Trial: Tennessee Evolution Case* (Dayton, TN, 1978 [1925]), 176.

3. Ibid., 178.

4. *Richmond* (VA) *Planet*, April 11, 1925, 1; April 18, 1925, 8.

5. *World's Most Famous Court Trial*, 197–98.

6. Henry Morris III, "The Unknown Creator," mass email from Institute for Creation Research, July 22, 2008.

7. Henry Morris III, "Satan's Strategic Plan," mass email from the Institute for Creation Research, June 27, 2008.

8. Morris, "The Unknown Creator."

9. Ibid.

10. Henry M. Morris III, "Creation, Conservation, and Consummation: Communicating the Full Gospel of Christ," *Acts & Facts*, August 2008, 5.

11. *Baltimore Afro-American*, July 4, 1925, 17.

12. One of several fascinating aspects of evolution's visual representations explicated in Constance Areson Clark, "'You Are Here': Missing Links, Chains of Being, and the Language of Cartoons," *Isis* 100 (September 2009): 580–81; see also Constance Areson Clark, *God or Gorilla: Images of Evolution in the Jazz Age* (Baltimore, 2008).

13. Chattanooga *Times*, July 6, 1925, n.p.

14. *Baltimore Evening Sun*, July 14, 1925, 1.

15. *World's Most Famous Court Trial*, 175.

16. "Nearly Two-Thirds of U.S. Adults Believe Human Beings Were Created by God," Harris Poll 52, July 6, 2005.

17. Lawrence W. Levine, *Defender of the Faith: William Jennings Bryan: The Last Decade, 1915–1925* (New York, 1965), 249; William Jennings Bryan, "The Prince of Peace" [ca. 1908], in Ray Ginger, ed., *William Jennings Bryan: Selections* (New York, 1967), 138–41.

18. Levine, *Defender of the Faith*, 250.

19. Arthur Kelly, *The Descent of Darwin: The Popularization of Darwinism in Germany, 1860–1914* (Chapel Hill, NC, 1981), 8–22; see also Walter Kaufmann, *Nietzsche: Philosopher, Psychologist, Antichrist*, 4th ed. (Princeton, 1974), 295–98.

20. Levine, *Defender of the Faith*, 261–62; Vernon Kellogg, *Headquarters Nights: A Record of Conversations and Experiences at the Headquarters of the German Army in France and Belgium* (Boston, 1917); Benjamin Kidd, *The Science of Power* (New York, 1918); see as well Gregg Mitman, "Evolution as Gospel: William Patten, the Language of Democracy, and the Great War," *Isis* 81 (September 1990): 446–63.

21. Kellogg, *Headquarters Nights*, 28, 40, and in general 23–30.

22. Kidd, *Science of Power*, 49.

23. Bryan, "Prince of Peace," 140.

24. The classic expression of this came in William Graham Sumner, *What Social Classes Owe to Each Other* (New York, 1883); Richard Hofstadter, *Social Darwinism in American Thought: 1860–1915* (Philadelphia, 1944); Donald C. Bellomy, "Social Darwinism Revisited," *Perspectives in American History*, n.s., 1 (1984): 1–130. See also Barry Werth, *Banquet at Delmonico's: Great Minds, the Gilded Age, and the Triumph of Evolution in America* (New York, 2009).

25. Gene Cohn, *Nashville Tennessean*, June 21, 1925, 11; see also George M. Marsden, "Fundamentalism as an American Phenomenon, A Comparison with English Evangelicalism," *Church History* 46 (June 1977): 215.

26. By far the best exegesis of these debates is Ronald L. Numbers, *The Creationists: From Scientific Creationism to Intelligent Design* (Cambridge, MA, 2006).

27. Ussher was no obscurantist, however; his use of biblical chronologies to determine the earth's age was fully a part of the seventeenth century's humanistic and scientific impulse.

28. For the best exposition of the extent of this sexual revolution, see Beth Bailey, *Sex in the Heartland* (Cambridge, MA, 1999).

29. On the rise of the New Right, see Lisa McGirr, *Suburban Warriors: The Origins of the New American Right* (Princeton, 2001); see also Jeffrey P. Moran, *Teaching Sex: The Shaping of Adolescence in the Twentieth Century* (Cambridge, MA, 2000), 156–93.

30. Numbers, *The Creationists*, 264–67; John L. Rudolph, *Scientists in the Classroom: The Cold War Reconstruction of American Science Education* (New York, 2002); Gerald Skoog, "Topic of Evolution in Secondary School Biology Textbooks, 1900–1977," *Science Education* 63 (1979): 621–40; Laura Engleman, ed., *The BSCS Story: A History of the Biological Sciences Curriculum* Study (Colorado Springs, 2001).

31. Henry M. Morris, *The Twilight of Evolution* (Grand Rapids, MI, 1963), 24, quoted in Michael Lienesch, *In the Beginning: Fundamentalism, the Scopes Trial, and the Making of the Evolution Movement* (Chapel Hill, NC, 2007), 214.

32. Much of my analysis of the alliance between antievolutionists and the New Right is indebted to arguments in Lienesch, *In the Beginning*, 214–19.

33. "Creation and the Feminist Movement," August 9, 2008, radio broadcast listed in *Acts and Facts*, August 2008, 16.

34. "Creation and God's Plan for the Family," August 16, 2008, radio broadcast listed in *Acts and Facts*, August 2008, 16.

35. Mass letter from Kelly L. Segraves, director of the Creation-Science Research Center (San Diego), March 1978, in Wilcox Collection of the Kansas Collection, Spencer Research Library, University of Kansas.

36. Promotional flyer for Mid-America League for Constitutional Government, Merriam, Kansas, n.d., in Wilcox Collection of the Kansas Collection, Spencer Research Library, University of Kansas.

37. John D. Morris, "Academic Freedom Battle Continues State by State," *Acts and Facts*, August 2008, 3.

38. Reported in *Newsweek*, June 29, 1987, 23. Coincidentally, in 2007 the conservative Club for Growth cited the same number for scientists who discount the evidence for global warming, and this figure made its way into the Minority Report of the U.S. Senate's 2009 Environment and Public Works Committee, recorded in "U.S. Senate Minority Report: More than 700 International Scientists Dissent over Man-Made Global Warming Claims: Scientists Continue to Debunk 'Consensus' in 2008 and 2009," U.S. Senate Environment and Public Works Committee, 2009, http://hatch.senate.gov/public/_files/USSenateEPWMinorityReport.pdf.

39. "Ranks of Scientists Doubting Darwin's Theory on the Rise," Center for Science and Culture, February 8, 2007, www.discovery.org/a/2732 (accessed April 29, 2010); "A Scientific Dissent from Darwinism," www.dissentfromdarwin.org/scientists (accessed April 29, 2010). The Discovery Institute had first

publicized a list of about one hundred scientists' names in 2001 with paid advertisements in the *New York Review of Books*, *New Republic*, and *Weekly Standard*, as noted at http://ncse.com/creationism/general/doubting-darwinism-creative-license (accessed September 10, 2011).

40. See, for example, John Ashton, ed., *In Six Days: Why Fifty Scientists Choose to Believe in Creation* (Green Forest, AR, 2001).

41. Christopher P. Toumey, *God's Own Scientists: Creationists in a Secular World* (New Brunswick, NJ, 1994.

42. Ibid., 233–36.

43. Ibid., 233–35.

44. Kenneth Miller phone interview with author, February 4, 2009.

45. See Center for Science and Culture website at www.discovery.org/csc/topQuestions.php; on Project Steve, see "Project Steve," October 2008, http://ncse.com/taking-action/project-steve (accessed September 8, 2011).

46. *Epperson et al. v. Arkansas*, 390 U.S. 941 (1968).

47. *Edwards v. Aguillard*, 482 U.S. 578 (1987).

48. Phillip E. Johnson, *Darwin on Trial* (Washington, DC, 1991).

49. Stephen Jay Gould, "Impeaching a Self-Appointed Judge," *Scientific American* 267 (July 1992): 119.

50. Ibid., 120.

51. Ibid., 119.

52. Barbara Forrest, "The Wedge at Work: How Intelligent Design Creationism Is Wedging Its Way into the Cultural and Academic Mainstream," in Robert T. Pennock, ed., *Intelligent Design Creationism and Its Critics* (Cambridge, MA, 2002), 8–9.

53. Ibid.

54. Ibid., 10–11.

55. Phillip E. Johnson, quoted in Ibid., 11.

56. Phillip E. Johnson interview with James M. Kushiner, 2000, www.arn.org/docs/johnson/le_berkeleysradical.htm (accessed August 10, 2009).

57. Ibid.

58. "The Wedge," unpublished memorandum from the Center for the Renewal of Science and Culture at the Discovery Institute, Seattle, WA, 1998, www.antievolution.org/features/wedge.html, and elsewhere (accessed November 4, 2008).

59. Ibid.

60. Phillip E. Johnson, *The Wedge of Truth: Splitting the Foundations of Naturalism* (Downers Grove, IL, 2000), 13–15.

61. Tim Stafford, "The Making of a Revolution: Law Professor Phillip Johnson Wants to Overturn the Scientific Establishment's 'Creation Myth,'" *Christianity Today*, December 8, 1997, www.ctlibrary.com/ct/1997/december8/7te016.html (accessed May 14, 2010).

62. ID's publication record is examined in Forrest, "The Wedge at Work," 17–24.

63. Barbara Forrest and Paul R. Gross, *Creationism's Trojan Horse: The Wedge of Intelligent Design* (New York, 2004).

64. "Opponents of Evolution Adopting a New Strategy," *New York Times*, June 4, 2008.

65. See, for example, the Zogby poll from September 21, 2001. Opinions on the subject, however, tend to be quite malleable depending on the wording of the question, and the Zogby polls in particular tend to overstate adherence to religion and creationism. See George Bishop, "Trends: Americans' Belief in God," *Public Opinion Quarterly* 63, no. 3 (Autumn 1999): 421–34.

66. *Tammy Kitzmiller, et al., v. Dover Area School District, et al.*, 400 F. Supp. 2d 707 (M.D. Pa. 2005). The ins and outs of the Dover trial are detailed in Edward Humes, *Monkey Girl: Evolution, Education, Religion, and the Battle for America's Soul* (New York, 2008).

67. Humes, *Monkey Girl*, 301. The Flying Spaghetti Monster had its genesis in Bobby Henderson's open letter to the Kansas State Board of Education protesting the board majority's attempts to limit the teaching of evolution in the public schools. The parody religion proliferated rapidly in the fertile fields of the internet, gaining numerous adherents—"Pastafarians"—who are required to present themselves as pirates. More detail available in Bobby Henderson, *The Gospel of the Flying Spaghetti Monster* (New York, 2006).

68. *Kitzmiller*, 730–31, 748–53.

69. Bill Buckingham, quoted in Humes, *Monkey Girl*, 60.

70. *Kitzmiller*, 721.

71. Ibid., 744.

72. Ibid., 745.

73. Ibid., 720.

74. Ibid., 745–46.

75. See, for example, the interview with the prominent Missouri antievolutionist John Calvert, in *Flock of Dodos: The Evolution—Intelligent Design Circus*, dir. Randy Olson, 2005, Prairie Starfish Productions.

76. Johnson, *Wedge of Truth*, 158.

77. Humes, *Monkey Girl*, 22–34, quotation on 34. One up-close examination of this "subculture" may be found in Randall Balmer, *Mine Eyes Have Seen the Glory: Evangelical Subculture in America*, expanded ed. (New York, 1993).

78. Figures taken from Lienesch, *In the Beginning*, 313, who derives them from www.charitynavigator.org.

79. NBC News poll conducted by Peter Hart and Bill McInturff, March 8–10, 2005; see "Poll Finds Americans Split on Creation Idea," *New York Times*, August 29, 1982. An overview of the polls can be found in "Reading the Polls on Evolution and Creationism," *Pew Research Center Poll Watch*, September 28, 2005.

80. *New York Times*, May 5, 2007, 10. The moment was reported with approval in Mark Looy, "The Republican Presidential Candidates on Evolution," Answers

in Genesis website, May 4, 2007, www.answersingenesis.org/arti-cles/2007/05/04/republican-candidates-evolution (accessed August 14, 2009).

81. Sam Brownback, "What I Believe about Evolution," *New York Times*, May 31, 2007, 19.

82. CBS News/*New York Times* poll, November 18–21, 2004; "Reading the Polls on Evolution and Creationism," *Pew Research Center Poll Watch*, September 28, 2005. See also the less robust Zogby poll of August 25–29, 2001.

83. Harris Poll, June 17–21, 2005.

84. On ID, see "Nearly Two-thirds of U. S. Adults Believe Human Beings Were Created by God," Harris Poll 52, July 6, 2005; CBS News/*New York Times* Poll, November 18–21, 2004.

85. *USA Today*/Gallup poll, June 1–3, 2007.

86. "'Intelligent Design' Costs Dover over $1,000,000," *NCSE Resource*, February 24, 2006, http://ncse.com/news/2006/02/intelligent-design-costs-dover-over-1000000-00899 (accessed September 8, 2011), 12.

87. Kansas City *Star*, October 13, 2005, cited in NCSE report "Antievolutionism Bad for Business," http://ncse.com/news/2005/10/antievolutionism-bad-business-kansas-00614 (accessed November 12, 2008).

88. "Opponents of Evolution Adopting a New Strategy," *New York Times*, June 4, 2008 (accessed November 21, 2008).

89. Glenn Branch and Eugenie C. Scott, "The Latest Face of Creationism in the Classroom," *Scientific American*, www.scientificamerican.com/article. cfm?id=the-latest-face-of-creationism (accessed November 1, 2009); Kenneth Miller phone interview with author, February 4, 2009.

90. Gordy Slack, "Inside the Creation Museum," Salon.com, May 31, 2007, www. salon.com/news/feature/2007/05/31/creation_museum (accessed November 11, 2008).

91. Carl Wieland, "AIG's Views on the Intelligent Design Movement," August 30, 2002,www.answersingenesis.org/docs2002/0830_IDM.asp (accessed November 29, 2008).

92. Ibid. Carl Wieland's relationship with AIG is explained in Numbers, *The Creationists*, 400–401. See also James J. S. Johnson, "The Failed Apologetic of the Wedge Strategy," *Acts and Facts*, July 2011, 10–11.

93. Georgia Purdom, "The Intelligent Design Movement: Does the Identity of the Creator Really Matter?" *Answers: Building a Biblical Worldview*, www.answersin-genesis.org/articles/am/v1/n1/intelligent-design-movement (accessed May 9, 2010).

94. Wieland, "ÁIG's Views."

95. Martin E. Marty, *A Nation of Behavors* (Chicago, 1976), 75–78.

96. John G. Kramer, "John G. Kramer, Biochemistry," in Ashton, ed., *In Six Days*, 54.

97. Lewis Black, *Red White and Screwed*, HBO Video, 2006.

98. The debate over the ways in which group structures interact with personal identity can be found in Michael A. Hogg, Deborah J. Terry, and Katherine M. White, "A Tale of Two Theories: A Critical Comparison of Identity Theory with Social Identity Theory," *Social Psychology Quarterly* 58, no. 4 (May 4, 1995): 255–69.

CHAPTER 5: CREATIONISM AND THE CAMPUS

1. This and following quotations are from Paulyn Cartwright and Bruce Lieberman, interview with author, Lawrence, Kansas, January 8, 2009.
2. James H. Leuba, *The Belief in God and Immortality: A Psychological, Anthropological and Statistical Study* (Boston, 1916), 213–20.
3. Ibid., 203–11, 283–88.
4. Ibid., 248–79.
5. William Jennings Bryan and Mary Baird Bryan, *The Memoirs of William Jennings Bryan* (Philadelphia, 1925), 479.
6. Phillip E. Johnson, *The Wedge of Truth: Splitting the Foundation of Naturalism* (Downers Grove, IL, 2000); see also Barbara Forrest, "The Wedge at Work: How Intelligent Design Creationism Is Wedging Its Way into the Cultural and Academic Mainstream," in Robert T. Pennock, ed., *Intelligent Design Creationism and Its Critics: Philosophical, Theological, and Scientific Perspectives* (Cambridge, MA, 2002), 31–32. In his treatment, Johnson makes much of an essay by one of his distant predecessors at Harvard, Philip E. Wentworth, who recounted his travails in "What College Did to My Religion," *Atlantic Monthly* 149, no. 6 (June 1932): 679–88.
7. David Caplovitz and Fred Sherrow, *The Religious Drop-Outs: Apostasy Among College Undergraduates* (Los Angeles, 1977).
8. Jeremy E. Uecker, Mark D. Regnerus, and Margaret L. Vaaler, "Losing My Religion: Social Sources of Religious Decline in Early Adulthood," *Social Forces* 85, no. 4 (2007): 1669.
9. Ibid., 1605.
10. Alexander W. Astin, "The Changing American College Student: Thirty-Year Trends, 1966–1996," *Review of Higher Education* 21, no. 1 (1998): 115–35, cited in Uecker, Regnerus, and Vaaler, 1669.
11. Uecker, Regnerus, and Vaaler, "Losing My Religion," 1669.
12. Ibid., 1683. Oddly, the authors do not include biology as one of the fields of study that would most threaten Christian beliefs.
13. H. R. Zuidema, "How to Rock a Campus Without Hiring," *Liberty* 79, no. 6 (1984): 17–18; on the possibility of religious discrimination among faculty, see Jerry Bergman, "Contemporary Suppression of the Theistic Worldview," *Journal of Creation* 9, no. 2 (August 1995): 267–75, reprinted at http://creation.com/contemporary-suppression-of-the-theistic-worldview (accessed September 15, 2009).

14. For one of many examples, see *4 Power Questions to Ask an Evolutionist*, DVD, dir. Mike Riddle, Answers in Genesis, 2008.

15. One of the most complete examinations is Lisa D. Pearce and Melinda Lundquist Denton, *A Faith of Their Own: Stability and Change in the Religiosity of America's Adolescents* (New York, 2011); see also Mark D. Regnerus and Jeremy E. Uecker, "Finding Faith, Losing Faith: The Prevalence and Context of Religious Transformations during Adolescence," *Review of Religious Research* 47, no. 3 (March 2006): 217–37.

16. Regnerus and Uecker, "Finding Faith, Losing Faith," 220.

17. Uecker, Regnerus, and Vaaler, "Losing My Religion," 1677–79 (italics in the original).

18. "Nearly Two-Thirds of U.S. Adults Believe Human Beings Were Created by God," Harris Poll 52, July 6, 2005.

19. Ibid. The Harris Poll reveals some puzzling anomalies even among college graduates, with only 31 percent believing in human evolution, but 53 percent agreeing that "man and apes have common ancestry." High school graduates showed a similar pattern, but skewed more heavily to the creationist side.

20. Leuba, *The Belief in God and Immortality*, 248–79.

21. Edward J. Larson and Larry Witham, "Scientists Are Still Keeping the Faith," *Nature* 386 (April 3, 1997): 435–36; Edward J. Larson and Larry Witham, "Leading Scientists Still Reject God," *Nature* 394 (July 23, 1998): 313. For a critique of the weaknesses of the follow-up survey, see Eugenie C. Scott, "Do Scientists Really Reject God?" *Reports of the National Center for Science Education* 18, no. 2 (1998): 24–25.

22. Elaine Howard Ecklund and Christopher P. Scheitle, "Religion Among Academic Scientists: Distinctions, Disciplines, and Demographics," *Social Problems* 54, no. 2 (2007): 289–307. Ecklund did find a surprising amount of interest in "spirituality" among her subjects, although this is obviously an exceedingly elastic category; Elaine Howard Ecklund, "Religion and Spirituality Among Scientists," *Contexts* 7, no. 1 (2008): 12–15.

23. Elaine Howard Ecklund, *Science vs. Religion: What Scientists Really Think* (New York, 2010), 52–53.

24. Ecklund and Scheitle, "Religion Among Academic Scientists," 304.

25. James Moore, "That Evolution Destroyed Darwin's Faith in Christianity—Until He Converted on His Deathbed," in Ronald L. Numbers, ed., *Galileo Goes to Jail and Other Myths About Science and Religion* (Cambridge, MA, 2009), 146–48; Moore traces the entire tale of Darwin's deathbed conversion in 142–51.

26. William Jennings Bryan, "Text of Bryan's Proposed Address in Scopes Case," in *World's Most Famous Court Trial: Tennessee Evolution Case* (Dayton, Tenn., 1978 [1925]), 328.

27. Ecklund, "Religion and Spirituality," 303. The same filial influence is also true for the religiously unaffiliated in the population at large.

28. Phillip E. Johnson, "Evolution as Dogma: The Establishment of Naturalism," *First Things* 6 (1990): 15–22, reprinted in Robert T. Pennock, ed., *Intelligent Design Creationism and Its Critics: Philosophical, Theological, and Scientific Perspectives* (Cambridge, MA, 2002), 61.

29. Ibid., 72.

30. Nicole Oresme, quoted in Ronald L. Numbers, "Science Without God: Natural Laws and Christian Beliefs," in David C. Lindberg and Ronald L. Numbers, eds., *When Science and Christianity Meet* (Chicago, 2003), 267.

31. Ibid., 268.

32. Richard Dawkins, *The Blind Watchmaker* (New York, 1966), 6.

33. For a thoughtful overview and partial repudiation of social constructionism that is rooted in the everyday practices of science, see David L. Hull, *Science as Process: An Evolutionary Account of the Social and Conceptual Development of Science* (Chicago, 1988); more direct repudiation is found in Noretta Koertage, ed., *A House Built on Sand: Exposing Postmodernist Myths About Science* (Oxford, 1998), and Norman Levitt and Paul R. Gross, *Higher Superstition: The Academic Left and its Quarrels with Science* (Baltimore, 1994).

34. *Tammy Kitzmiller, et al., v. Dover Area School District, et al.*, 400 F. Supp. 2d 707 (M.D. Pa. 2005), October 24 morning testimony.

35. Phillip E. Johnson, *Darwin on Trial* (Downers Grove, IL, 1993), 86.

36. Testimony in *Kitzmiller*.

37. Thomas Kuhn, *The Structure of Scientific Revolutions* (Chicago, 1962). The debates and literature that Kuhn's work spawned are too voluminous to trace here. For the observation that scientists do not recognize "anomalies" until *after* a paradigm shifts, see Alan Lightman and Owen Gingerich, "When Do Anomalies Begin?" *Science* 255, no. 5045 (February 7, 1992): 690–95.

38. See discussion in Ronald L. Numbers, *The Creationists: From Scientific Creationism to Intelligent Design* (Cambridge, MA, 2006), 274–75.

39. Stephen Jay Gould, "Nonoverlapping Magisteria," *Natural History* 106 (March 1997): 16–22; Stephen Jay Gould, *Rocks of Ages: Science and Religion in the Fullness of Life* (New York, 2002).

40. Johnson, *Wedge of Truth*, 98–99.

41. Howard J. Van Till writes of this destruction of a middle ground as a collaborative process between episodic creationists and evolutionary naturalists in "The Creation: Intelligently Designed or Optimally Equipped?" in Robert T. Pennock, ed., *Intelligent Design Creationism and Its Critics: Philosophical, Theological, and Scientific Perspectives* (Cambridge, MA, 2002).

42. Scott, "Do Scientists Really Reject God?" 490–92.

43. Stephen Jay Gould, "Impeaching a Self-Appointed Judge," *Scientific American*, July 1992, 118.

44. Niles Eldredge and Stephen Jay Gould, "Punctuated Equilibria: An Alternative to Phyletic Gradualism," in T. J. M. Schopf, ed., *Models in Paleobiology* (San

Francisco, 1972), 82–115; A. Somit and S. A. Peterson, eds., *The Punctuated Equilibrium Debate in the Natural and Social Sciences* (Ithaca, NY, 1992).

45. Linda Heuman, "The Evolution of Ken Miller," *Brown Alumni Magazine*, November-December 2005, www.brownalumnimagazine.com/november/december-2005/the-evolution-of-ken-miller.html (accessed February 9, 2009).

46. John F. Ashton, ed., *In Six Days: Why Fifty Scientists Choose to Believe in Creation* (Green Forest, Ark., 2000).

47. John P. Marcus, "John P. Marcus," in Ashton, ed., *In Six Days*, 172.

48. As an example, see John K. G. Kramer, "John K. G. Kramer," in Ashton, ed., *In Six Days*, 46.

49. Dan Cray, "God vs. Science," *Time.com*, November 5, 2006, www.time.com/time/magazine/article/0,9171,1555132-3,00.html (accessed November 12, 2009).

50. Ibid.

51. Francis S. Collins, *The Language of God: A Scientist Presents Evidence for Belief* (New York, 2007).

52. Denis O. Lamoureux, "Evangelicals Inheriting the Wind: The Phillip E. Johnson Phenomenon," in Phillip E. Johnson, Denis O. Lamoureux, et al., *Darwinism Defeated? The Johnson-Lamoureux Debate on Biological Origins* (Vancouver, 1999), 9.

53. Ibid., 12. For a very informal confirmation of this assertion at the faculty level, see John C. Sutherland, "Evangelical Biologists and Evolution," *Science*, 309, no. 5731 (July 1, 2005): 51.

54. Lamoureux, "Evangelicals Inheriting the Wind," 45.

55. Ibid., 38.

56. Ibid., 39, 70.

57. Ibid., 42–43.

58. Mark A. Noll, *The Scandal of the Evangelical Mind* (Leicester, UK, 1994), 45.

59. Keith B. Miller, "Design and Purpose Within an Evolving Creation," in Johnson, Lamoureux, et al., *Darwinism Defeated*, 108–9.

60. Howard J. Van Till, telephone interview with author, November 23, 2009.

61. Ibid.

62. Lamoureux, "Evangelicals Inheriting the Wind," 70.

63. Loren Wilkinson, "Does Methodological Naturalism Lead to Metaphysical Naturalism?" in Johnson, Lamoureux, et al., *Darwinism Defeated*, 173.

64. Aubrey L. Moore, *Science and Faith* (London, 1889), 184, cited in Wilkinson, "Does Methodological Naturalism," 173.

65. Vincent Rossmeier, "Can't Darwin and God Get Along?" Salon.com, July 1, 2008, www.salon.com/books/atoms_eden/2008/07/01/saving_darwin (accessed November 11, 2009).

66. Howard J. Van Till, "Intelligent Design: The Celebration of Gifts Withheld?" in Johnson, Lamoureux, et al., *Darwinism Defeated*, 84–85.

67. Ibid., 84.
68. Ibid., 88.
69. Ibid.
70. Phillip E. Johnson, "What Is Darwinism?" in *Man and Creation: Perspectives on Science and Theology* (Hillsdale, MI, 1992), www.arn.org/docs/johnson/wid. htm (accessed September 18, 2009).
71. Phillip E. Johnson radio interview with James C. Dobson, September 15, 1997, quoted in Phillip E. Johnson, "Final Response to Denis O. Lamoureux," in Johnson, Lamoureux, et al., *Darwinism Defeated*, 78–79.
72. Howard J. Van Till, telephone interview with author, November 23, 2009.
73. Ibid.
74. Harry Boonstra, *Our School: Calvin College and the Christian Reformed Church* (Grand Rapids, Michigan, 2001), 117. See as well Howard J. Van Till, Davis A. Young, and Clarence Menninga, *Science Held Hostage: What's Wrong with Creation Science and Evolutionism* (Downers Grove, IL, 1988).
75. Davis A. Young, *Christianity and the Age of the Earth* (Grand Rapids, MI, 1982)
76. Howard J. Van Till, telephone interview with the author, November 23, 2009.
77. Howard J. Van Till, *The Fourth Day: What the Bible and the Heavens Are Telling Us About the Creation* (Grand Rapids, MI, 1986), 66.
78. E. B. Verhulst, "Editor's Corner," *Kerux: The Calvin Seminary Student Newspaper*, September 29, 1989, 1.
79. The denomination was also wrestling with the question of dancing.
80. Howard J. Van Till, phone interview.
81. "Report of the Ad Hoc Committee," February 8, 1988, 1, copy in the possession of Eric Verhulst.
82. Ibid., 4.
83. Ibid.
84. Ibid., 5.
85. Untitled open letter to the faculty and body of Calvin Theological Seminary, May 26, 1988, 1, copy in the possession of Eric Verhulst.
86. Ibid., 5.
87. E. B. Verhulst, "Editor's Corner," *Kerux*, September 29, 1989, 1–2.
88. See, for example, Clarence Menninga, letter to the editor, *Kerux*, October 13, 1989, 3.
89. Howard J. Van Till interview.
90. Howard J. Van Till, "From Calvinism to Freethought," presented May 24, 2006, for the Freethought Association of West Michigan. Thanks to Howard J. Van Till for sharing this document with me.
91. Howard J. Van Till and Phillip E. Johnson, "God and Evolution: An Exchange," *First Things*, June-July 1993, 31–38.
92. Howard J. Van Till, email communication with author, November 26, 2009.

93. "Ohio Scientists' Intelligent Design Poll," NCSE website, October 15, 2002, http://ncse.com/creationism/general/ohio-scientists-intelligent-design-poll (accessed February 6, 2009).

94. Michael Lienesch, *In the Beginning: Fundamentalism, the Scopes Trial, and the Making of the Antievolution Movement* (Chapel Hill, NC, 2007), 236.

95. Theodosius Dobzhansky, "Nothing in Biology Makes Sense Except in the Light of Evolution," *American Biology Teacher* 35 (March 1973): 125–29.

96. Heuman, "Evolution of Ken Miller."

97. Miller phone interview with author, February 4, 2009.

98. Ibid.

99. Heuman, "Evolution of Ken Miller."

100. Miller phone interview. Morris's hopes for converting Rhode Island to the creationist cause could not have been very high in the first place.

101. Ibid.

102. Ibid.

103. Marcel Chotkowski LaFollette, *Reframing Scopes: Journalists, Scientists, and Lost Photographs from the Trial of the Century* (Lawrence, KS, 2008).

104. The following narrative is derived largely from Hee-Joo Park, "The Politics of Anti-Creationism: The Committees of Correspondence," *Journal of the History of Biology* 35 (2000): 349–70.

105. Ibid., 354.

106. Ibid., 365.

107. Glenn Branch email communication with author, February 19, 2009.

108. Ibid.

109. Ibid.

110. Ibid.

111. See Lee Raine, John Horrigan, et al., "The Internet and Email Aid Users in Maintaining Their Social Networks and Provide Pathways to Help When People Face Big Decisions," Pew Internet and American Life Project, January 25, 2006, www.pewinternet.org/Reports/2006/The-Strength-of-Internet-Ties.aspx (accessed November 11, 2010).

112. Nick Matzke email communication with author, May 18, 2010.

113. Wesley Elsberry phone interview with author, May 19, 2010.

114. Matzke email communication with author, May 18, 2010.

115. Ibid.

116. From Wesley Elsberry's self-introduction to the American Scientific Affiliation discussion forum in 1997, www.asa3.org/archive/evolution/199703/0031.html (accessed May 20, 2010).

117. Wesley Elsberry phone interview with author, May 19, 2010.

118. Ibid.

119. Matzke email communication with author, May 18, 2010.

120. www.talkorigins.org/origins/other-links-cre.html and www.talkorigins.org/origins/other-links-evol.html (both accessed May 30, 2010). Very rough estimates of the relative volume of traffic on these sites can be found through Alexa.com, www.alexa.com/siteinfo/answersingenesis.org.

121. Walter Lippmann, *American Inquisitors: A Commentary on Dayton and Chicago* (New York, 1928), 66.

Index